thinking
SKILLS
&

EYE IQ CUE

VISUAL TOOLS FOR RAISING INTELLIGENCE

OLIVER CAVIGLIOLI   IAN HARRIS   BILL TINDALL

Published by Network Educational Press Ltd
PO Box 635
Stafford
ST16 1BF
t: 01785 225515
f: 01785 228566
e: enquiries@networkpress.co.uk

Editor: Gina Walker
Page layout: Neil Hawkins
Illustration and design: Oliver Caviglioli
Overview maps: Carol Hariram
Printed in Great Britain by MPG Books, Cornwall, Bodmin.

Thinking Skills and Eye Q Posters

A set of eight vibrant posters is available, in A2 size, which depicts all the visual tools described in this book. The posters are perfect to help stimulate thinking skills and accelerate learning in your classroom. Contact Network Educational Press for details.

Price £19.95 + VAT

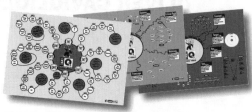

(Non returnable)

'The human mind is not, as philosophers would have you think, a debating hall, but a picture gallery.'

D. E. Harding (1998)

TL.

This book is due for return on or before the last date shown below.

B/23946

Acknowledgements

Oliver:

To my mother, Constance, for always encouraging me.

To my family, Lyn, Pascal, Roma and Francesca, for accommodating my pursuits.

Ian:

Thank you to Lorraine, my partner, for the beautiful ways she finds to remind me how simple life really is.

Thank you also to all those teachers and managers that have taken the time to write and send examples of the fabulous ways they have translated our books into practice – in particular, Jo and 'Dick the Fish' in the South West, and Gerry and Trevor in Scotland.

Bill:

To my mother and father, who launched me on my learning journey and have supported me at every turn.

To my wife, Janet, and my children and grandchildren who have brought so much richness to our shared lives.

And with thanks to all those pupils, students and colleagues who have challenged, encouraged, inspired and taught me a great deal about myself and the world. I am grateful to the teachers and mentors I have met through their books and in person. But for these human and humane contacts my life in education might have been a dull one.

Contents

introduction		the content	P7
		the structure	P9
section 1 context	CHAPTER 1	background	P13
	CHAPTER 2	the iDesk model	P21
	CHAPTER 3	the knowledge age	P27
section 2 visuals	CHAPTER 4	visual tools and computers	P33
	CHAPTER 5	visual literacy	P39
	CHAPTER 6	tools to learn	P47
section 3 meaning	CHAPTER 7	schemas	P53
	CHAPTER 8	holographic–linear	P61
	CHAPTER 9	constructing knowledge	P69
section 4 language	CHAPTER 10	support for language	P77
	CHAPTER 11	reading	P85
	CHAPTER 12	writing	P93
section 5 thinking	CHAPTER 13	thinking skills	P99
	CHAPTER 14	questions	P105
	CHAPTER 15	thinking in action	P113
section 6 learning	CHAPTER 16	active learning	P123
	CHAPTER 17	styles of learning	P131
	CHAPTER 18	ability range	P137
section 7 lexicon	CHAPTER 19	lexicon	P143

Foreword

A multi-media world breeds sophisticated visual learners. Children who've been exposed from their earliest years to TV, video and computer displays respond naturally – and eagerly – to pictures, diagrams and other visual models. Yet in education we've been slow to recognise the potential of visual teaching strategies to enhance and accelerate children's learning.

Having recently conducted work for the National Literacy Strategy on using visual planning for cross-curricular writing (simple 'skeletons', on which children can organise their thoughts before starting to write), I'm convinced that this potential is enormous. When teachers or learners arrange their ideas on a timeline, spidergram or other visual skeleton, they are 'making thinking visible'.

This 'big picture' representation – which can be talked around and thought about – is an excellent preparation for writing. It allows children to sort out the content and organisation of their work first, before the difficult task of forcing their understanding into the linear straitjacket of written language. In fact, when you put a visual model in the centre of the teaching process, the boundaries between 'literacy', 'learning' and 'thinking skills' begin to seem increasingly artificial.

However, if we are to make maximum use of visual teaching strategies, we need first to be aware of the range of techniques and devices available to us. The skills involved must be defined, described and clarified. *Thinking Skills and Eye Q* addresses this task with enormous clarity, combining a theoretical perspective ('what is behind our understanding – how does the mind work?') with the practical considerations that underlie all good teaching. I believe it is a very important book, which teachers of all age groups will find a valuable and stimulating resource.

Sue Palmer, Literacy writer and trainer

the content **P7**

the structure **P9**

overview

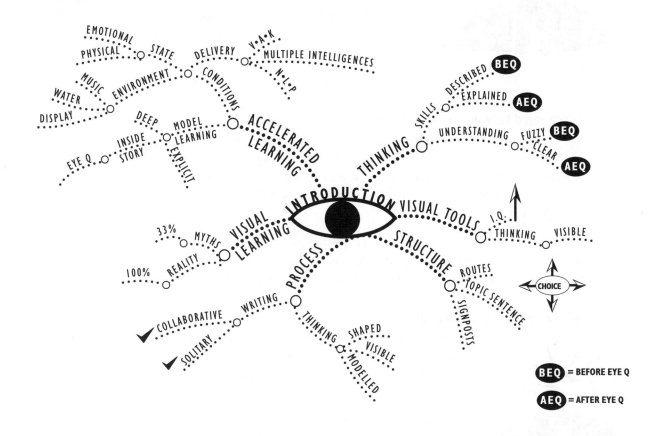

The content

<table>
<tr><td>preview</td><td>

■ There has been a great deal of fuzzy thinking about thinking skills.

■ Accelerated Learning deals with the conditions for learning.

■ All learners are visual learners.

■ Visual tools make thinking visible.

■ *Eye Q* raises your IQ

■ Visual tools need to be identified, labelled, organised and taught.

</td></tr>
</table>

There has been a great deal of fuzzy thinking about thinking skills.

So, you have attended several thinking skills courses. You have even taught a thinking skills programme to your students. More recently, you have highlighted the opportunities for challenging students' thinking in the context of your subject. You have understood, therefore, and agreed with the move from thinking skills to thinking schools. Infusion is your byword.

But, after all this manoeuvring, you are still not clear what thinking actually is. Yes, you can identify the various levels of thinking in several taxonomies. You are familiar with competencies ranging from systematic search to syllogisms. Cognitive conflict and metacognition are actively promoted in your lessons. Yet, underneath all the surface descriptions of the different types of thinking, operating at various levels, supported by a string of strategies and applied across a range of contexts, thinking itself remains unexamined.

Eye Q aims to analyse, reveal and explain the basis of thought.

Accelerated Learning deals with the conditions for learning.

Your students are well watered, oxygenated from their Brain Gym, and relaxed thanks to ambient music. You have developed a positive learning environment with warm, respectful relationships, and vibrant, visual classrooms. Your teaching incorporates visual, auditory and kinaesthetic modalities. Children have opportunities to demonstrate their prowess across a range of intelligences. Your skilful use of neuro-linguistic programming principles promotes success.

Yet, while you confidently apply these highly effective Accelerated Learning techniques, are you clear what is actually happening in the heads of your students when they are learning? Can you articulate your sense of what the 'ah ha!' moment – when a learner grasps a concept – actually consists of?

All learners are visual learners.

When people learn to drive, do they manage to do so with their eyes closed? Do companies spend millions of pounds on advertising in the expectation that only a third of the population will notice, still less be influenced by, billboards and television? Can you easily and successfully communicate complex diagrams just by talking about them?

Our brains, as Robert Ornstein points out in *New World, New Mind* (Ornstein and Ehrlich, 1991), are the evolutionary product of humans living for millennia in conditions far removed from what we know as civilisation. They became finely tuned to detect rapidly what was wanting to eat us, and what we wanted to eat. For humans, visual proficiency correlated directly with life span. No one could afford to opt out because using their eyes was not their preferred modality!

These conditions shaped the structure and processes of our brains. We retain this overwhelmingly visual orientation.

causal visual tool | fishbone diagram | lexicon link | page 218

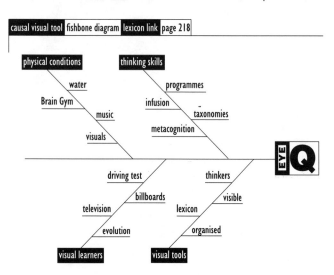

Visual tools make thinking visible.

When we think, we organise our thoughts in particular ways. We treat our thoughts much as we treat real objects – we manipulate them, move them about and even forget where we put them. The only difference with our thoughts-as-objects is that we cannot see them. They are invisible. As such, we have a correspondingly lower awareness of them, much like our forgetfulness of any physical object permanently hidden from view.

Much of the trouble students have with thinking is due to its invisible nature. When people can see what they are thinking, they immediately become better thinkers. When they no longer have to strain to remember the specific locational arrangement of their thoughts in their heads, their mental energy is released to examine the combination of thoughts themselves. This is known as high-level, reflective thinking.

Visual tools make students' thinking visible. Beware, because they make your thinking visible too. When thinking is visible, it also becomes public and interactive.

Eye Q raises your IQ.

Thinking can be transformed from being a private, abstract and invisible act, to one that is public, concrete and visible. Visual tools are cues for your eyes. With such cues, your thinking is stimulated, challenged and supported.

The basis of intelligence is thinking. Behind all the various models of intelligence lies the act of thinking. By becoming better thinkers through the eye cues of visual tools, students raise their intelligence.

Visual tools need to be identified, labelled, organised and taught.

Humans have always used marks to depict their thoughts. We now have a vast array of maps, diagrams, charts and matrices available to us. However, their uses are spread around a range of disciplines – mathematics, information architecture, logic, business and illustration, for example.

In education there is no categorisation, or 'lexicon', of visual tools. They have never been 'gathered together'. Teachers need to know what tools are available, to be able to name them, to understand their different functions, to appreciate the match of tools to contexts, and to find them in an organised filing system. *Eye Q* contains this first-ever comprehensive lexicon of visual tools for teachers.

The structure

> **preview**
> - Traditionally, books are not well designed for readers.
> - In *Eye Q*, there are several views and routes available.
> - Your navigation through sections and chapters is signposted.
> - The architecture of each chapter is made visible with topic sentences in bold.
> - Visual tools illustrate the points made in the text.

Traditionally, books are not well designed for readers.

When a book is produced, much emphasis is often placed on the authors – their backgrounds, their aspirations, their values. Much less emphasis is placed on the readers. This is not the case with other items for sale. Designers behind new furniture, appliances and buildings are not lauded in this way. The emphasis is not on them, but on their products.

Products are designed with the user in mind. Information architects design information pathways for computer users, to make the content accessible and easily manipulated. Books have not moved with the times – they do not, in general, display the same attention to the experience of the reader.

When reading a book, do you find that you use a highlighter to pick out key points, or make notes in the margin? Readers frequently have to add organising structures and orientational signposts to the text for their own benefit. But such work is often unnecessary as the author probably had these same principles and signposts in her original plans. They then disappeared when the plans were converted to text.

Eye Q is written with you, the reader, in mind. It has been designed to make your reading easier, more flexible, more organised and more memorable. Illustrations, visual tools, chapter structures, topic sentences, Previews and Reviews, as well as suggested reading routes, all combine to create a book designed with the end user in mind.

In *Eye Q*, there are several views and routes available.

Many books tell their readers that there is no obligation to read from cover to cover in linear fashion. As if people follow such sequential patterns anyway! Yet, after such an invitation, there are no structures designed into the book to make flexible reading excursions easy, connected and fruitful. Any meandering from a linear progression through the book is entirely at the reader's mental expense. It is the reader alone who is expected to do all the work.

While it is true that it can only be the reader who creates meaning from the text, there are, nonetheless, design principles available to make your reading more comfortable, more exciting and more 'intelligent'. *Eye Q* both invites you to read through in a non-linear way and supports you in doing so.

Your navigation through sections and chapters is signposted.

There are seven sections to the book. Sections 1 to 6 each contain three chapters, while section 7 comprises a single chapter providing the lexicon of visual tools.

At the start of every chapter, at the top of the page, there is a drop-down menu. This shows which chapter you are about to read, in which section. It also shows what has preceded this point, and what follows. There is also a table giving a brief summary of each chapter in the whole book. In the table, the chapter you are about to read is highlighted. This table is displayed at the beginning of every chapter, with the highlighted summary changing as you proceed, in whatever fashion, through the book. Using this orientational support, you can see where you have gone and where you might want to go next. The table also reinforces your reading experience by summarising the content and visually offering you conceptual connections.

Each chapter begins with an Overview – a model map that shows you the organising principles of the content in a graphic format (for example, see page 13). Then there is a Preview, in which the major topic sentences of the chapter are assembled in sequence. This allows you to read the key points of the chapter in around only ten sentences. Normally, when you skim-read a chapter, you are aiming to find these important sentences while you flick through the pages, which can be very hit-and-miss. This Preview device gives you a 'skim-on-a-plate'.

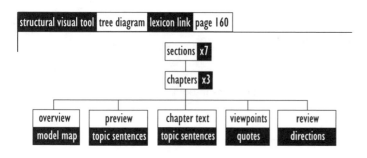

After the main body of text in each chapter, there follows a Viewpoint section. Here you will find a series of quotations that were influential in the authors' thinking when working on the chapter. These quotations are included under a separate heading in order to give the reader a wider perspective on the content without crowding the main text.

Lastly, there is a Review section to each chapter. Here, you are invited to consider certain points raised, to answer questions about your own thinking or to reflect on your practice. You may even be invited to imagine adapting your practice.

The architecture of each chapter is made visible with topic sentences in bold.

When writers compose their texts, there are a certain number of main points to be made. These are mostly hidden in the text and it is up to the reader to find them. Why?

Eye Q presents these main points explicitly, in sentence form. Each chapter is composed of around ten topic sentences. They appear at the beginning of each chapter, as a Preview. Then, in the text itself, they appear in bold print. They are written in such a way that, together, they themselves form a coherent and contracted text.

You can, therefore, simply read the Preview of a chapter, or read the text more thoroughly, coming across the topic sentences as you do so. While reading the text, you can read some parts fully and some with a lighter touch by bounding from one bold-typed topic sentence to the next. This kind of 'textual triple-jumping' also allows a subliminal gathering of information.

Visual tools illustrate the points made in the text.

Throughout the book, visual tools are used to illustrate the points made in the text. This spatial display of ideas not only helps to explain the concepts within the text, but will also help you to become familiar with the visual tools described in the lexicon (chapter 19) and the ways in which they can be used.

Each time a visual tool is used, its name is given, along with the category to which it belongs. As the category of visual tool directly relates to the type of thinking involved, each example will engage you in considering the different perspectives available from different types of thought. The medium is the message.

causal visual tool | critical path analysis | lexicon link | page 224

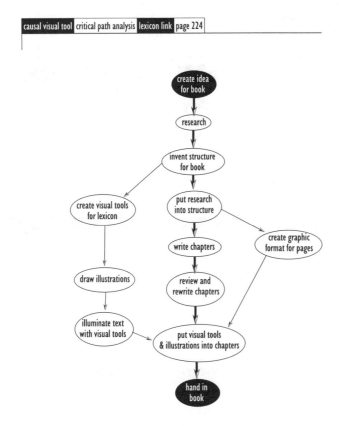

temporal visual tool | GANTT chart | lexicon link | page 214

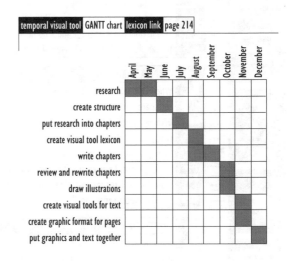

ROUTE MAP FOR YOUR READING

SECTION 1 — CONTEXT

CHAPTER ONE — BACKGROUND

The primary assertion is that we are all *Eye Q* experts. Throughout history, humans have used an assortment of visual tools to reflect and communicate knowledge. Current knowledge creation dynamics are based on this same notion. The 'inside story' of learning is obtained by looking both inside (cognitive psychology) and outside (Accelerated Learning).

CHAPTER TWO — THE iDESK MODEL

Most of our activities are not based on a theory of learning. Consequently, there is little sense of meaning or coherence. The iDesk model is holistic. It connects thinking, feeling and doing. Finally, it links these faculties to the environment and the individual. Visual tools impact all areas of the iDesk model, and all components interact with each other. Serious schools need models.

CHAPTER THREE — THE KNOWLEDGE AGE

We are living in the knowledge age with a need for more knowledge workers. These new types of workers require new, extended mental skills and knowledge tools. Visual tools are central in creating and communicating knowledge. Schools need to learn from business theory and practice with regard to intellectual capital and the use of visual tools.

SECTION 2 — VISUALS

CHAPTER FOUR — VISUAL TOOLS AND COMPUTERS

We are learning that the use of computers can reinforce poor learning habits. The attraction of the screen can degenerate into visual 'candyfloss'. This turns computer users into consumers. Behind the screen lies a knowledge structure. Visual tools make this explicit and turn consumers into explorers of knowledge. Clarity about visual literacy will support this.

CHAPTER FIVE — VISUAL LITERACY

In our culture, the visual—verbal polarity may well be more divisive than the sciences—arts gulf. There are historical, philosophical reasons for the low value placed on visuals. Visual literacy, nonetheless, is an established discipline. All visual content exists in the spatial dimension. Space is our first and primary frontier. The spatial metaphor shapes our understanding.

CHAPTER SIX — TOOLS TO LEARN

The successes of our civilisation are based on tools. We have created these tools and they, in turn, end up shaping our behaviour. Using new tools causes new learning to take place. Habitual use of tools changes our habits. The most effective use of tools happens when accompanied with theory. Visual tools impact on learning habits. New eras need new tools.

SECTION 3 — MEANING

CHAPTER SEVEN — SCHEMAS

We all have schemas. They are personal and unique and are based on how we view the world. In business they are termed mental models. Their organisation represents how we think and shape our behaviour. All students have these mental maps but are unaware of them — as are teachers. Making schemas visible allows students and teachers to see what they are thinking.

CHAPTER EIGHT — HOLOGRAPHIC—LINEAR

Every day, every student, in every lesson has to turn linear communication (what she reads or hears) into what is termed her holographic understanding. Schemas are holographic in structure — definitely not linear. The student then has to turn her new, enlarged understanding back into linear format. This process has, until now, been an unknown phenomenon.

CHAPTER NINE — CONSTRUCTING KNOWLEDGE

All our students construct knowledge — even the very youngest and the least able. Knowledge cannot be delivered. It has to be created each time by the individual, for knowledge is created not discovered. This view of learning is called constructivism. Understanding this process stimulates teachers to make learning more meaningful and motivating for all students.

SECTION 4 — LANGUAGE

CHAPTER TEN — SUPPORT FOR LANGUAGE

It is normally thought that visuals 'compete' with words. With visual tools, this is not true. Visual tools exist in the overlapping area between words and pictures. If you examine language, you realise that images play a big part in stimulating thought and supporting planning. They help the organisation of our language, which normally has to take place in the unseen interior of our heads.

CHAPTER ELEVEN — READING

Reading is active. Readers' interrogation of text is shaped by their own schemas. They have to adapt their existing schemas in order to absorb text into meaningful messages. Visual tools can reveal the hidden structure and meaning of a text. Just as computer software can show you what your voice looks like, visual tools can show you what your thinking looks like.

CHAPTER TWELVE — WRITING

Writing is difficult. Students' difficulties and fears stem from not knowing what to write. Visual tools make planning explicit, easy and empowering. Through the use of visual tools, students can model the planning that excellent writers do 'in their heads'. Planning in linear fashion is too difficult for most. The schematic nature of visual tools matches the way the brain naturally works.

SECTION 5 — THINKING

CHAPTER THIRTEEN — THINKING SKILLS

When we think, we are either thinking of objects (in space) or events (in time). Our thoughts become 'thought—objects'. Just as we manipulate real, physical objects in space, so we move our 'thought—objects' in our inner space. This is thinking. It is, however, invisible and demands much short term memory. Visual tools make thinking visible, easier and obvious.

CHAPTER FOURTEEN — QUESTIONS

Questions are more powerful than answers. They directly determine our focus and thinking. Young children are wonderful questioners — young scientists. Schools have conditioned students to demand only questions. This severely limits their thinking and learning. Visual tools are themselves questions. They demand investigation. Their visible nature makes questioners of all students.

CHAPTER FIFTEEN — THINKING IN ACTION

There is a link between text, thinking and visual tools. The nature of different types of text (genres) demand different types of thinking. All thinking is the manipulation of 'thought—objects'. Visual tools show students what this looks like. Matching types of visual tools to specific genres and linking them to the National Curriculum thinking skills is a powerful matrix.

SECTION 6 — LEARNING

CHAPTER SIXTEEN — ACTIVE LEARNING

You don't have to leave your seat to be actively learning. Active doesn't mean kinaesthetic! Active learning involves becoming engrossed, relating new material to personal prior knowledge, and creating meaning. Active learning needs to be encouraged by teachers. It is what is demanded of business. Visual tools stimulate and challenge active learning from students.

CHAPTER SEVENTEEN — STYLES OF LEARNING

Learning style labels can be dangerous. They can limit rather than stimulate expansion. Behind their often surface description lies a common cognitive activity — putting the detail into the big picture. Visual tools meet the needs of all learners, involving them in visual, verbal, analytic and holistic thinking. They also promote the four essential skills of learning.

CHAPTER EIGHTEEN — ABILITY RANGE

We have many labels for our pupils — from the gifted and talented to SEN. Behind all these labels there lies the act of meaning making. Visual tools show students what understanding looks like. This gives confidence to them all. It allows the least able to see their intelligence and supports the more able to organise and communicate their sometimes erratic thinking.

SECTION 7 — LEXICON

CHAPTER NINETEEN — LEXICON

CATEGORIES OF VISUAL TOOLS

- structural thinking — Structural Visual Tools
- differential thinking — Differential Visual Tools
- representational thinking — Representational Visual Tools
- temporal thinking — Temporal Visual Tools
- causal thinking — Causal Visual Tools
- numerical thinking — Numerical Visual Tools
- organisational thinking — Organisational Visual Tools
- individual thinking — Individual Visual Tools

There are seven types of visual tools related to seven types of thinking. The eighth is a hybrid of all seven. Within each category, there is a variety of visual tools. Visual tools within the categories achieve slightly different results, at different levels of complexity to suit age, ability and the nature of the tasks set. Each visual tool is described, its workings explained and ideas given for introducing it to students. Differences between similar visual tools are clarified. Each visual tool is illustrated both in templated format and as a hand-drawn example in use. The context for each hand-drawn visual tool is a well known story.

CH1 | background | P13

CH2 | the iDesk model | P21

CH3 | the knowledge age | P27

overview

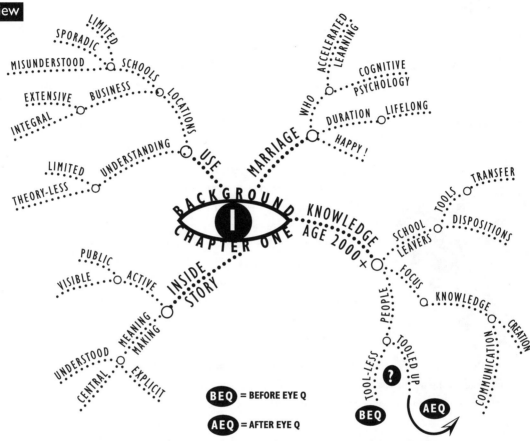

BEQ = BEFORE EYE Q

AEQ = AFTER EYE Q

preview

- We are all *Eye Q* experts – we just aren't aware of it yet.

- Human beings have always used visual tools and they are commonplace in cultures throughout the world.

- Whether conscious of the fact or not, we all devote most of our mental energy to visually interpreting our surroundings.

- Narrative stimulates the production of internal 'pictures' in the brain.

- History has shown that the capacity to interpret and represent the world through written language was largely restricted to the elite, who held power through their ability to access knowledge.

- Everyone needs to know how to create and use knowledge.

- *Eye Q* is a visual tool kit for life-long learning.

- Accelerated Learning gives us only part of the story about how we learn.

- Visual tools give us the 'inside story' of how learners construct meaning.

- The educational world is ready for, and needs, access to visual tools.

We are all *Eye Q* experts – we just aren't aware of it yet.

Look at something. Do it now. Look at something else. Keep doing this until you notice that a thought always follows visual attention. What you look at shapes your thoughts. What you look at acts as a visual cue for your thinking. *Eye Q* builds on what is natural – it brings to the surface natural thinking processes that are normally so deeply buried that we do not know we have them. *Eye Q* is a ground-breaking book!

structural visual tool | single bubble | lexicon link | page 152

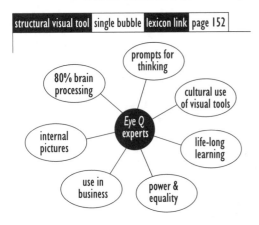

Human beings have always used visual tools and they are commonplace in cultures throughout the world.

No one knows where, or for what purpose, someone first got the idea of drawing a sketch. Perhaps it was drawn in order to communicate something to someone else, or to capture some thoughts that were personal to the individual. Historians believe that cave paintings were drawn not solely to represent but also to prompt or 'cue' thoughts. Things may not have changed that much. In the business world, particularly in Japan, the use of visual tools is an everyday occurrence. Visual tools are used for project development and management purposes, to plan and deliver presentations, as a Total Quality Management tool and for decision making and problem solving purposes.

Next time you walk down the high street or read a newspaper have a look at how visual structures are used in displays and advertisements to get across ideas and to conjure up desire. Advertisers know you do not have time to stand and read a long narrative. So they must use the limited attention time and space available to maximum advantage, if they are to communicate highly complex messages and emotions effectively. Consider the sheer volume of information that has been condensed into a few words and lines. Look at how the space has been used. As another example, think what a road atlas might look like if the information within it were represented not by icons, lines and single words but by linear text.

Typographers, along with information architects, illustrators and graphic artists, have mastered the use of visual and spatial relationships. They have learned how to use visual tools to help them grasp, and then communicate, complex ideas simply and effectively.

Whether conscious of the fact or not, we all devote most of our mental energy to visually interpreting our surroundings.

From the moment we are born, in order to survive, we need to make sense of our visual world. Even a blind person has to use other external senses to create internal 'visualisations'. Look around you now. It is likely that what you are looking at are objects – 'things' – and that you spend a lot of your time interacting with these 'things'. You too are, as far as the universe is concerned, a 'thing'.

As you will see in section 6, Thinking, we make sense of the visual world by discriminating (separating) and patterning (joining) aspects of the world around us. Some of the time our thinking is concerned with realities of everyday life. The remainder is spent forming virtual-world relationships and re-organising real-life experiences into virtual frameworks of interpretation in our heads. This is called thinking.

All of our time is spent building, re-organising and communicating these interpretations. All this is concerned with objects (either real or otherwise) and their interaction with each other. We operate and exist in a world that is visual, both externally and internally. That is why some scientists believe that around 80% of your brain is engaged in visual processing at any one time.

Narrative stimulates the production of internal 'pictures' in the brain.

This is corroborated by listeners' and readers' accounts following exposure to a passage of text, delivered either verbally or on paper. Those who reported creating internal 'pictures' during exposure showed greater understanding of the text than those who did not. Language becomes 'embodied' into visual frameworks. Using such frameworks, the 'picture makers' seem to grasp and respond to the text more fully – and, therefore, understand more – than those who do not create internal images. Conversely, good writers are adept at describing the images in their minds.

Eye Q argues that the formation of images and metaphors shapes our understanding and actions. Visual tools can make this process explicit and can help all learners access verbal linguistic territories that might otherwise be 'out of bounds'.

(For more detail on this, see chapters 5, 10, 11 and 12.)

History has shown that the capacity to interpret and represent the world through written language was largely restricted to the elite, who held power through their ability to access knowledge.

Throughout history, literacy has been the domain of, and a tool for, the minority in power. Where it was made available to the masses it was often used to persuade or indoctrinate, or to encourage views in support of the status quo. Illustrations were used to represent and reinforce the messages in the text. For the vast majority of the masses, however, the text itself was impenetrable. The language was unfamiliar, the surface grammar complex and the visual metaphors being represented by linear text inaccessible.

Theoretically, we are now entering an age of equality. However, within this age of equality, an inability to understand linear text continues to prevent some people from being 'equal' to those who have a good understanding.

Have you ever tried to read a legal document? Why is it that we never see visual tools used as part of any legal documentation? Courtroom juries, who go through days of linear dialogue, are asking for visual tools to be introduced to help them access and summarise the information being given. Read this paragraph again, this time thinking about learners in classrooms. The analogy is clear. The case for the prosecution is made.

Everyone needs to know how to create and use knowledge.

Individuals create knowledge from the stimuli, information and data that they receive. We need to be clear that this is an act of creation. Knowledge is not 'out there', waiting to be gathered up (see section 3, Meaning).

Furthermore, all learners need to know not only how to create knowledge but also how to use it, and how to communicate it effectively to others. The need for learners to know how to create, use and communicate knowledge is common to both education and business.

In their book examining best business practice, Nonaka and Takeuchi talk of the increased demand from companies for individuals that they describe as 'knowledge workers'. Such workers are able to turn information into knowledge and are able to communicate this knowledge effectively. Nonaka and Takeuchi make the distinction between workers being passive receivers and passers on of information and workers that are active and actually do something with information.

'[First] Knowledge, unlike information, is about beliefs and commitment. Knowledge is a function of a particular stance, perspective or intention. Second, knowledge, unlike information, is about action. It is always knowledge 'to some end'. And third, knowledge, unlike information, is about meaning. It is context specific and relational.'

I. Nonaka and H. Takeuchi (1995)

To enable learners to create knowledge from the linear information with which they are presented, we need to show them how to 'unlock the pictures' that are held within written and spoken texts. In this way, all learners can deal with the demand to be 'knowledge workers'. This demand will not be met unless visual tools are used, taught and modelled – not just in the business world but in all stages of education. The solution to the problem is to condense knowledge creation and knowledge communication into a visual format.

There is not as great a difference between visual formats and linear text as you might imagine. Both can say the same thing since both are representations of meaning. Visual tools are the 'open sesame!' of language.

Eye Q is a visual tool kit for life-long learning.

The tools to help learners to create knowledge are available but, until now, they have normally been used as something separate or as an 'extra' to linear text. In section 7, the visual tools are brought together as a 'lexicon' of techniques, which can be used as an intrinsic part of pre-school, school and post-school learning.

Teaching is a profession. A 'theory-less' profession is, after all, an oxymoron. Without a theory of learning, teaching becomes, at the very best, a weaker profession. Sometimes we resist listening to or attending to theory, believing perhaps that it is not relevant to the reality of classroom practice. In fact, theory and practice are intrinsically linked, as Edmiston, a thinking skills author, points out.

'Thinking skills are the practical outworkings of theory. When teachers can get a grip of the underlying theory, their teaching is transformed.'

A. Edmiston (2000)

In the 1960s and 1970s constructivism was a popular theory of learning, but by the late 1980s it had gone out of favour, perhaps because it was a 'tool-less' theory. *Eye Q* supports the return of constructivist theory. The difference is that now, by using visual tools, we can share with learners what the construction of knowledge looks like. *Eye Q* provides a theory for learning that gets to the heart of how we learn and successfully bridges the gap between theory and practice.

Accelerated Learning gives us only part of the story about how we learn.

Accelerated Learning is promoted under the banner of 'learning how to learn'. It places emphasis on developing stimulating environments and positive personal states in order to optimise learning. Charged by an interest in 'how

the brain works', schools have learned how to create visually stimulating environments. Teachers focus on creating safe and challenging cultures and on fostering self-esteem. Communication takes place in a multi-sensory way and accesses the multiple intelligences of students. Teachers have become experts at meeting learners' physiological needs and some have even integrated ambient music into learning.

These and other strategies certainly make learning more likely to happen. It is interesting to note, however, that while teachers are now focusing on the 'process of learning', the term 'Accelerated Learning' has not, so far, included any models of, or strategies for, the actual processes of thinking and learning that occur within the learner's mind. It does not provide a model of cognition.

Ask some colleagues what they understand by the term 'learning how to learn' or 'Accelerated Learning' and their answers will probably relate to the conditions for learning. In short, it is not strictly true to say that Accelerated Learning is about 'learning how to learn' – a more accurate description might be 'learning how to make learning more likely'.

Cognitive psychology tackles the inside story of how human beings create meaning for themselves.

Without an embedded and underlying theory of learning, the teaching profession will continue to look for 'quick fixes' or 'tips' that may have a limited shelf life and will continue to seek answers by constantly moving from one seemingly new idea to the next. As Guy Claxton of Bristol University points out:

> 'Clever mental techniques – devices that 'tap' the resources of the right hemisphere as if it were a barrel of beer – miss the point if they leave in place the same questing, restless attitude of mind.'
>
> *G. Claxton (1999)*

Visual tools give us the 'inside story' of how learners construct meaning.

Visual tools support a theory of learning called 'constructivism' (see section 3, Meaning). As the name suggests, constructivism asserts that meaning is something that learners 'build up' or create for themselves; meaning is not and cannot be 'given' by a teacher.

Some teaching methods can best be described as no more than 'dissemination of information' – the teacher talks and the learner is a passive receiver of a linear sequence of words. 'Active learning' is very different. As you will see in section 6, Learning, it has very little to do with physical action – that is, getting up and moving around. Rather, active learning is concerned with dialogue and interaction between teacher and learners. Visual tools make the private thinking of teachers and learners public and available to each other. They support interaction and active learning. They are the constructivist's tool kit.

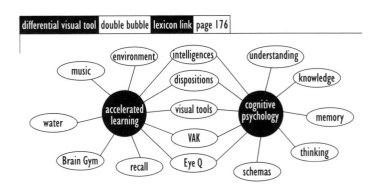

The educational world is ready for, and needs, access to visual tools.

It is time that the phrase 'learning how to learn' was examined – that the 'inside story' of learning was investigated. There is a missing set of tools that can do for the mind what Accelerated Learning has already done for the culture, environment and psycho-physical state of the learner.

The *Eye Q* tool kit is needed in schools now. Whether you are a manager, teacher or student you are involved in an organisation that specialises in understanding and ensuring that knowledge creation takes place. These tools are for you.

Although visual tools have been available for some time, until now they have lacked a rationale or theory for their use. They have not been organised in a consistent and accessible way. Through reading this book, you will understand the need for these tools, they will become accessible to you and – hopefully – you will transfer your personal learning back to your place of learning. You will increase your 'eye cue'!

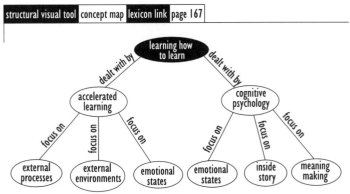

viewpoints

early literacy

'You could argue that map-making was one of the first and most distinctive forms of literacy ... It's a tremendously efficient way of recording complex information.'

S. Coughlan (2000)

cognitive repertoire

'The ability to distil out your everyday experience in useful maps and models of the world around us is very down-to-earth; so mundane that it is, in many ways, the unsung hero of the cognitive repertoire.'

G. Claxton (1997)

shaping perception

'Because (most) maps represent spatial information from a plain or oblique perspective and at a relatively small scale, they can afford a fundamentally different way of perceiving and thinking about spatial information than can be gained from direct experience in the world. For example, it is easier to conceive of a set of stars as forming a constellation if we first see the locations on a chart.'

D. Uttal and L. S. Tan (2000)

knowledge structures

'Teachers who help students to see the theories of knowledge which shape their subjects are not indulging in a philosophical luxury, some 'extra' for the very able. Quite the reverse.'

C. Counsell (2000)

visible and intelligible

'The visible and the intelligible are, indeed, virtually interchangeable and synonymous terms.'

D. E. Harding (1998)

visuals

'I have always thought it a pity that the world is run by literary blokes because the visual side is so much more powerful and constructive.'

E. de Bono (1996)

visual awareness

Next time you read the newspaper, go shopping or take a bus, heighten your visual awareness and wonder at the range, use and impact of visuals in contemporary culture.

internal cinema

Stop. Simply stop now. Notice how your mind wanders. Watch your own internal cinema as it joins objects, thoughts and events together for your personal viewing.

misunderstanding

The next time a child misunderstands you, consider the possibility that it is because she can't see what you are talking about.

visual–verbal relationship

The next time you read a book, notice how you form pictures in your mind. The next time you look at an image, notice how you form words in your mind. Visual tools operate in the domain where the visual and verbal overlap.

theory

What would you say if someone asked you 'How do children learn?' or 'How do children make sense of the world?' How useful for you, as a teacher, would it be if you had a theory of learning?

ROUTE MAP FOR YOUR READING

SECTION 1 — CONTEXT

CHAPTER ONE — BACKGROUND

The primary assertion is that we are all Eye Q experts. Throughout history, humans have used an assortment of visual tools to reflect and communicate knowledge. Current knowledge creation dynamics are based on this same notion. The 'inside story' of learning is obtained by looking both inside (cognitive psychology) and outside (Accelerated Learning).

CHAPTER TWO — THE iDESK MODEL

Most of our activities are not based on a theory of learning. Consequently, there is little sense of meaning or coherence. The iDesk model is holistic. It connects thinking, feeling and doing. Finally, it links these faculties to the environment and the individual. Visual tools impact all areas of the iDesk model, and all components interact with each other. Serious schools need models.

CHAPTER THREE — THE KNOWLEDGE AGE

We are living in the knowledge age with a need for more knowledge workers. These new types of workers require new, extended mental skills and knowledge tools. Visual tools are central in creating and communicating knowledge. Schools need to learn from business theory and practice with regard to intellectual capital and the use of visual tools.

SECTION 2 — VISUALS

CHAPTER FOUR — VISUAL TOOLS AND COMPUTERS

We are learning that the use of computers can reinforce poor learning habits. The attraction of the screen can degenerate into visual 'candyfloss'. This turns computer users into consumers. Behind the screen lies a knowledge structure. Visual tools make this explicit and turn consumers into explorers of knowledge. Clarity about visual literacy will support this.

CHAPTER FIVE — VISUAL LITERACY

In our culture, the visual–verbal polarity may well be more divisive than the sciences–arts gulf. There are historical, philosophical reasons for the low value placed on visuals. Visual literacy, nonetheless, is an established discipline. All visual content exists in the spatial dimension. Space is our first and primary frontier. The spatial metaphor shapes our understanding.

CHAPTER SIX — TOOLS TO LEARN

The successes of our civilisation are based on tools. We have created these tools and they, in turn, end up shaping our behaviour. Using new tools causes new learning to take place. Habitual use of tools changes our habits. The most effective use of tools happens when accompanied with theory. Visual tools impact on learning habits. New eras need new tools.

SECTION 3 — MEANING

CHAPTER SEVEN — SCHEMAS

We all have schemas. They are personal and unique and are based on how we view the world. In business they are termed mental models. Their organisation represents how we think and shape our behaviour. All students have these mental maps but are unaware of them — as are teachers. Making schemas visible allows students and teachers to see what they are thinking.

CHAPTER EIGHT — HOLOGRAPHIC–LINEAR

Every day, every student, in every lesson has to turn linear communication (what she reads or hears) into what is termed her holographic understanding. Schemas are holographic in structure — definitely not linear. The student then has to turn her new, enlarged understanding back into linear format. This process has, until now, been an unknown phenomenon.

CHAPTER NINE — CONSTRUCTING KNOWLEDGE

All our students construct knowledge — even the very youngest and the least able. Knowledge cannot be delivered. It has to be created each time by the individual, for knowledge is created not discovered. This view of learning is called constructivism. Understanding this process stimulates teachers to make learning more meaningful and motivating for all students.

SECTION 4 — LANGUAGE

CHAPTER TEN — SUPPORT FOR LANGUAGE

It is normally thought that visuals 'compete' with words. With visual tools, this is not true. Visual tools exist in the overlapping area between words and pictures. If you examine language, you realise that images play a big part in stimulating thought and supporting planning. They help the organisation of our language, which normally has to take place in the unseen interior of our heads.

CHAPTER ELEVEN — READING

Reading is active. Readers' interrogation of text is shaped by their own schemas. They have to adapt their existing schemas in order to absorb text into meaningful messages. Visual tools can reveal the hidden structure and meaning of a text. Just as computer software can show you what your voice looks like, visual tools can show you what your thinking looks like.

CHAPTER TWELVE — WRITING

Writing is difficult. Students' difficulties and fears stem from not knowing what to write. Visual tools make planning explicit, easy and empowering. Through the use of visual tools, students can model the planning that excellent writers do 'in their heads'. Planning in linear fashion is too difficult for most. The schematic nature of visual tools matches the way the brain naturally works.

SECTION 5 — THINKING

CHAPTER THIRTEEN — THINKING SKILLS

When we think, we are either thinking of objects (in space) or events (in time). Our thoughts become 'thought–objects'. Just as we manipulate real, physical objects in space, so we move our 'thought–objects' in our inner space. This is thinking. It is, however, invisible and demands much short term memory. Visual tools make thinking visible, easier and obvious.

CHAPTER FOURTEEN — QUESTIONS

Questions are more powerful than answers. They directly determine our focus and thinking. Young children are wonderful questioners — young scientists. Schools have conditioned students to demand only questions. This severely limits their thinking and learning. Visual tools are themselves questions. They demand investigation. Their visible nature makes questioners of all students.

CHAPTER FIFTEEN — THINKING IN ACTION

There is a link between text, thinking and visual tools. The nature of different types of text (genres) demand different types of thinking. All thinking is the manipulation of 'thought–objects'. Visual tools show students what this looks like. Matching types of visual tools to specific genres and linking them to the National Curriculum thinking skills is a powerful matrix.

SECTION 6 — LEARNING

CHAPTER SIXTEEN — ACTIVE LEARNING

You don't have to leave your seat to be actively learning. Active doesn't mean kinaesthetic! Active learning involves becoming engrossed, relating new material to personal prior knowledge, and creating meaning. Active learning needs to be encouraged by teachers. It is what is demanded of business. Visual tools stimulate and challenge active learning from students.

CHAPTER SEVENTEEN — STYLES OF LEARNING

Learning style labels can be dangerous. They can limit rather than stimulate expansion. Behind their often surface description lies a common cognitive activity — putting the detail into the big picture. Visual tools meet the needs of all learners, involving them in visual, verbal, analytic and holistic thinking. They also promote the four essential skills of learning.

CHAPTER EIGHTEEN — ABILITY RANGE

We have many labels for our pupils — from the gifted and talented to SEN. Behind all these labels there lies the act of meaning making. Visual tools show students what understanding looks like. This gives confidence to them all. It allows the least able to see their intelligence and supports the more able to organise and communicate their sometimes erratic thinking.

SECTION 7 — LEXICON

CHAPTER NINETEEN — LEXICON

CATEGORIES OF VISUAL TOOLS

- structural thinking — Structural Visual Tools
- differential thinking — Differential Visual Tools
- representational thinking — Representational Visual Tools
- temporal thinking — Temporal Visual Tools
- causal thinking — Causal Visual Tools
- numerical thinking — Numerical Visual Tools
- organisational thinking — Organisational Visual Tools
- individual thinking — Individual Visual Tools

There are seven types of visual tools related to seven types of thinking. The eighth is a hybrid of all seven. Within each category, there is a variety of visual tools. Visual tools within the categories achieve slightly different results, at different levels of complexity to suit age, ability and the nature of the tasks set. Each visual tool is described, its workings explained and ideas given for introducing it to students. Differences between similar visual tools are clarified. Each visual tool is illustrated both in templated format and as a hand-drawn example in use. The context for each hand-drawn visual tool is a well known story.

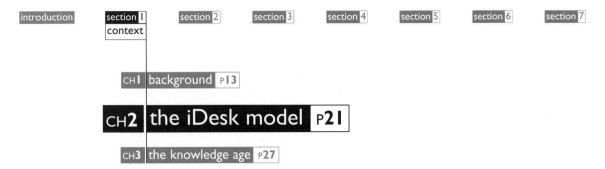

CH1 background P13

CH2 the iDesk model P21

CH3 the knowledge age P27

overview

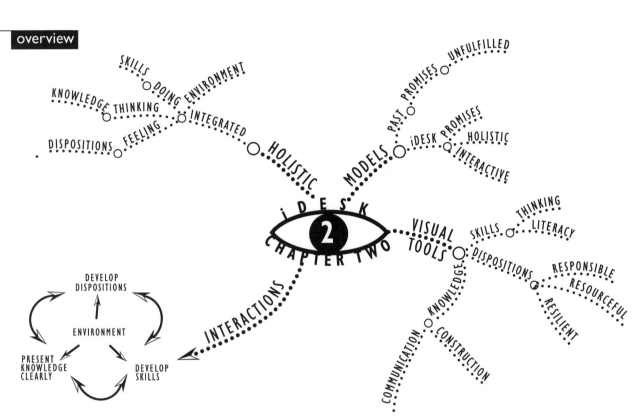

preview

■ There is a lack of a model of learning to make coherent sense of the developments in education.

■ We have all learned to chant the mantra 'make connections' to our learners, but our initiatives don't connect.

■ Models should be built on a holistic view of learners.

■ The iDesk model integrates learners' faculties and their environment.

■ The constituent parts of the iDesk model interact with each other.

■ Students need to understand what understanding is and how to achieve it.

■ Visual tools impact all areas of the iDesk model.

■ There are implications for schools that take learning seriously.

There is a lack of a model of learning to make coherent sense of the developments in education.

Schools are developing rapidly. They respond to government initiatives as well as exploring new approaches such

as Accelerated Learning, emotional intelligence, thinking skills, educational kinesiology, multiple intelligences and so on. Yet, there doesn't seem to be a model into which these developments fit.

Initiatives from the government are heavily slanted towards encouraging students to build up their knowledge, with some emphasis on skills. Accelerated Learning – an umbrella term for many learning strategies – emphasises the importance of environment and childrens' dispositions to learning. The use of visual tools places great emphasis on both skills *and* knowledge.

Schools are 'collecting' these developments, but without a model with which to integrate them. It is hard to imagine how they form a coherent strategy towards a holistic and intelligible vision of learning.

We have all learned to chant the mantra 'make connections' to our learners, but our initiatives don't connect.

Learning, you have come to realise, is about making connections. You feel reassured that the research coming out from neuroscience is validating this realisation. Students are exhorted, coached and trained in making links and relationships between discrete pieces of information. Such conceptual links are the very basis of meaning and understanding.

If, however, schools were to be questioned about the conceptual connections between their developments and projects, and were asked to articulate those connections against a known and well-communicated model of learning, how would they do? Are the relative values of proposed developments discussed against such a model of learning? Do audits evaluate the contributions of projects against a balanced development towards this model of learning?

Models should be built on a holistic view of learners.

Learners, being human beings, engage in thinking, feeling and acting. That, after all, is what we humans do. And we do it in classrooms. Any education that does not address these three human forms of learning will produce

unbalanced and, often, disengaged and disenchanted learners. By engaging and integrating all three, learning can become a meaningful experience. The basis for this reasoning is very simple – treat students as human beings, addressing the domains of experience particular to all human beings, and you are more likely to get a balanced, integrated and satisfied response from the students.

In addition to thinking, feeling and acting, students operate in specific environments. These environments have profound influences on childrens' thoughts, feelings and actions. Included in the term 'environment' are classrooms, the local community, the school premises in general, and – above all – the adults in them.

The results of this interaction of the environment with students' thinking, feeling and acting are the individual experiences of each student. And, we must always

remember, it is only individuals who create knowledge. Not institutions, cohorts or year groups, but individuals. This is vital to accept if you are fully to appreciate the assertion of Joseph Novak, a long-time promoter of an integrated model of learning:

> '... the central purpose of education is to empower learners to take charge of their own meaning making. Meaning making involves thinking, feeling, and acting, and all three of these aspects must be integrated for significant new learning, and especially new knowledge creation.'
>
> *J. D. Novak (1998)*

The iDesk model integrates learners' faculties and their environment.

The iDesk model brings all these fundamental aspects of learning together into a simple model of learning. You will see that the individual is central and around her are the three human domains of experience – thinking, feeling and acting. Other terms can be substituted for thinking, feeling and acting. 'Thinking' can be represented by the concept of 'knowledge'. 'Feeling' can be represented by the concept of 'disposition'. 'Acting' can be represented by the concept of 'skills'. They all operate within an environment – an ecology – which interacts with the individual.

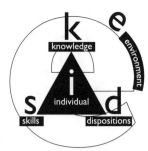

Hold on, you may be saying at this point! This all sounds very familiar. Isn't this model just a re-hash of our traditional 'knowledge, skills and understanding'? And didn't Sir Christopher Ball cleverly turn it around by calling it the ASK curriculum, where A stood for 'attitude' (the most important, and substitute term for 'understanding'), S for 'skills' and K for 'knowledge'?

Yes – certainly, this model has resonance in other theories. The iDesk model, however, makes clearer the basis for the trio of human faculties, and it relates them to the environment that shapes and responds to them.

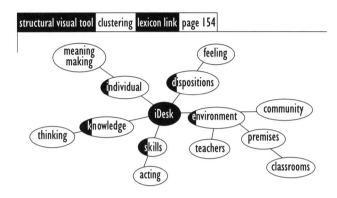

structural visual tool | clustering | lexicon link | page 154

The constituent parts of the iDesk model interact with each other.

There is a dynamic between the elements of the iDesk model. It is this interaction that holds much promise in evaluating the impact of various developments in schools on the individual learner.

When a learner is well disposed to learning, the learning of skills and the creation of knowledge are positively and fundamentally affected. When a poorly disposed learner manages to learn new skills, her confidence rises and her disposition to learn regains some of its natural enthusiasm. When knowledge is presented in an ordered, structured and attractive way, the disinclined learner can become more disposed to learning.

While the last point may not seem very likely, research has proved the effectiveness of this interrelation. Jere Brophy (1998) has surveyed much research showing that teachers' structuring of knowledge is highly motivational to students. They value it when key concepts are readily identified and the relevance of the content communicated is made explicit. Perhaps surprisingly, these strategies are more popular and motivating than teachers' attempts to entertain, and to 'dumb-down' the content.

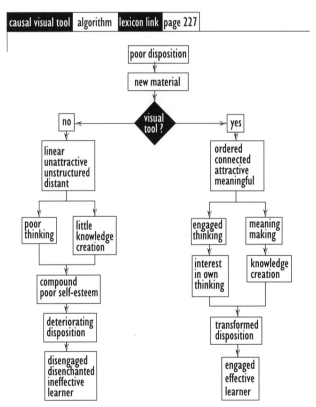

causal visual tool | algorithm | lexicon link | page 227

Students need to understand what understanding is and how to achieve it.

When students understand something, they don't know what it was they did in order to understand it – which means that when they later come across new material they don't understand, they haven't got a known strategy with which to work on it. This causes enormous problems for children. They close down their exploration and risk-taking in terms of forming hypotheses about the new material. Worse still, as Carol Dweck (1995) has amply researched, they create negative judgements about their worth based on unvoiced, internal and unconscious theories about intelligence.

However, if students knew what they did when they successfully understood new material, they would have the confidence to repeat, elaborate or modify their strategy. Visual tools are not only a strategy for understanding, they are a strategy made *visible*. Students can literally *see* what they do in order to understand new material.

This awareness of what is entailed in successful learning is called metacognition. As Jane Healy makes clear, metacognition involves:

'... 'strategies', the mental processes that learners can deliberately recruit to help themselves learn or understand something new.'

J. M. Healy (1999)

This is probably not new to you. Back in the 1970s, Jerome Bruner claimed that:

'Children should be at least as self-conscious about their strategies of thought as they are about their attempts to commit things to memory. They should be conscious, too, of the tools of thought – causal explanation, categorisation, and the rest.'

J. S. Bruner (1971)

Visual tools impact all areas of the iDesk model.

Esteemed as Jerome Bruner is, and as insightful as his writings are, we are still hearing the plea for metacognition decades later. How will students ever achieve it if they cannot see their strategies at work?

Visual tools are strategies made visible. When students are competent and confident in a range of visual tools, they are fearless in the face of new material. They know that they have previously been successful in deconstructing new material to identify the key concepts. They know they have a set of cognitive tools that work. They know they will work again. This confidence allows students to ride the edges of their comfort zones.

Intelligence is like a muscle that grows with exercise (Claxton, 1999). Like the tools in a gym, used to increase muscular strength, so visual tools increase thinking strength. Students armed with a set of thinking tools reinforce their belief systems, and become well disposed to learning. They grasp the structures of knowledge and feel familiar with such notions – because they can see them.

There are implications for schools that take learning seriously.

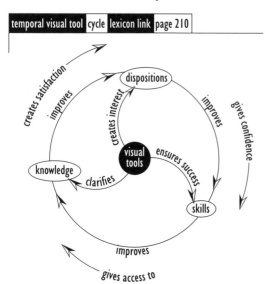

temporal visual tool | cycle | lexicon link | page 210

If you want to see your students develop positive intellectual dispositions and skills in the creation of personal knowledge, then you have got to engage in the same process as your students. You must:

'... maintain an open window on your own thinking processes. Reveal – vocalise – your own thinking ... What you model in the classroom will have the dominant impact on students.'

G. A. Woditsch (1991)

Schools have to consistently, coherently and continuously promote the explicit nature of understanding and thinking. They must give teachers and students the language with which to communicate and internalise crucial distinctions. This language must stem from a model of learning that integrates all aspects of human experience. Visual tools offer an unparalleled opportunity to promote the nature of thinking in this way.

connections

'There is general agreement about what needs to be done to enable students to construct meaningful knowledge ... content needs to be represented as networks of connected information structured around powerful ideas.'

J. Brophy (1998)

considering alternatives

'Deliberately employing mapping tools causes us to restrain our impulsivity, to suspend our judgements, to generate and consider alternatives, and to attend empathically to others' perspectives.'

A. L. Costa (1996)

mediators

'Tools serve as mediational means, i.e. they – metaphorically speaking – stand between the individual and the world.'

R. Saljo (1998)

chess masters

'... the superior playing skills of chess masters stem from their ability to perceive the chess board as an organised whole rather than as a collection of individual pieces.'

A. Baddeley (1994)

knowledge

'Information ... is acquired by being told, whereas knowledge can be acquired by thinking.'

T. Roszak (1986)

review

initiatives

Draw four columns on a sheet of paper. Label them Dispositions, Environment, Skills and Knowledge. Now consider the extent to which initiatives in your school are impacting on them. Map them out.

research

Start to consider what impact Brophy's and Dweck's research could have on your classroom practice. How might visual tools help you in responding positively to it?

not knowing

Are your students happy about not knowing or not understanding something? What impact might having a tool kit available have on their confidence to approach new, difficult material?

strategies

What strategies and tools do your students currently have available to them for the learning process?

modelling

Start to consider, as you read through the rest of the book, how you might model the use of visual tools in your classroom.

ROUTE MAP FOR YOUR READING

SECTION 1 — CONTEXT

CHAPTER ONE BACKGROUND
The primary assertion is that we are all *Eye Q* experts. Throughout history, humans have used an assortment of visual tools to reflect and communicate knowledge. Current knowledge creation dynamics are based on this same notion. The 'inside story' of learning is obtained by looking both inside (cognitive psychology) and outside (Accelerated Learning).

CHAPTER TWO THE iDESK MODEL
Most of our activities are not based on a theory of learning. Consequently, there is little sense of meaning or coherence. The iDesk model is holistic. It connects thinking, feeling and doing. Finally, it links these faculties to the environment and the individual. Visual tools impact all areas of the iDesk model, and all components interact with each other. Serious schools need models.

CHAPTER THREE THE KNOWLEDGE AGE
We are living in the knowledge age with a need for more knowledge workers. These new types of workers require new, extended mental skills and knowledge tools. Visual tools are central in creating and communicating knowledge. Schools need to learn from business theory and practice with regard to intellectual capital and the use of visual tools.

SECTION 2 — VISUALS

CHAPTER FOUR VISUAL TOOLS AND COMPUTERS
We are learning that the use of computers can reinforce poor learning habits. The attraction of the screen can degenerate into visual 'candyfloss'. This turns computer users into consumers. Behind the screen lies a knowledge structure. Visual tools make this explicit and turn consumers into explorers of knowledge. Clarity about visual literacy will support this.

CHAPTER FIVE VISUAL LITERACY
In our culture, the visual–verbal polarity may well be more divisive than the sciences–arts gulf. There are historical, philosophical reasons for the low value placed on visuals. Visual literacy, nonetheless, is an established discipline. All visual content exists in the spatial dimension. Space is our first and primary frontier. The spatial metaphor shapes our understanding.

CHAPTER SIX TOOLS TO LEARN
The successes of our civilisation are based on tools. We have created these tools and they, in turn, end up shaping our behaviour. Using new tools causes new learning to take place. Habitual use of tools changes our habits. The most effective use of tools happens when accompanied with theory. Visual tools impact on learning habits. New eras need new tools.

SECTION 3 — MEANING

CHAPTER SEVEN SCHEMAS
We all have schemas. They are personal and unique and are based on how we view the world. In business they are termed mental models. Their organisation represents how we think and shape our behaviour. All students have these mental maps but are unaware of them — as are teachers. Making schemas visible allows students and teachers to see what they are thinking.

CHAPTER EIGHT HOLOGRAPHIC—LINEAR
Every day, every student, in every lesson has to turn linear communication (what she reads or hears) into what is termed her holographic understanding. Schemas are holographic in structure — definitely not linear. The student then has to turn her new, enlarged understanding back into linear format. This process has, until now, been an unknown phenomenon.

CHAPTER NINE CONSTRUCTING KNOWLEDGE
All our students construct knowledge — even the very youngest and the least able. Knowledge cannot be delivered. It has to be created each time by the individual, for knowledge is created not discovered. This view of learning is called constructivism. Understanding this process stimulates teachers to make learning more meaningful and motivating for all students.

SECTION 4 — LANGUAGE

CHAPTER TEN SUPPORT FOR LANGUAGE
It is normally thought that visuals 'compete' with words. With visual tools, this is not true. Visual tools exist in the overlapping area between words and pictures. If you examine language, you realise that images play a big part in stimulating thought and supporting planning. They help the organisation of our language, which normally has to take place in the unseen interior of our heads.

CHAPTER ELEVEN READING
Reading is active. Readers' interrogation of text is shaped by their own schemas. They have to adapt their existing schemas in order to absorb text into meaningful messages. Visual tools can reveal the hidden structure and meaning of a text. Just as computer software can show you what your voice looks like, visual tools can show you what your thinking looks like.

CHAPTER TWELVE WRITING
Writing is difficult. Students' difficulties and fears stem from not knowing what to write. Visual tools make planning explicit, easy and empowering. Through the use of visual tools, students can model the planning that excellent writers do 'in their heads'. Planning in linear fashion is too difficult for most. The schematic nature of visual tools matches the way the brain naturally works.

SECTION 5 — THINKING

CHAPTER THIRTEEN THINKING SKILLS
When we think, we are either thinking of objects (in space) or events (in time). Our thoughts become 'thought–objects'. Just as we manipulate real, physical objects in space, so we move our 'thought–objects' in our inner space. This is thinking. It is, however, invisible and demands much short term memory. Visual tools make thinking visible, easier and obvious.

CHAPTER FOURTEEN QUESTIONS
Questions are more powerful than answers. They directly determine our focus and thinking. Young children are wonderful questioners — young scientists. Schools have conditioned students to demand only questions. This severely limits their thinking and learning. Visual tools are themselves questions. They demand investigation. Their visible nature makes questioners of all students.

CHAPTER FIFTEEN THINKING IN ACTION
There is a link between text, thinking and visual tools. The nature of different types of text (genres) demand different types of thinking. All thinking is the manipulation of 'thought–objects'. Visual tools show students what this looks like. Matching types of visual tools to specific genres and linking them to the National Curriculum thinking skills is a powerful matrix.

SECTION 6 — LEARNING

CHAPTER SIXTEEN ACTIVE LEARNING
You don't have to leave your seat to be actively learning. Active doesn't mean kinaesthetic! Active learning involves becoming engrossed, relating new material to personal prior knowledge, and creating meaning. Active learning needs to be encouraged by teachers. It is what is demanded of business. Visual tools stimulate and challenge active learning from students.

CHAPTER SEVENTEEN STYLES OF LEARNING
Learning style labels can be dangerous. They can limit rather than stimulate expansion. Behind their often surface description lies a common cognitive activity — putting the detail into the big picture. Visual tools meet the needs of all learners, involving them in visual, verbal, analytic and holistic thinking. They also promote the four essential skills of learning.

CHAPTER EIGHTEEN ABILITY RANGE
We have many labels for our pupils — from the gifted and talented to SEN. Behind all these labels there lies the act of meaning making. Visual tools show students what understanding looks like. This gives confidence to them all. It allows the least able to see their intelligence and supports the more able to organise and communicate their sometimes erratic thinking.

SECTION 7 — LEXICON

CHAPTER NINETEEN LEXICON

CATEGORIES OF VISUAL TOOLS

- structural thinking — Structural Visual Tools
- differential thinking — Differential Visual Tools
- representational thinking — Representational Visual Tools
- temporal thinking — Temporal Visual Tools
- causal thinking — Causal Visual Tools
- numerical thinking — Numerical Visual Tools
- organisational thinking — Organisational Visual Tools
- individual thinking — Individual Visual Tools

There are seven types of visual tools related to seven types of thinking. The eighth is a hybrid of all seven. Within each category, there is a variety of visual tools. Visual tools within the categories achieve slightly different results, at different levels of complexity to suit age, ability and the nature of the tasks set. Each visual tool is described, its workings explained and ideas given for introducing it to students. Differences between similar visual tools are clarified. Each visual tool is illustrated both in templated format and as a hand-drawn example in use. The context for each hand-drawn visual tool is a well known story.

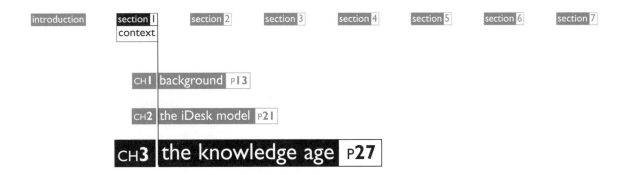
overview

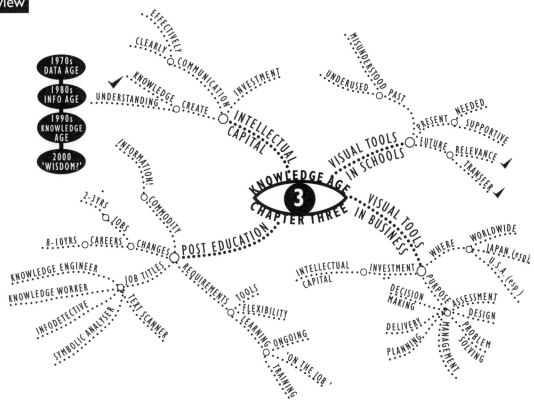

preview

- Knowledge is the gold that we try to distil from teachers and students in schools.

- Visual tools reflect our use of language.

- Visual tools are already an established part of business practice and of our everyday culture.

- Twenty-first century knowledge workers need tools to help them create knowledge.

- Knowledge workers need mental knowledge tools to increase their value to their organisation.

- Tools simplify and make obvious knowledge creation processes and enable them to be shared effectively.

- In education we need to model or mirror what the business world already does and knows.

Knowledge is the gold that we try to distil from teachers and students in schools.

We all have more information than is useful to us. Information needs to be organised in order that it can be understood. It then becomes knowledge and only then does is it powerful and valuable.

Nonaka and Takeuchi (1995), in their seminal book *The Knowledge Creating Company*, predict that organisations that learn how best to utilise knowledge will be the most successful in the twenty-first century. As Czerniawska puts it:

'... knowledge is, in effect, the gold which organisations – rather like 16th Century alchemists – are trying to distil from the raw materials of their organisation.'

F. Czerniawska (1997)

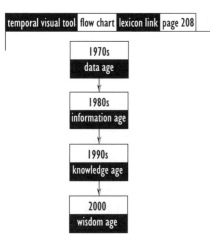

temporal visual tool flow chart lexicon link page 208

1970s
data age

1980s
information age

1990s
knowledge age

2000
wisdom age

The organisations that best harness this capacity to turn information into knowledge and understanding will be deemed to be wise.

The challenge for education is firstly to harness the knowledge-creating potential of its staff and students, and secondly to show them how to use not just what they know but how they know. Visual tools help you share what you know you know. Sometimes visual tools can even help you articulate and share what you did not know you knew!

Visual tools reflect our use of language.

The Japanese, in particular, are leading the way in using visual tools. This is not surprising when we realise that physical and concrete images of objects are indispensable for Japanese expression. As Nonaka and Takeuchi explain:

'An essential epistemological pattern for the Japanese is to think visually and manipulate tangible images. These images, irrespective of whether they belong in the world of reality or the imagination, are all realistic to the speaker because they exist as a reality within the mind of the speaker the moment they are spoken. Even when the speaker narrates a past experience, the concrete images of the experience are revived within himself or herself.'

I. Nonaka and H. Takeuchi (1995)

Put simply, the Japanese language is characterised by visual concepts that are highly context-specific in terms of both time and space. As explained in section 5, Thinking, Japanese language closely reflects the way all human beings think in order to make sense of their world.

Visual tools are an established part of Japanese business culture. The Japanese use visual tools for self-assessment, for collaborative decision-making and to help them build highly visual information management and knowledge creation systems.

Children come to school with a very similar profile of visual–verbal inter-relationship. The current system tends not to address this but, instead, lead children into a linear way of learning, based almost entirely on words.

Visual tools are already an established part of business practice and of our everyday culture.

Model mapping is commonly used to aid the problem-solving and decision-making process. It is widely used by managers for planning and delivering presentations and for the management of meetings. Companies use mapping software for interactive conferencing.

In newspapers, on billboards and in shops, we see advertisers use visual tools to capture our attention and explain relatively complex ideas in a few seconds. Flowscapes are used by manufacturers as part of their product design process. Venn diagrams and double bubble maps are used to show and identify similarities and differences among individuals and client groups. Flow charts and fishbone diagrams are used to plan and manage multi-agency projects. Systems diagrams are used by organisations wanting to examine how effectively the individual parts of the system are working together. (All these tools are described in detail in section 7, from page 143 onwards.)

Visual tools are being used in some schools, especially in the USA and Japan, but their application is limited through a misunderstanding of their nature. Consequently, their use can degenerate into templated worksheets.

Twenty-first century knowledge workers need tools to help them create knowledge.

Predictions made in the 1970s are coming true. In the next decade students leaving education can expect to change their jobs every two to three years and their careers every eight to ten. Workers in the twenty-first century, more than ever before, will be dealing with information. There will be more of it than ever, coming faster than ever, from a wider range of sources. To avoid information overload, or information anxiety, workers will have to develop strategies to deal with the onslaught.

In education we can gain some sense of what will be required of our charges by observing the language being used to describe the twenty-first century workforce (Stewart, 1998). Tell your students that they will be 'info detectives', 'knowledge workers', 'knowledge engineers' and 'symbolic analysis workers' and gauge their reaction! Tell them that they will need to become expert 'text scanners', 'information managers', team players and learners who embrace change and welcome 'reframing'. They will be expected and required to learn not just in the training room or on external courses but in the workplace, and in their life generally. Their employer will see their competencies, capabilities, skills and strategic assets as the source of sustainable competitive advantage. Ask them if they might be interested in some tools to help them achieve all this!

Knowledge workers need mental knowledge tools to increase their value to their organisation.

Businesses are investing heavily in building up what they call their 'intellectual capital'. Intellectual capital has two parts to its definition. Part one is 'the capacity to turn discreet pieces of data or information or stimulus into knowledge and understanding'. Part two is 'the capacity to communicate this new knowledge effectively to others'.

Businesses regard the ability to unleash their employees' intellectual capital as the key to success. The link to visual tools is made clear by Stewart, a business writer, when he argues that:

> 'Intelligence becomes an asset when some useful order is created out of free floating brain power – that is, when it is captured in a way that allows it to be described, shared and exploited; and when it can be deployed to do something that could not be done if it remained scattered around like so many coins in the gutter.'
>
> *T. A. Stewart (1998)*

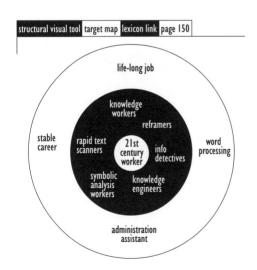

structural visual tool | target map | lexicon link | page 150

The use of visual tools in the business world is commonplace because businesses have realised that visual tools support them in increasing their intellectual capital. In education we need to do the same.

Tools simplify and make obvious knowledge creation processes and enable them to be shared effectively.

Visual tools show and reflect what we do, cognitively, when we understand. In section 3, Meaning, and in section 5, Thinking, you will have an opportunity to develop your understanding in this area. Visual tools give the learner a way forward when confronted, and confused, by new material. Confusion is an unwillingness to simply accept that you do not know what to do, or where to start – as Guy Claxton puts it:

'... learning is what you learn to do when you do not know what to do'.

G. Claxton (1999)

We all like to know what to do. Visual tools bring what we do in a state of unconscious competence into the domain of consciousness. More importantly, a visual tool kit is a place to go when we do not know what to do. Businesses have visual tool kits – so should education.

In education we need to model or mirror what the business world already does and knows.

Look at the first part of the definition of intellectual capital again – 'the capacity to turn discreet pieces of data or information or stimulus into knowledge and understanding'. Isn't this exactly what teachers, through exploration and explanation, support students in doing?

Now look at the second part again – 'the capacity to communicate this new knowledge effectively to others'. Isn't this exactly what teachers ask learners to do in schools?

Visual tools address both parts, by both helping learners to create knowledge from the information they receive, and making this process explicit, available and understandable to others.

Business writers Clarke and Clegg argue that:

'In knowledge-based business, learning and innovation are the critical drivers of business development.'

T. Clarke and S. Clegg (2000)

The same can surely be said for schools. Visual tools bridge the gap between school and work. The tools needed by workers in the twenty-first century are not hand tools – twenty-first century workers need mental knowledge tools.

viewpoints

data

'Data, data everywhere, but not a thought to think.'

T. Roszak (1986)

information overload

'Managers and professionals need to develop strategies to cope with information overload. They must stop gathering information just because it is available, and remember that learning creates knowledge and that we learn for a purpose.'

M. Funes and N. Johnson (1998)

tools

'Unless students have a tool kit of thinking and problem-solving skills which match the feast of information so readily available, they may emerge from their meal bloated with techno-garbage, information junk food.'

M. McKenzie (1996)

life-long tools

'... these [visual tools] are not merely tools for students to use today but in their future lives.'

D. Hyerle (2000)

assimilation

'Our dominant objective must be to teach for map learning. We must help our students relate the material they need to know to what they already know.'

R. N. Caine and G. Caine (1991)

environment

'Visual information, as much as language, is part of that environment with which the whole person (mind and body) interacts.'

M. Lake (1994)

cause and effect

'The old common sense was an understanding of cause and effect in the complicated world of discrete events. The next common sense is a description of cause and effect in a world of interweavings.'

M. Lissack and J. Roos (1999)

review

visual tools
How wide is the use of visual tools in your school?

post school
How prepared are your students for an adult world in which the use of visual tools is becoming increasingly commonplace?

the bridge to work
Start to consider the possibility that visual tools are a very practical way of bridging the gap between school and work practices.

intellectual capital
What would increased access to visual tools do to your school's intellectual capital (that includes you, by the way)?

ROUTE MAP FOR YOUR READING

SECTION 1 — CONTEXT

CHAPTER ONE BACKGROUND
The primary assertion is that we are all Eye Q experts. Throughout history, humans have used an assortment of visual tools to reflect and communicate knowledge. Current knowledge creation dynamics are based on this same notion. The 'inside story' of learning is obtained by looking both inside (cognitive psychology) and outside (Accelerated Learning).

CHAPTER TWO THE iDESK MODEL
Most of our activities are not based on a theory of learning. Consequently, there is little sense of meaning or coherence. The iDesk model is holistic. It connects thinking, feeling and doing. Finally, it links these faculties to the environment and the individual. Visual tools impact all areas of the iDesk model, and all components interact with each other. Serious schools need models.

CHAPTER THREE THE KNOWLEDGE AGE
We are living in the knowledge age with a need for more knowledge workers. These new types of workers require new, extended mental skills and knowledge tools. Visual tools are central in creating and communicating knowledge. Schools need to learn from business theory and practice with regard to intellectual capital and the use of visual tools.

SECTION 2 — VISUALS

CHAPTER FOUR VISUAL TOOLS AND COMPUTERS
We are learning that the use of computers can reinforce poor learning habits. The attraction of the screen can degenerate into visual 'candyfloss'. This turns computer users into consumers. Behind the screen lies a knowledge structure. Visual tools make this explicit and turn consumers into explorers of knowledge. Clarity about visual literacy will support this.

CHAPTER FIVE VISUAL LITERACY
In our culture, the visual—verbal polarity may well be more divisive than the sciences—arts gulf. There are historical, philosophical reasons for the low value placed on visuals. Visual literacy, nonetheless, is an established discipline. All visual content exists in the spatial dimension. Space is our first and primary frontier. The spatial metaphor shapes our understanding.

CHAPTER SIX TOOLS TO LEARN
The successes of our civilisation are based on tools. We have created these tools and they, in turn, end up shaping our behaviour. Using new tools causes new learning to take place. Habitual use of tools changes our habits. The most effective use of tools happens when accompanied with theory. Visual tools impact on learning habits. New eras need new tools.

SECTION 3 — MEANING

CHAPTER SEVEN SCHEMAS
We all have schemas. They are personal and unique and are based on how we view the world. In business they are termed mental models. Their organisation represents how we think and shape our behaviour. All students have these mental maps but are unaware of them — as are teachers. Making schemas visible allows students and teachers to see what they are thinking.

CHAPTER EIGHT HOLOGRAPHIC—LINEAR
Every day, every student, in every lesson has to turn linear communication (what she reads or hears) into what is termed her holographic understanding. Schemas are holographic in structure — definitely not linear. The student then has to turn her new, enlarged understanding back into linear format. This process has, until now, been an unknown phenomenon.

CHAPTER NINE CONSTRUCTING KNOWLEDGE
All our students construct knowledge — even the very youngest and the least able. Knowledge cannot be delivered. It has to be created each time by the individual, for knowledge is created not discovered. This view of learning is called constructivism. Understanding this process stimulates teachers to make learning more meaningful and motivating for all students.

SECTION 4 — LANGUAGE

CHAPTER TEN SUPPORT FOR LANGUAGE
It is normally thought that visuals 'compete' with words. With visual tools, this is not true. Visual tools exist in the overlapping area between words and pictures. If you examine language, you realise that images play a big part in stimulating thought and supporting planning. They help the organisation of our language, which normally has to take place in the unseen interior of our heads.

CHAPTER ELEVEN READING
Reading is active. Readers' interrogation of text is shaped by their own schemas. They have to adapt their existing schemas in order to absorb text into meaningful messages. Visual tools can reveal the hidden structure and meaning of a text. Just as computer software can show you what your voice looks like, visual tools can show you what your thinking looks like.

CHAPTER TWELVE WRITING
Writing is difficult. Students' difficulties and fears stem from not knowing what to write. Visual tools make planning explicit, easy and empowering. Through the use of visual tools, students can model the planning that excellent writers do 'in their heads'. Planning in linear fashion is too difficult for most. The schematic nature of visual tools matches the way the brain naturally works.

SECTION 5 — THINKING

CHAPTER THIRTEEN THINKING SKILLS
When we think, we are either thinking of objects (in space) or events (in time). Our thoughts become 'thought—objects'. Just as we manipulate real, physical objects in space, so we move our 'thought—objects' in our inner space. This is thinking. It is, however, invisible and demands much short term memory. Visual tools make thinking visible, easier and obvious.

CHAPTER FOURTEEN QUESTIONS
Questions are more powerful than answers. They directly determine our focus and thinking. Young children are wonderful questioners — young scientists. Schools have conditioned students to demand only questions. This severely limits their thinking and learning. Visual tools are themselves questions. They demand investigation. Their visible nature makes questioners of all students.

CHAPTER FIFTEEN THINKING IN ACTION
There is a link between text, thinking and visual tools. The nature of different types of text (genres) demand different types of thinking. All thinking is the manipulation of 'thought—objects'. Visual tools show students what this looks like. Matching types of visual tools to specific genres and linking them to the National Curriculum thinking skills is a powerful matrix.

SECTION 6 — LEARNING

CHAPTER SIXTEEN ACTIVE LEARNING
You don't have to leave your seat to be actively learning. Active doesn't mean kinaesthetic! Active learning involves becoming engrossed, relating new material to personal prior knowledge, and creating meaning. Active learning needs to be encouraged by teachers. It is what is demanded of business. Visual tools stimulate and challenge active learning from students.

CHAPTER SEVENTEEN STYLES OF LEARNING
Learning style labels can be dangerous. They can limit rather than stimulate expansion. Behind their often surface description lies a common cognitive activity — putting the detail into the big picture. Visual tools meet the needs of all learners, involving them in visual, verbal, analytic and holistic thinking. They also promote the four essential skills of learning.

CHAPTER EIGHTEEN ABILITY RANGE
We have many labels for our pupils — from the gifted and talented to SEN. Behind all these labels there lies the act of meaning making. Visual tools show students what understanding looks like. This gives confidence to them all. It allows the least able to see their intelligence and supports the more able to organise and communicate their sometimes erratic thinking.

SECTION 7 — LEXICON

CHAPTER NINETEEN LEXICON

CATEGORIES OF VISUAL TOOLS

- structural thinking — Structural Visual Tools
- differential thinking — Differential Visual Tools
- representational thinking — Representational Visual Tools
- temporal thinking — Temporal Visual Tools
- causal thinking — Causal Visual Tools
- numerical thinking — Numerical Visual Tools
- organisational thinking — Organisational Visual Tools
- individual thinking — Individual Visual Tools

There are seven types of visual tools related to seven types of thinking. The eighth is a hybrid of all seven. Within each category, there is a variety of visual tools. Visual tools within the categories achieve slightly different results, at different levels of complexity to suit age, ability and the nature of the tasks set. Each visual tool is described, its workings explained and ideas given for introducing it to students. Differences between similar visual tools are clarified. Each visual tool is illustrated both in templated format and as a hand-drawn example in use. The context for each hand-drawn visual tool is a well known story.

CH**4** | visual tools and computers P**33**

CH5 visual literacy P39

CH6 tools to learn P47

overview

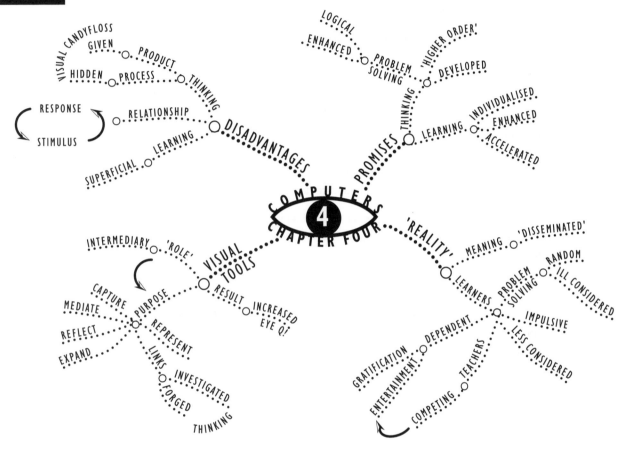

preview

■ Computers have offered many promises to accelerate learning and develop thinking skills.

■ Being accomplished at particular programs didn't necessarily amount to much, after all.

■ We should be learning lessons from the mistakes of our initial love affair with computers.

■ The visual attraction of the screen has many disadvantages.

■ Ironically, the visual characteristics of the screen obscure the possibilities of making knowledge visible.

■ Visual candyfloss can be avoided.

■ Visual tools can make our use of computers more intelligent.

■ Access to progression will come through greater clarity about the distinctions within visual literacy and visual tools.

Computers have offered many promises to accelerate learning and develop thinking skills.

A new age of information technology in which learning would be transformed has been heralded several times. Freed from the tyranny of whole-class teaching, learners, according to many ICT advisors, would be free to learn at their own pace. The interactivity of the programs, along with the visual seduction of the screen, were assured to win over students to engage in more extended, higher order thinking. It was, perhaps, assumed that the ultimate visual tool had arrived.

The reality is very different from this advertising hype. In her best-selling book, *A Failure to Connect*, Jane Healy (1999) lists the failures of the computer dream so far. Students are not becoming more sophisticated learners. Far from it. Instead, they are becoming more impulsive and less considered, more dependent on immediate sensory gratification and less resilient to difficulties, more random and less logical in their problem solving, more isolated and less conversant about their on-screen learning, more visually dependent and less verbally proficient.

Being accomplished at particular programs didn't necessarily amount to much, after all.

Many people assumed that because there was often a great deal of novelty and complexity involved in learning new programs, much useful learning was taking place. Not so. Even with such esteemed 'educational' programs as Logo, mastery of the detailed procedural instructions was confused with intellectual progress. The success, consequently, and not surprisingly, did not transfer to other contexts.

Just as Latin was once considered to be the best thinking skills programme available to students because of its inherent complexity and logic, so computers have taken on this role. Yet, just as Latin failed to prove its effective transfer, so computers are failing to transform our students' cognitive abilities. If anything, they are in danger of feeding a dependency, or consumerist intellectual culture.

We should be learning lessons from the mistakes of our initial love affair with computers.

The ability to create extended associations through surfing the Internet and by hypertext links does not represent a leap in thinking on the part of the computer user. Guy Claxton, one of the most astute commentators on learning, observed this when he wrote that:

> 'Access to avalanches of information, loosely interconnected by threads of casual associations, does not of itself bring about the transformation of that information into knowledge, nor the development of the requisite skills and dispositions for doing so.'
>
> *G. Claxton (1999)*

Computers, once thought of as the ultimate visual tool, do not easily support the learner in creating meaning. They are often relegated to being no more than sophisticated disseminators of information. Software programmers are

now in the same 'more, better, different' culture of forever having to surpass the entertainment factor of their preceding 'educational' programs. Within this paradigm, teachers will always be competing with computers.

An underlying cause for this situation is that computer users are, for the most part, mere consumers. As consumers, students expect the computer to do the thinking. There is an assumption that because of the computer's capacity to process large amounts of data, it is 'clever' and the user is not. We forget that it was humans who created computers and the software that goes with them. It was software developers who engaged in deep thinking – away from their screens. And that is the crucial point. Thinking takes place, for the most part, away from the screen. It is the conversations with others about the activity on screen that challenge and develop thinking.

structural visual tool | concept map | lexicon link | page 167

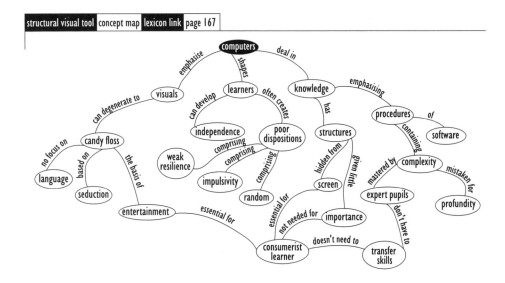

Yet, as Healy (1999) detailed so clearly, habitual use of computers seems to encourage a diminished disposition and capacity to talk to others that is hindering the development of thinking and learning. Talking involves so much more than simply responding to what has been termed the 'visual candyfloss' of the screen.

The visual attraction of the screen has many disadvantages.

There is no doubt our students live in a very visually orientated world. It makes little sense to expect students to be engaged in a curriculum that doesn't reflect, to some extent, this level of visual sophistication. Teachers up and down the country will give you detailed accounts of how many disenchanted students become entranced by the computer screen.

Operating in a visual stimulus–response relationship with a computer does not, however, automatically qualify as learning. An attraction to, and absorption with particular programs does not in itself testify to their value.

The visual attraction of the screen hides the thinking behind it. To engage merely with the surface visual signposts, or 'candyfloss', is to become a consumer. To think about the structures that the visual signposts refer to, is to become a learner.

Ironically, the visual characteristics of the screen obscure the possibilities of making knowledge visible.

The visual stimulus–response relationship between user and screen often leads to mere surface learning. When the types of visuals used on screen are no more than signposts for immediate action, they don't make explicit the hierarchically organised knowledge structure that lies behind the screen.

differential visual tool | double bubble | lexicon link | page 176

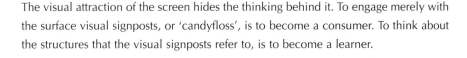

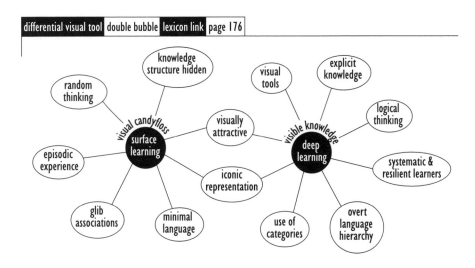

Behind every program, however zany it may appear on screen, lies an ordered structure. It was the software developers who engaged in deep thinking in order to create this knowledge structure. Yet their products, mostly, do not make this explicit or available to the user. It simply offers a surface ease and stimulation to the eyes. A visual opportunity is being lost.

Visual candyfloss can be avoided.

Behind every screen lie large amounts of thinking. And most of that thinking took place in traditional ways – conversations with others and work on paper. Just look at this piece of advice to potential builders of websites taken from a computer magazine:

'Your first challenge is to draft a broad organisational scheme for your site's contents. You need to find logical ways to group your information, so readers can quickly find what they need. For this, you'll want to create a site tree – a diagram of how your site's pages are linked together.'

MacUser (2001)

Behind every screen lies the organisational thinking of the creator. If we want our students to develop their thinking, then they must have access to the same visual tools that are used by the software developers. Later on in the advice to web builders, above, there is reference to other visual systems used to categorise, sequence and communicate information. Visual tools are for creators of knowledge. Consumers don't need them.

Visual tools can make our use of computers more intelligent.

Visual tools can become the intermediary between screen and user. This avoids the seductive pull of the consumerist response. Instead of giving an immediate, impulsive response, the student becomes engaged in exploring the significance of the on-screen information. The on-screen information can be made explicit and expanded by the use of visual tools.

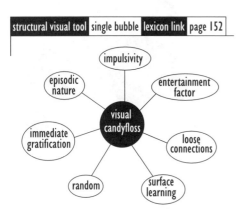

Visual tools offer students the opportunity to link information into coherent patterns. They can 'join' items into groups and relate the groups in certain ways. For example, evidence could be collected together from various sources – including computer-based resources – and shaped into a fishbone diagram (see page 218). This diagram both illustrates and stimulates causal thinking. So rather than simply listing events, the learner is forced to assemble 'discrete' facts into a reasoned argument. The visual tool forces thinking to occur. It supports, reflects and records the thinking that has occurred.

In this context, computers can fulfil many of their initial promises. They can handle the so-called 'left brain' work of detail and information processing, so freeing up the right brain for creative work. They can provide the right brain with the big picture by exploiting the visual–spatial holographic dimension that best mirrors the human thinking processes.

Access to progression will come through greater clarity about the distinctions within visual literacy and visual tools.

As valuable as Jane Healy's research into the deteriorating learning habits of computer users is to us, it is still confused regarding its notion of visual literacy. Healy puts all visuals into the same category, making no distinction between mere visual labelling (signposts) and stimulation (candyfloss), and the visual representation of the relationships between these items in an organised structure of knowledge.

Unless we recognise the interconnected nature of our visual and verbal worlds we tend to relegate visuals and substitute them for language and reason (Postman, 1992). Yet Jerome Bruner, decades previously, noted that:

'This is not to say that highly evolved images do not go beyond immediate time and given place. Maps and flow charts are iconic in nature, but they are images that translate prior linguistic and mathematical renderings into a visual form.'

J. Bruner (1968)

When we become more educated with regards to visuals we are able to discriminate between the representation of physical relationships and the representation of conceptual relationships.

viewpoints

visual thinkers

'They think visually, spatially and laterally. They work with flair and abandon. Where are these skills in the national curriculum?'

S. Bowers (2001)

ideas

'The mind thinks with ideas, not with information.'

T. Roszak (1986)

hypertext

'The question about hypertext that people fail to ask is, who creates the hyperlinks?'

P. Gilster (1997)

'I saw how the computer could mirror the way my brain worked – not thinking in a linear way, but jumping from idea to idea.'

N. Paine (2000)

blind spot

'There are many computer programs to help with spelling and a wide range of reading difficulties: how much software teaches visual literacy? Why this blind spot?'

A. Peacock (2000)

review

behind the screen

How much do students understand the visual structures implicit in software programs?

thinking structures

Just as students need access to the thinking behind the computer screen, they also need access to the structure of your thinking, as their teacher. Consider how visual tools could support you in giving students such access.

computer use

Reflect on the use of computers in your school, in light of the points made in this chapter. How much computer time is meaningful learning and how much is given over to mere visual candyfloss?

ROUTE MAP FOR YOUR READING

SECTION 1 — CONTEXT

CHAPTER ONE — BACKGROUND

The primary assertion is that we are all Eye Q experts. Throughout history, humans have used an assortment of visual tools to reflect and communicate knowledge. Current knowledge creation dynamics are based on this same notion. The 'inside story' of learning is obtained by looking both inside (cognitive psychology) and outside (Accelerated Learning).

CHAPTER TWO — THE iDESK MODEL

Most of our activities are not based on a theory of learning. Consequently, there is little sense of meaning or coherence. The iDesk model is holistic. It connects thinking, feeling and doing. Finally, it links these faculties to the environment and the individual. Visual tools impact all areas of the iDesk model, and all components interact with each other. Serious schools need models.

CHAPTER THREE — THE KNOWLEDGE AGE

We are living in the knowledge age with a need for more knowledge workers. These new types of workers require new, extended mental skills and knowledge tools. Visual tools are central in creating and communicating knowledge. Schools need to learn from business theory and practice with regard to intellectual capital and the use of visual tools.

SECTION 2 — VISUALS

CHAPTER FOUR — VISUAL TOOLS AND COMPUTERS

We are learning that the use of computers can reinforce poor learning habits. The attraction of the screen can degenerate into visual 'candyfloss'. This turns computer users into consumers. Behind the screen lies a knowledge structure. Visual tools make this explicit and turn consumers into explorers of knowledge. Clarity about visual literacy will support this.

CHAPTER FIVE — VISUAL LITERACY

In our culture, the visual–verbal polarity may well be more divisive than the sciences–arts gulf. There are historical, philosophical reasons for the low value placed on visuals. Visual literacy, nonetheless, is an established discipline. All visual content exists in the spatial dimension. Space is our first and primary frontier. The spatial metaphor shapes our understanding.

CHAPTER SIX — TOOLS TO LEARN

The successes of our civilisation are based on tools. We have created these tools and they, in turn, end up shaping our behaviour. Using new tools causes new learning to take place. Habitual use of tools changes our habits. The most effective use of tools happens when accompanied with theory. Visual tools impact on learning habits. New eras need new tools.

SECTION 3 — MEANING

CHAPTER SEVEN — SCHEMAS

We all have schemas. They are personal and unique and are based on how we view the world. In business they are termed mental models. Their organisation represents how we think and shape our behaviour. All students have these mental maps but are unaware of them — as are teachers. Making schemas visible allows students and teachers to see what they are thinking.

CHAPTER EIGHT — HOLOGRAPHIC–LINEAR

Every day, every student, in every lesson has to turn linear communication (what she reads or hears) into what is termed her holographic understanding. Schemas are holographic in structure — definitely not linear. The student then has to turn her new, enlarged understanding back into linear format. This process has, until now, been an unknown phenomenon.

CHAPTER NINE — CONSTRUCTING KNOWLEDGE

All our students construct knowledge — even the very youngest and the least able. Knowledge cannot be delivered. It has to be created each time by the individual, for knowledge is created not discovered. This view of learning is called constructivism. Understanding this process stimulates teachers to make learning more meaningful and motivating for all students.

SECTION 4 — LANGUAGE

CHAPTER TEN — SUPPORT FOR LANGUAGE

It is normally thought that visuals 'compete' with words. With visual tools, this is not true. Visual tools exist in the overlapping area between words and pictures. If you examine language, you realise that images play a big part in stimulating thought and supporting planning. They help the organisation of our language, which normally has to take place in the unseen interior of our heads.

CHAPTER ELEVEN — READING

Reading is active. Readers' interrogation of text is shaped by their own schemas. They have to adapt their existing schemas in order to absorb text into meaningful messages. Visual tools can reveal the hidden structure and meaning of a text. Just as computer software can show you what your voice looks like, visual tools can show you what your thinking looks like.

CHAPTER TWELVE — WRITING

Writing is difficult. Students' difficulties and fears stem from not knowing what to write. Visual tools make planning explicit, easy and empowering. Through the use of visual tools, students can model the planning that excellent writers do 'in their heads'. Planning in linear fashion is too difficult for most. The schematic nature of visual tools matches the way the brain naturally works.

SECTION 5 — THINKING

CHAPTER THIRTEEN — THINKING SKILLS

When we think, we are either thinking of objects (in space) or events (in time). Our thoughts become 'thought–objects'. Just as we manipulate real, physical objects in space, so we move our 'thought–objects' in our inner space. This is thinking. It is, however, invisible and demands much short term memory. Visual tools make thinking visible, easier and obvious.

CHAPTER FOURTEEN — QUESTIONS

Questions are more powerful than answers. They directly determine our focus and thinking. Young children are wonderful questioners — young scientists. Schools have conditioned students to demand only questions. This severely limits their thinking and learning. Visual tools are themselves questions. They demand investigation. Their visible nature makes questioners of all students.

CHAPTER FIFTEEN — THINKING IN ACTION

There is a link between text, thinking and visual tools. The nature of different types of text (genres) demand different types of thinking. All thinking is the manipulation of 'thought–objects'. Visual tools show students what this looks like. Matching types of visual tools to specific genres and linking them to the National Curriculum thinking skills is a powerful matrix.

SECTION 6 — LEARNING

CHAPTER SIXTEEN — ACTIVE LEARNING

You don't have to leave your seat to be actively learning. Active doesn't mean kinaesthetic! Active learning involves becoming engrossed, relating new material to personal prior knowledge, and creating meaning. Active learning needs to be encouraged by teachers. It is what is demanded of business. Visual tools stimulate and challenge active learning from students.

CHAPTER SEVENTEEN — STYLES OF LEARNING

Learning style labels can be dangerous. They can limit rather than stimulate expansion. Behind their often surface description lies a common cognitive activity — putting the detail into the big picture. Visual tools meet the needs of all learners, involving them in visual, verbal, analytic and holistic thinking. They also promote the four essential skills of learning.

CHAPTER EIGHTEEN — ABILITY RANGE

We have many labels for our pupils — from the gifted and talented to SEN. Behind all these labels there lies the act of meaning making. Visual tools show students what understanding looks like. This gives confidence to them all. It allows the least able to see their intelligence and supports the more able to organise and communicate their sometimes erratic thinking.

SECTION 7 — LEXICON

CHAPTER NINETEEN — LEXICON

CATEGORIES OF VISUAL TOOLS

- structural thinking – Structural Visual Tools
- differential thinking – Differential Visual Tools
- representational thinking – Representational Visual Tools
- temporal thinking – Temporal Visual Tools
- causal thinking – Causal Visual Tools
- numerical thinking – Numerical Visual Tools
- organisational thinking – Organisational Visual Tools
- individual thinking – Individual Visual Tools

There are seven types of visual tools related to seven types of thinking. The eighth is a hybrid of all seven. Within each category, there is a variety of visual tools. Visual tools within the categories achieve slightly different results, at different levels of complexity to suit age, ability and the nature of the tasks set. Each visual tool is described, its workings explained and ideas given for introducing it to students. Differences between similar visual tools are clarified. Each visual tool is illustrated both in templated format and as a hand-drawn example in use. The context for each hand-drawn visual tool is a well known story.

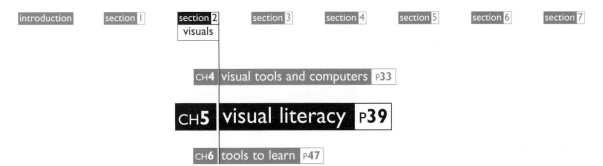

CH4 visual tools and computers P33

CH5 visual literacy P39

CH6 tools to learn P47

overview

REALITY   TRUTH
REASON ...... MIND
DICHOTOMY   BODY
APPEARANCE
EMOTIONS
IRRATIONALITY

INTEGRATE   MIND   BODY
ACCEPT

POST MODERN
PHILOSOPHY

DEVELOPMENT OF MIND

VISUAL LITERACY
CHAPTER FIVE
5

VISUAL VERBAL

LOCATION OF VISUAL TOOLS

DIFFERENT — DIFFERENT
TYPES — TYPES
OF — OF
VISUAL — VISUAL
TOOLS — TOOLS
REFLECTED BY

TAXONOMIES

VISUAL TOOLS DOMAINS

VISUAL PROCESSING

BELIEF   1/3 LEARNERS

REALITY   ALL   INCLUDING BLIND

VISUAL
VERBAL   OVERLAP
SPATIAL   ALWAYS

30+ AREAS   BRAIN   85% ENGAGED

preview

- The visual–verbal distinction threatens to be a greater cultural divide than the ubiquitous science and arts division.

- There are major philosophical reasons behind the devaluing of visual literacy.

- A major part of the brain's activity is processing visual information.

- Visual literacy is a discipline.

- There are several taxonomies of visual displays.

- Visuals always operate within a spatial context.

- Space is our first frontier and, as such, influences our language and thinking.

- The mind works in two different ways: in linear and non-linear modes.

The visual–verbal distinction threatens to be a greater cultural divide than the ubiquitous science and arts division.

We live in an increasingly visual world. Just take a look at the emphasis placed on visuals in advertising. Notice the visual sophistication of magazines. Watch children's television. Work on a computer. Peer closer at all these and you will find the use of tables, icons, charts, maps, diagrams and a whole array of different types of illustrations.

Children are growing up in this world. They are familiar and comfortable with it. It is a modality to which they respond with enthusiasm and within which they learn. Once in schools, alas, things are different. We make students operate in a different modality – listening. Teachers, on the whole, are not knowledgeable about visuals or confident with their use. This discrepancy between the visual orientation of the outside world and the verbal emphasis in classrooms will expand unless we take action. Without an education on the uses of visual strategies, we are causing a major cultural divide.

There are major philosophical reasons behind the devaluing of visual literacy.

Karin Murris (1992), creator of her own pictorial Philosophy for Children programme, has elegantly identified historical tracks of thought that have resulted in our current feelings about visual literacy. She found that the division between mind and body is mirrored in the polarity of rationality and emotion. From Descartes' mind–body dichotomy, we have tended to group rationality with the mind, and with words, concepts and meaning. Images, by contrast, are related to the body – to perception and feeling, irrationality and emotion. Through words, the intellect is able to detect invisible and unchanging truths. By attending to pictures, we are merely offered the concrete and the visible – that which is perceived with the body's mundane senses. And as Plato repeatedly told us, such perception is only an illusion.

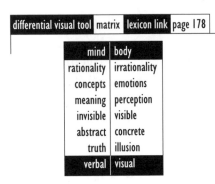

| differential visual tool | matrix | lexicon link | page 178 |

mind	body
rationality	irrationality
concepts	emotions
meaning	perception
invisible	visible
abstract	concrete
truth	illusion
verbal	visual

Post-modernist philosophers have managed to liberate themselves from such false and constricting views. They realise that we are whole human beings and that the body's messages are included in what is termed the mind. We understand the world by organising our experiences as if they were real physical objects operating in a spatial domain – and, therefore, visible. Being able to manipulate these 'entities', we can then reason about them.

A major part of the brain's activity is processing visual information.

The philosophical development described above relates well to the information we are receiving about how our brains work. They work primarily in a visual capacity. In fact, according to Robert Sylwester (1995), up to around 85% of any human brain's activity is involved in processing visual information. So, whether you have beliefs, even sophisticated beliefs, about your preferred modality (visual, auditory, kinaesthetic), you need to come to terms with this fact.

Even students without any sight use their visual modality! David Hyerle (1996), author and trainer on visual tools, recounts how he came to realise this surprising phenomenon. At a conference he was leading, a member of the audience pointed out that the visual tools being explored would not work with his students. They had no sight. Hyerle was taken aback, realising that he had met a first, but valid, objection to the utilisation of visual tools for every learner. He resolved to keep in contact with the teacher and, some months later, he visited the school. The teacher welcomed him and announced enthusiastically that he wanted to apologise because the visual tools were working just fine with all his students. What David Hyerle found were blind students working with visual tools that had been processed through an embossing machine. The students were feeling the embossed, raised lines of the diagrams and internalising their layout. They were using their visual–spatial capacities.

Visual literacy is a discipline.

If 'The visible and the intelligible are, indeed, virtually synonymous terms' (Harding, 1998), then visual literacy is about using the visual modality for thinking, and for communicating those thoughts to others. If 'Pattern seeking is a natural and important part of every act of visual thought' (McKim, 1972), then there is such a thing as visual intelligence (Hoffman, 1998). If 'Visual literacy is really training for visual thinking' (Hortin, 1980), then there are different types of visuals for different types of thinking.

There are several taxonomies of visual displays.

Visual displays are initially divided by the pictorial–verbal distinction. The pictorial spectrum is related to 'reality', while the verbal is associated with 'abstraction' (McKim, 1972).

Pictorial 'reality' is represented by two categories:

- concrete graphic languages

- orthographic projection, isometric and oblique projection, perspective projection, rough three-dimensional mock-ups, and appearance or working models.

Verbal 'abstraction' is also represented by two categories:

- abstract graphic languages

- charts, graphs, diagrams and schematics.

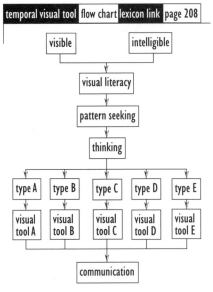

We want to look in the overlapping space where pure pictorial representation and words meet – where we visualise the verbal and verbalise the visual (Braden, 1983). We want to do so because:

> **'Visual thinking is often driven more strongly by the conceptual knowledge we use to organise our images than by the contents of the images themselves.'**
>
> *S. Pinker (1997)*

Focusing on the visual–verbal category, we find nine types of visual display, according to Moore and Dwyer (1994):

1 information mapping

2 multi-level writing

3 pattern notes

4 outline graphics

5 matrix displays

6 flowcharts

7 schematic diagrams

8 logic diagrams

9 hierarchical displays and models.

These structured combinations of text, pictures and graphic design can be alternatively categorised according to their function of 'infography' (Petterson, 1989):

1 instructional graphics

2 presentation graphics

3 explanatory graphics

4 new graphics

5 locating graphics

6 exhibition graphics.

Visuals always operate within a spatial context.

The emphasis on the visual–verbal overlap is important in demolishing the false, and unnecessary, polarity between the word and the image. There is yet another distinction, however, that lies behind and supports both: space.

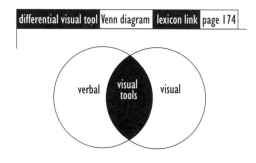

| differential visual tool | Venn diagram | lexicon link | page 174 |

verbal — visual tools — visual

When we think of the visual modality, we don't give very much consideration to the spatial dimension in which it operates. But the object of our visualisation is always placed, situated, in relation to other objects or its background.

When we think of skills relating to space, we don't emphasise the intrinsically visual component. Orientation in space is visually determined. As we saw earlier, this is true even for those without sight (page 40). Visualisation can only operate in a spatial dimension. To fully understand our use of visuals, we need to understand space and its influence on our thinking.

Space is our first frontier and, as such, influences our language and thinking.

So Captain Kirk got it wrong – space is our first, not our final, frontier. We navigate space, obviously, from birth. By relating ourselves to our environment and by relating objects to other objects, we create meaning from our

world. This process is fundamental. Because it is part of the very structure of our existence, it is difficult to distance ourselves from it and identify it as a phenomenon.

It is so central to our understanding of the world that it shapes our thinking and language. George Lakoff and Mark Johnson (1980) have written how we are unaware of our ordinary conceptual systems, how they are fundamentally metaphorical in nature, and how space is one of the fundamental metaphors. Examine the language we use, and you will see that relationships between ideas, from the most abstract concepts to everyday notions, are predicated on spatial relationships. In fact, this last sentence was such an example. The word 'between' is a spatial, orientational metaphor. It transforms the notions of 'ideas' into objects that are spatially related. Other spatial metaphors include 'up–down', 'front–back', 'on–off', 'deep–shallow' and 'central–peripheral'. Taking just one of these – up–down – we can see how readily we deal with all kinds of concepts using orientational language:

■ happy is up, and sad is down

■ conscious is up, and unconscious is down

■ health and life is up, and sickness and death are down

■ having control is up, being subject to control is down

- more is up, and less is down

- high status is up, and low status is down

- good is up, and bad is down

- virtue is up, and depravity is down.

These are just examples of one of the orientational metaphors we live by. It is not too difficult, now, for you to imagine the overwhelming influence space has in giving us our basic structures for understanding and communicating. For these very reasons, the power of visual tools resides centrally in their capacity to signify spatial relationships. Because the fact is, whether we demonstrate our orientational metaphors through visual means or not, this spatial arrangement of ideas takes place in our heads anyway! We all use such metaphors, built from our basic domains of experience, with which to think.

The mind works in two different ways: in linear and non-linear modes.

One way in which the mind works is the linear mode. From this mode, we construct lists, taxonomies, instructions, descriptions. Memory built from this mode is called taxon memory. We often take this mode to be the only way in which our minds work, but in fact we also use a non-linear mode. This is spatial in nature, giving the 'big picture', identifying relationships, creating meaning. Memory built from this mode is called locale memory. One is not better than the other. They are simply different modes of thinking.

When we learn things spontaneously, without effort, we are working in locale mode. Yet, a very large part of schooling does not utilise this mode. Visual tools tap into the overlooked but very natural locale mode, because of their inherent and explicit spatial nature. This is why visual tools are so very effective. In a book summarising long-term research into the best teaching methods, Marzano and co-workers point out that:

'Representing similarities and differences in graphic or symbolic form enhances students' understanding of and ability to use knowledge.'

R. J. Marzano and co-workers (2001)

Such strategies help *all* learners – not only so-called 'visual learners'. They do so because we *all* operate in a spatial domain, we *all* use language that relies on spatial metaphors and we *all* operate in the locale mode. Most of the human brain's work involves the processing of visual information. So, if, as Flory (1978) made very clear:

- a visual language exists

- people can and do think visually

- people can and do learn visually

- people can and should express themselves visually'

then what specific strategies are schools pursuing to promote visual literacy?

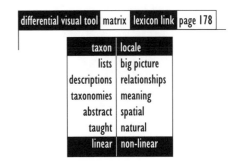

differential visual tool	matrix	lexicon link	page 178

taxon	locale
lists	big picture
descriptions	relationships
taxonomies	meaning
abstract	spatial
taught	natural
linear	**non-linear**

viewpoints

print

'The growing question, of course, is whether so-called 'visual literacies' could replace print. Will instruction manuals of the future rely on pictures and diagrams instead of words?'

J. M. Healy (1999)

visual sophistication

'Television has conditioned everyone at being very good at discerning what an image is 'getting at' within a few frames.'

N. Poyner (1996)

space

'The way we arrange or manipulate things in space can make our cognitive lives easier. Scrabble-players and anagram-solvers use real space to support their thinking. By physically ordering and reordering the letters, different possibilities are encouraged to make themselves known.'

G. Claxton (1999)

painting

'Painting is just another way of keeping a diary.'

Pablo Picasso

vision

'Every man takes the limits of his own field of vision for the limits of the world.'

Arthur Schopenhaur, nineteenth century philosopher

reflection

'We don't see things as they are, we see things as we are.'

Anais Nin

audit

Do a visual audit of your school or classroom. How many of the visual tools in the section 7 (page 143) do you already use?

opinion

What was your view on the use of visuals? Did you have a view before you started reading *Eye Q*?

space

Spend some time noticing what you look at in the external world. Notice how everything you look at exists in space. Now spend some time noticing your internal visualisations. Again, you will realise, they exist in space – your inner space.

metaphors

Listen to conversations, or read a variety of texts. Notice how many of the words used are not to be taken literally. They are words directly describing physical objects in space – 'in', 'part of, 'under', 'joining', 'distanced from', 'far', and so on – and part of the spatial metaphor.

ROUTE MAP FOR YOUR READING

SECTION 1 — CONTEXT

CHAPTER ONE BACKGROUND
The primary assertion is that we are all Eye Q experts. Throughout history, humans have used an assortment of visual tools to reflect and communicate knowledge. Current knowledge creation dynamics are based on this same notion. The 'inside story' of learning is obtained by looking both inside (cognitive psychology) and outside (Accelerated Learning).

CHAPTER TWO THE iDESK MODEL
Most of our activities are not based on a theory of learning. Consequently, there is little sense of meaning or coherence. The iDesk model is holistic. It connects thinking, feeling and doing. Finally, it links these faculties to the environment and the individual. Visual tools impact all areas of the iDesk model, and all components interact with each other. Serious schools need models.

CHAPTER THREE THE KNOWLEDGE AGE
We are living in the knowledge age with a need for more knowledge workers. These new types of workers require new, extended mental skills and knowledge tools. Visual tools are central in creating and communicating knowledge. Schools need to learn from business theory and practice with regard to intellectual capital and the use of visual tools.

SECTION 2 — VISUALS

CHAPTER FOUR VISUAL TOOLS AND COMPUTERS
We are learning that the use of computers can reinforce poor learning habits. The attraction of the screen can degenerate into visual 'candyfloss'. This turns computer users into consumers. Behind the screen lies a knowledge structure. Visual tools make this explicit and turn consumers into explorers of knowledge. Clarity about visual literacy will support this.

CHAPTER FIVE VISUAL LITERACY
In our culture, the visual–verbal polarity may well be more divisive than the sciences–arts gulf. There are historical, philosophical reasons for the low value placed on visuals. Visual literacy, nonetheless, is an established discipline. All visual content exists in the spatial dimension. Space is our first and primary frontier. The spatial metaphor shapes our understanding.

CHAPTER SIX TOOLS TO LEARN
The successes of our civilisation are based on tools. We have created these tools and they, in turn, end up shaping our behaviour. Using new tools causes new learning to take place. Habitual use of tools changes our habits. The most effective use of tools happens when accompanied with theory. Visual tools impact on learning habits. New eras need new tools.

SECTION 3 — MEANING

CHAPTER SEVEN SCHEMAS
We all have schemas. They are personal and unique and are based on how we view the world. In business they are termed mental models. Their organisation represents how we think and shape our behaviour. All students have these mental maps but are unaware of them — as are teachers. Making schemas visible allows students and teachers to see what they are thinking.

CHAPTER EIGHT HOLOGRAPHIC–LINEAR
Every day, every student, in every lesson has to turn linear communication (what she reads or hears) into what is termed her holographic understanding. Schemas are holographic in structure — definitely not linear. The student then has to turn her new, enlarged understanding back into linear format. This process has, until now, been an unknown phenomenon.

CHAPTER NINE CONSTRUCTING KNOWLEDGE
All our students construct knowledge — even the very youngest and the least able. Knowledge cannot be delivered. It has to be created each time by the individual, for knowledge is created not discovered. This view of learning is called constructivism. Understanding this process stimulates teachers to make learning more meaningful and motivating for all students.

SECTION 4 — LANGUAGE

CHAPTER TEN SUPPORT FOR LANGUAGE
It is normally thought that visuals 'compete' with words. With visual tools, this is not true. Visual tools exist in the overlapping area between words and pictures. If you examine language, you realise that images play a big part in stimulating thought and supporting planning. They help the organisation of our language, which normally has to take place in the unseen interior of our heads.

CHAPTER ELEVEN READING
Reading is active. Readers' interrogation of text is shaped by their own schemas. They have to adapt their existing schemas in order to absorb text into meaningful messages. Visual tools can reveal the hidden structure and meaning of a text. Just as computer software can show you what your voice looks like, visual tools can show you what your thinking looks like.

CHAPTER TWELVE WRITING
Writing is difficult. Students' difficulties and fears stem from not knowing what to write. Visual tools make planning explicit, easy and empowering. Through the use of visual tools, students can model the planning that excellent writers do 'in their heads'. Planning in linear fashion is too difficult for most. The schematic nature of visual tools matches the way the brain naturally works.

SECTION 5 — THINKING

CHAPTER THIRTEEN THINKING SKILLS
When we think, we are either thinking of objects (in space) or events (in time). Our thoughts become 'thought–objects'. Just as we manipulate real, physical objects in space, so we move our 'thought–objects' in our inner space. This is thinking. It is, however, invisible and demands much short term memory. Visual tools make thinking visible, easier and obvious.

CHAPTER FOURTEEN QUESTIONS
Questions are more powerful than answers. They directly determine our focus and thinking. Young children are wonderful questioners — young scientists. Schools have conditioned students to demand only questions. This severely limits their thinking and learning. Visual tools are themselves questions. They demand investigation. Their visible nature makes questioners of all students.

CHAPTER FIFTEEN THINKING IN ACTION
There is a link between text, thinking and visual tools. The nature of different types of text (genres) demand different types of thinking. All thinking is the manipulation of 'thought–objects'. Visual tools show students what this looks like. Matching types of visual tools to specific genres and linking them to the National Curriculum thinking skills is a powerful matrix.

SECTION 6 — LEARNING

CHAPTER SIXTEEN ACTIVE LEARNING
You don't have to leave your seat to be actively learning. Active doesn't mean kinaesthetic! Active learning involves becoming engrossed, relating new material to personal prior knowledge, and creating meaning. Active learning needs to be encouraged by teachers. It is what is demanded of business. Visual tools stimulate and challenge active learning from students.

CHAPTER SEVENTEEN STYLES OF LEARNING
Learning style labels can be dangerous. They can limit rather than stimulate expansion. Behind their often surface description lies a common cognitive activity — putting the detail into the big picture. Visual tools meet the needs of all learners, involving them in visual, verbal, analytic and holistic thinking. They also promote the four essential skills of learning.

CHAPTER EIGHTEEN ABILITY RANGE
We have many labels for our pupils — from the gifted and talented to SEN. Behind all these labels there lies the act of meaning making. Visual tools show students what understanding looks like. This gives confidence to them all. It allows the least able to see their intelligence and supports the more able to organise and communicate their sometimes erratic thinking.

SECTION 7 — LEXICON

CHAPTER NINETEEN LEXICON

CATEGORIES OF VISUAL TOOLS

- structural thinking — Structural Visual Tools
- differential thinking — Differential Visual Tools
- representational thinking — Representational Visual Tools
- temporal thinking — Temporal Visual Tools
- causal thinking — Causal Visual Tools
- numerical thinking — Numerical Visual Tools
- organisational thinking — Organisational Visual Tools
- individual thinking — Individual Visual Tools

There are seven types of visual tools related to seven types of thinking. The eighth is a hybrid of all seven. Within each category, there is a variety of visual tools. Visual tools within the categories achieve slightly different results, at different levels of complexity to suit age, ability and the nature of the tasks set. Each visual tool is described, its workings explained and ideas given for introducing it to students. Differences between similar visual tools are clarified. Each visual tool is illustrated both in templated format and as a hand-drawn example in use. The context for each hand-drawn visual tool is a well known story.

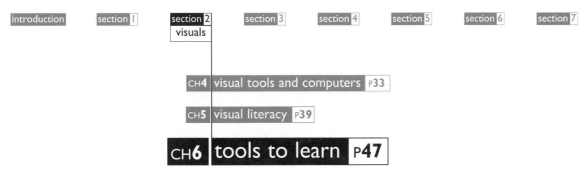
overview

FLEXIBLE
RESOURCED
HABITS PERFORMANCE OUTCOMES
SHAPE
INITIATE THINKING
DEVELOP
REFLECT
REPRESENT
TOOLS
CHAPTER SIX
6
PURPOSES THINKING
FOCUS
ORGANISE
DELIVER
LEARNING
LIFE-LONG
TRANSFER
REASON
TEACHERS
MODELLERS SUPPORTED PROFESSIONALLY
EMOTIONALLY
EXPLANATION
EXPLICIT
VISIBLE

preview

- We are all tool users.

- While we create and shape the tools we use, they soon come to shape us.

- Tools make success more likely.

- Tools have many purposes.

- Our use of tools is often indiscriminate.

- Using new tools causes learning to happen.

- Using tools habitually changes our habits.

- New eras need new tools.

We are all tool users.

It is bracing to consider that without tools, we wouldn't be far different from our cave-dwelling ancestors. As Smitsman observes:

> 'Much of today's so-called 'intelligence' stems from tool use and would no longer exist if the tools that sustain the mental capacities disappeared.'
>
> *A. W. Smitsman (2000)*

So when the tools are missing, we are in trouble. Management author Jensen has this to say on the subject:

> 'Even with a shared vision, more employees than you may care to admit don't have the tools or training to do what is expected of them. Clarity about the use of tools and adequate levels of training is critical. But clarity comes second. Investing in the tools comes first.'
>
> *E. Jensen (2000)*

Is your school investing in effective tools?

While we create and shape the tools we use, they soon come to shape us.

If you look back over the last twenty-four hours, you will notice that most of your activities were occupied with, if not driven by, tools. You probably can't think of anything you did that did not involve or take advantage of tools in some way. They have come to shape your life.

We have, then, a very interesting relationship with tools. We created them and are reliant on them for most of what we call a civilised life. The very basis of our intelligence is predicated on tool use. Without tools, we wouldn't be 'forced' to expand our thinking – we would still be as prehistoric cave dwellers.

Yet we don't have enough of them to achieve the success we want. And, interestingly, we don't have a very sophisticated framework with which to understand them.

Tools make success more likely.

Imagine you are faced with a plumbing crisis at home – one in which you need to respond personally and immediately. How confident would you feel without tools? How reasoned would your thinking be? How much energy would be devoted to calming your emotions rather than dealing with the problem? Do you think these might be the same responses your students have when faced with similarly daunting knowledge problems?

Knowledge is the main context for students' work. They have to be able to chart it, explore it and report on it. For that, they need tools.

> 'If a person knows how to use a map or navigational tool of some sort, extensive travel will not only be more successful, it also becomes more likely.'
>
> *M. Gauvain (1995)*

Teachers and students need tools for the job of developing knowledge workers.

Tools have many purposes.

Tools for '…knowledge work include anything that clarifies, focuses, organises and delivers information' (Jensen, 2001). They are, therefore, complex tools that help to simplify things.

These 'more complex tools include symbols and symbol systems of all kinds, such as the number system, the drawing system, taxonomies to categorise objects and events' (Smitsman, 2000). This, you will now realise, is an exact description of most visual tools!

Just as we substitute alternative, near-equivalent words for those we cannot find, so tools must also be 'substitutable'. Jerome Bruner made this point very well when he pointed out how carpenters without a chisel can adapt and use other tools – such as the edge of a plane, a pocket knife or even a sharp stone – to do the same job. The danger in identifying specific tools for particular uses is a rapid descent into 'functional fixedness' (Bruner, 1971). Tools are not, themselves, fixed – only our perceptions of them are fixed. For example, you could choose a Venn diagram to represent two overlapping sets of information, or you could use a double bubble (pages 174 and 176). When visual tools are used only in the form of templates, on worksheets for example, their 'substitutability' or flexibility is diminished along, eventually, with the generative thinking power of the user.

Our use of tools is often indiscriminate.

In general, people don't have a lexicon of tools, much less a theory about them. Without a theory, our use of visual tools is indiscriminate and not as efficient as it could be. Peter Senge, in his work on systems thinking (1990 and 1994) writes of the consequences of 'theoryless' tools. He admits, of course, that the first quality of a tool is its usefulness. However, without a theory we are not likely to build up a knowledge that allows us to generalise about them – something that can be very evident with the theoryless use of visual tools in schools.

A lack of theory means that reasoned and flexible tool use and transfer is unlikely. Not knowing *why* tools work in specific contexts with particular contents limits your capacity both to reap maximum benefit from their use and to create variations of them.

Without an underlying theory, your capacity to notice the limitations of specific tools is greatly diminished. Inappropriate, or even counter-productive, use may not only be missed but actually reinforced. As Senge points out:

> '… in our rush to solve practical problems [the tendency is to] grab at ready-made solutions that neither address the fundamental causes of a problem nor stretch our thinking.'
>
> *P. Senge and co-workers (1994)*

Does this sound familiar regarding the ad hoc use of visual tools in schools?

Using new tools causes learning to happen.

Buckminster Fuller – inventor, information architect and philosopher – said that the best way to have an impact on people's thinking is not to teach them *what* or *how* to think, but to give them new tools to use. Out of their explorations will come new thinking patterns. Thinking is shaped by the nature of the tool (Saljo, 1998), in remarkable ways. One of the most moving examples of this is that of Casper Hauser. Born in Germany two centuries ago, Casper spent his first sixteen years away from all human contact, locked in a cupboard. With the gradual introduction of language (humankind's most elevated tool), Casper's world transformed. His subsequent writings reveal how the tool of language literally changed the world before his very eyes. Tools transform.

Tools stand in between the world and the individual. They, therefore, mediate between the two. And the more complex and sophisticated the tool, the more meaningful and inter-related the world appears to the tool user. Marks on an X-ray image that are chaotic and unintelligible to a non-tool user are highly meaningful to a regular tool user (the radiographer). Tools enable and structure new practices and thought processes (Pollard, 1999).

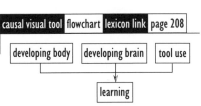

causal visual tool | flowchart | lexicon link | page 208

developing body | developing brain | tool use

learning

Using tools habitually changes our habits.

In a fascinating study on the effects of the use of an abacus, Stigler (1984, 1986) found out how tools shape habits. Chinese children's use of an abacus showed that they employed a 'mental abacus' when calculating in their head. This led both to better mental calculation skills and to better conceptual understanding of the number system. Simply moving bits of wood along string did this! A tool is an external, symbolic representation, and as such, its repeated use gradually becomes internalised by the user.

Having seen tool use from this perspective, you will be ready to consider Smitsman's comment that:

'... tool use is as important to development as growth of the body and brain.'

A. W. Smitsman (2000)

This is a remarkable assertion, and one that educators need to take seriously. Just as schools are taking seriously the significance of brain research and the need for body movement, so they need quickly to assess the central and crucial impact of tool use.

New eras need new tools.

New tools are not always readily accepted. Back in the thirteenth and fourteenth centuries, Italian merchants encountered the Hindu–Arabic numeral system and found it much more efficient than the Roman numerals they were using. Adoption, however, was not smooth. There was opposition by those who promoted the continuation of the current tool (the Roman numerals).

Even recently, we have seen similar responses to change. The introduction of the calculator to aid mathematical activity met with very strong, and emotional, responses.

In this rapidly developing knowledge age, the prosperity of our country is dependent on having highly skilled knowledge workers. These workers must be able to think flexibly and creatively and for that they need knowledge tools. Our job in education is to provide both the contexts for developing thinking, and the confidence and competence in using knowledge tools. Both can be supplied using visual tools.

| causal visual tool | flowscape | lexicon link | page 234 |

1 We are all tool users.
2 While we create and shape the tools we use, they soon come to shape us.
3 Tools make success more likely.
4 Tools have many purposes.
5 Our use of tools is often indiscriminate.
6 Using new tools causes learning to happen.
7 Using tools habitually changes our habits.
8 New eras need new tools.

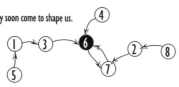

viewpoints

tool use

'Man is a tool-using animal. Without tools he is nothing, with tools he is all.'

Thomas Carlyle, nineteenth century Scottish critic

evolution

'... the evolution of human brain function has changed principally in response to the linkage between human beings and different tool systems.'

J. Bruner (1988)

productivity

'You cannot mandate productivity, you must provide the tools to let people become their best.'

Steve Jobs, former head of Apple Computer

Venn diagrams

'Someone who has mastered the use of formal logic or of what are known as Venn diagrams is better equipped to distinguish between the validity of an argument and the plausibility of its conclusions. It can be tricky to sort out in your head the logic of syllogisms such as 'some police officers are freemasons; no liars are freemasons; therefore no police officers are liars'. But by representing the three 'sets' as overlapping circles in a Venn diagram it becomes visually obvious that the conclusion is invalid. But such tools, if they are to be of practical value, have to be used not just in examination rooms but spontaneously and appropriately – and they are often not.'

G. Claxton (1999)

introducing tools

'Today, many executives are articulating a new philosophy revolving around 'empowering people'. But few organisations are working hard to introduce tools and methods to actually help to make more intelligent decisions.'

P. Senge, R. Ross, B. Smith, C. Roberts and A. Kleiner (1994)

review

audit

Consider how many tools you have at home and work. How many of those at work support either the delivery of information or the creation of meaning?

possibilities

Think of a time when learning to use a tool made something possible that previously seemed unattainable.

classrooms

Think of some classroom scenarios in which either you or a student experienced difficulty in communicating effectively. How might a tool have helped?

learning teachers

How willing are you to learn to use new electrical tools when they come on the market? How willing are you to go through the learning necessary to use these tools effectively?

ROUTE MAP FOR YOUR READING

CONTEXT — SECTION 1

CHAPTER ONE BACKGROUND

The primary assertion is that we are all *Eye Q* experts. Throughout history, humans have used an assortment of visual tools to reflect and communicate knowledge. Current knowledge creation dynamics are based on this same notion. The 'inside story' of learning is obtained by looking both inside (cognitive psychology) and outside (Accelerated Learning).

CHAPTER TWO THE iDESK MODEL

Most of our activities are not based on a theory of learning. Consequently, there is little sense of meaning or coherence. The iDesk model is holistic. It connects thinking, feeling and doing. Finally, it links these faculties to the environment and the individual. Visual tools impact all areas of the iDesk model, and all components interact with each other. Serious schools need models.

CHAPTER THREE THE KNOWLEDGE AGE

We are living in the knowledge age with a need for more knowledge workers. These new types of workers require new, extended mental skills and knowledge tools. Visual tools are central in creating and communicating knowledge. Schools need to learn from business theory and practice with regard to intellectual capital and the use of visual tools.

VISUALS — SECTION 2

CHAPTER FOUR VISUAL TOOLS AND COMPUTERS

We are learning that the use of computers can reinforce poor learning habits. The attraction of the screen can degenerate into visual 'candyfloss'. This turns computer users into consumers. Behind the screen lies a knowledge structure. Visual tools make this explicit and turn consumers into explorers of knowledge. Clarity about visual literacy will support this.

CHAPTER FIVE VISUAL LITERACY

In our culture, the visual–verbal polarity may well be more divisive than the sciences–arts gulf. There are historical, philosophical reasons for the low value placed on visuals. Visual literacy, nonetheless, is an established discipline. All visual content exists in the spatial dimension. Space is our first and primary frontier. The spatial metaphor shapes our understanding.

CHAPTER SIX TOOLS TO LEARN

The successes of our civilisation are based on tools. We have created these tools and they, in turn, end up shaping our behaviour. Using new tools causes new learning to take place. Habitual use of tools changes our habits. The most effective use of tools happens when accompanied with theory. Visual tools impact on learning habits. New eras need new tools.

MEANING — SECTION 3

CHAPTER SEVEN SCHEMAS

We all have schemas. They are personal and unique and are based on how we view the world. In business they are termed mental models. Their organisation represents how we think and shape our behaviour. All students have these mental maps but are unaware of them — as are teachers. Making schemas visible allows students and teachers to see what they are thinking.

CHAPTER EIGHT HOLOGRAPHIC–LINEAR

Every day, every student, in every lesson has to turn linear communication (what she reads or hears) into what is termed her holographic understanding. Schemas are holographic in structure — definitely not linear. The student then has to turn her new, enlarged understanding back into linear format. This process has, until now, been an unknown phenomenon.

CHAPTER NINE CONSTRUCTING KNOWLEDGE

All our students construct knowledge — even the very youngest and the least able. Knowledge cannot be delivered. It has to be created each time by the individual, for knowledge is created not discovered. This view of learning is called constructivism. Understanding this process stimulates teachers to make learning more meaningful and motivating for all students.

LANGUAGE — SECTION 4

CHAPTER TEN SUPPORT FOR LANGUAGE

It is normally thought that visuals 'compete' with words. With visual tools, this is not true. Visual tools exist in the overlapping area between words and pictures. If you examine language, you realise that images play a big part in stimulating thought and supporting planning. They help the organisation of our language, which normally has to take place in the unseen interior of our heads.

CHAPTER ELEVEN READING

Reading is active. Readers' interrogation of text is shaped by their own schemas. They have to adapt their existing schemas in order to absorb text into meaningful messages. Visual tools can reveal the hidden structure and meaning of a text. Just as computer software can show you what your voice looks like, visual tools can show you what your thinking looks like.

CHAPTER TWELVE WRITING

Writing is difficult. Students' difficulties and fears stem from not knowing what to write. Visual tools make planning explicit, easy and empowering. Through the use of visual tools, students can model the planning that excellent writers do 'in their heads'. Planning in linear fashion is too difficult for most. The schematic nature of visual tools matches the way the brain naturally works.

THINKING — SECTION 5

CHAPTER THIRTEEN THINKING SKILLS

When we think, we are either thinking of objects (in space) or events (in time). Our thoughts become 'thought–objects'. Just as we manipulate real, physical objects in space, so we move our 'thought–objects' in our inner space. This is thinking. It is, however, invisible and demands much short term memory. Visual tools make thinking visible, easier and obvious.

CHAPTER FOURTEEN QUESTIONS

Questions are more powerful than answers. They directly determine our focus and thinking. Young children are wonderful questioners — young scientists. Schools have conditioned students to demand only questions. This severely limits their thinking and learning. Visual tools are themselves questions. They demand investigation. Their visible nature makes questioners of all students.

CHAPTER FIFTEEN THINKING IN ACTION

There is a link between text, thinking and visual tools. The nature of different types of text (genres) demand different types of thinking. All thinking is the manipulation of 'thought–objects'. Visual tools show students what this looks like. Matching types of visual tools to specific genres and linking them to the National Curriculum thinking skills is a powerful matrix.

LEARNING — SECTION 6

CHAPTER SIXTEEN ACTIVE LEARNING

You don't have to leave your seat to be actively learning. Active doesn't mean kinaesthetic! Active learning involves becoming engrossed, relating new material to personal prior knowledge, and creating meaning. Active learning needs to be encouraged by teachers. It is what is demanded of business. Visual tools stimulate and challenge active learning from students.

CHAPTER SEVENTEEN STYLES OF LEARNING

Learning style labels can be dangerous. They can limit rather than stimulate expansion. Behind their often surface description lies a common cognitive activity — putting the detail into the big picture. Visual tools meet the needs of all learners, involving them in visual, verbal, analytic and holistic thinking. They also promote the four essential skills of learning.

CHAPTER EIGHTEEN ABILITY RANGE

We have many labels for our pupils — from the gifted and talented to SEN. Behind all these labels there lies the act of meaning making. Visual tools show students what understanding looks like. This gives confidence to them all. It allows the least able to see their intelligence and supports the more able to organise and communicate their sometimes erratic thinking.

LEXICON — SECTION 7

CHAPTER NINETEEN LEXICON

CATEGORIES OF VISUAL TOOLS

- structural thinking — Structural Visual Tools
- differential thinking — Differential Visual Tools
- representational thinking — Representational Visual Tools
- temporal thinking — Temporal Visual Tools
- causal thinking — Causal Visual Tools
- numerical thinking — Numerical Visual Tools
- organisational thinking — Organisational Visual Tools
- individual thinking — Individual Visual Tools

There are seven types of visual tools related to seven types of thinking. The eighth is a hybrid of all seven. Within each category, there is a variety of visual tools. Visual tools within the categories achieve slightly different results, at different levels of complexity to suit age, ability and the nature of the tasks set. Each visual tool is described, its workings explained and ideas given for introducing it to students. Differences between similar visual tools are clarified. Each visual tool is illustrated both in templated format and as a hand-drawn example in use. The context for each hand-drawn visual tool is a well known story.

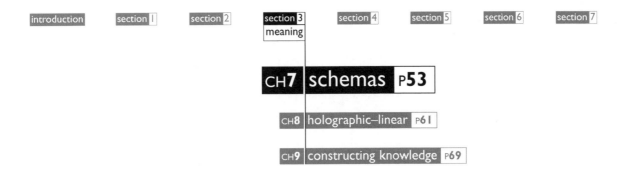

CH7 | schemas | P53

CH8 | holographic–linear | P61

CH9 | constructing knowledge | P69

overview

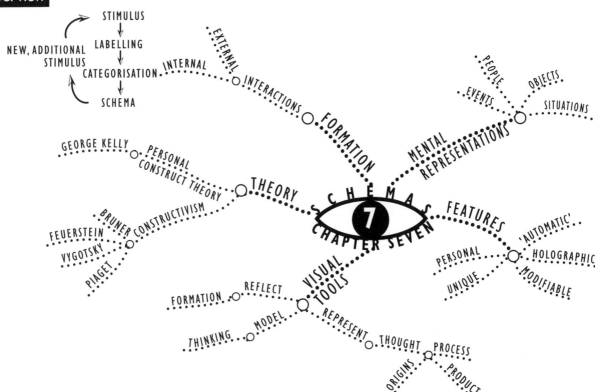

preview

- Everyone has a mental model of the world.

- Schemas are personal and unique.

- Schemas are formed by our external and internal interactions with the world.

- Learning is an ongoing process, a journey through life.

- Personal construct theory is at the heart of discussions about learning in the twenty-first century.

- Schemas are mental representations of people, objects, situations and events.

- We continually and automatically update our schemas as we navigate through life.

- 'Self-schema' is knowledge of our inner space.

- Schemas operate without us being aware of them.

- As teachers, we need to see the links between the individual's schema and the life of the classroom.

Everyone has a mental model of the world.

Imagine you have thirty young people seated in front of you. It's early in the morning, so they should be at their most receptive. You are about to launch into something new – uncharted territory – but a quick scan of the sea of faces tells you they need to be drawn together, to become more focused. Clearly some of them aren't quite 'there' with you – but where are they? Might they be 'in their own private little worlds'?

Well, yes, because thirty children plus one teacher means that the room contains thirty-one worlds. At least, that is the number of world models, or schemas, present. 'Schema' is a term psychologists use to describe the mental model of the world that exists inside the head of each and every person.

You may, or may not, be familiar with this term but you will certainly have an understanding of the elements of a schema, since they are ever-present in the classroom. Schemas are the packages of information and understanding in our heads. They are manifested in our actions and thoughts. Schemas directly influence every aspect of our behaviour.

Schemas are personal and unique.

To begin with, each newborn baby is gifted with a great deal of 'know-how', hard-wired in the brain. She has a 'blueprint' to begin making sense of human faces and language from her earliest days. She has the potential for receiving vast amounts of information through sensory experiences. Most importantly, she has the ability to transform those experiences into representations of the world.

We are all born with a range of predispositions. Some infants are calm and easy going, others fractious and unsettled – always 'on the go'. Not only will individual young learners perceive matters differently, as they mature they will seek out different forms of experience. Their emotional brains will cause them to respond in certain ways to situations in which they find themselves and to recreate those situations for themselves. This is what we mean by aptitude: a tendency towards a certain type of learning.

Our emotional state influences our learning. Who we become depends upon the schemas we assemble. No two people think in exactly the same way. Our schemas have been shaped by the experiences we have actively sought and by our reactions to those that have been offered. This is why some students appear highly motivated while others seem to need prompts and additional support.

Schemas are formed by our external and internal interactions with the world.

We do not live in the world passively. Our surroundings change. We change. As we begin to travel – both physically and mentally – we are able to explore more of our environment. We create our own moments and experiences. Our feelings, emotions and understanding are modified as a direct result of our dealings with other people, with animals, with possessions. After each new experience we add to our store of memories what the experience means to us. It is these memories that create our schemas.

According to Tulving (1983), memory comes in two forms. These are episodic memory and semantic memory. The first is directly related to the passage of time in our lives. It is, in a sense, our autobiography. Here we store personal events from the past – our past. The second, semantic memory, is vital for survival since it deals with the running of our daily lives. It encompasses a range of knowledge from knowing how much to spend on housekeeping to finding our way around town.

differential visual tool | matrix | lexicon link | page 178

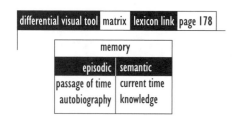

memory	
episodic	semantic
passage of time	current time
autobiography	knowledge

However, interaction between these memory banks is continuous since behind each semantic meaning lies an event or experience. Also, every episodic memory is supported by semantic recall. Visual and verbal memories are stored side by side. Visual tools enable us to recreate and recall memories more fully since they offer us holographic representation (chapter 8).

Learning is an ongoing process, a journey through life.

Any journey is made simpler if we travel with a map. Maps provide us with an impression of how the world might appear. They are not the real world. So it is with schemas. Each individual's mapping of the world is unique. These maps, contained in our heads, vary enormously and in direct relation to the strategies we employ while making them.

By making use of visual tools, we can recreate our maps in the public domain and compare and contrast them with the maps of fellow travellers and mapmakers. We can, if we wish, zoom in and pay particular attention to the detail of sections of these maps. Our schemas, our filing cabinets, contain maps for a range of terrains and destinations. Schemas are the contents of our minds. As Professor Susan Greenfield puts it:

> '... it is in this personalisation of the brain, crafted over the long years of childhood and continuing to evolve throughout life, that a unique pattern of connections between brain cells creates what might best be called a 'mind'... the mind should not be regarded as an airy-fairy alternative to the physical brain but, at the same time, it is something more than a generic lump of grey matter. My particular definition of mind will be that it is the seething morass of cell circuitry that has been configured by personal experiences and is constantly being updated as we live out each moment.'

S. Greenfield (2000)

Personal construct theory is at the heart of discussions about learning in the twenty-first century.

The psychologist George Kelly (1955) was influential in the development of constructivist theories. He believed that personal constructs were of primary importance in human development and emphasised the nature of their cognitive growth. In the same way that we construct objects from wood, we need an array of tools to build our knowledge and understanding from the thoughts and questions we have.

Kelly described individuals as scientists who hypothesised about the world. He offered the suggestion that people lived out their lives as intuitive scientists, observing, formulating hypotheses and continually testing them out and evaluating them. Like scientists, individuals can go amiss, their schemas may be built on shaky foundations and they may need a great deal of persuasion to adapt themselves to new situations.

Recent research into cognitive development, using electronic technology to observe and record babies' reactions in experimental situations, demonstrates Kelly's remarkable perception of the learning process. In *How Babies Think*, Gopnik, Meltzoff and Kuhl develop the links between how young learners go about the business of learning and how the scientist conducts his enquiries. They explain that they consider scientists to be nothing more than big children. In other words, for scientists, the meaningful playfulness that so epitomises the quality of early learning is not allowed to atrophy. Rather it is retained and exploited:

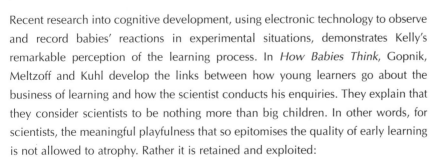

temporal visual tool | cycle | lexicon link | page 210

> 'Children create and revise theories in the same way that scientists create and revise theories. This idea seems to explain at least some types of cognitive development very well. We call it the theory theory. (The theory is that children have theories of the world.) ... Scientists, like babies, have rich, complex, abstract, coherent representations of the world. They have theories. The theories translate the input – the evidence scientists gather – into a more abstract representation of reality.'

A. Gopnik, A. Meltzoff and P. Kuhl (1999)

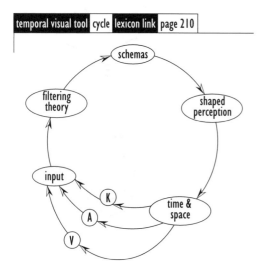

temporal visual tool | cycle | lexicon link | page 210

These theories are initiated in early childhood as we link and communicate our visual, spatial and temporal world through words. They remain with us and are subjected to challenges and reshaping throughout our lives. Maintaining and updating our schemas is life-long learning.

Visual tools are essential in this process. Students need to possess a comprehensive tool kit if they are to assemble their concepts from the raw materials they encounter. In order to construct knowledge and understanding they need to be able to seek out connections and relationships on their own. They need to join and fix the building blocks.

Schemas are mental representations of people, objects, situations and events.

While we are developing our schemas we spend our time classifying, labelling, categorising, generalising. We gradually acquire a sense or understanding of what belongs where. We learn about hierarchies and realise that we can use one word to describe a range of objects. We use the word 'shopping', for example, rather than create an unnecessary itemised list. We see patterns and consistency in the world and these observations affect our expectations. We form preconceptions and develop our predispositions.

As adults, we support our own children in developing their schemas. We watch amazed as they correctly label the household furry friend as a 'cat' and then howl with laughter as they give the same name to dogs, pigs, horses – anything with a tail, fur and four legs, in fact. This child has perceived a regularity – the fur, the tail and the legs – and has labelled it 'cat'. 'Cat' has become a concept. From these perceived regularities, schemas develop.

One of the first words Sarah learned as a two-year-old was 'drink'. Her parents would then try to 'guess the drink' she wanted, as they bought her milk, water, juice or tea. Sometimes they would get it right first time, sometimes

they would bring her the 'wrong' drink and have it pushed away. They helped Sarah by asking her 'What drink do you want Sarah? Do you want water? Do you want juice?' They were helping her create meaning for herself. Six months of 'guess the drink' resulted in Sarah developing the vocabulary that enabled her to answer the question 'What drink do you want Sarah?' with the word 'tea', 'water', 'milk' or 'juice'. Soon after this breakthrough, Sarah was able to request hot or cold milk, apple or orange juice and interestingly Mummy's or Daddy's tea – she did not have the vocabulary to ask for Earl Grey or Camomile but she knew that they tasted different!

As a three-year-old, Sarah added different categories to her schema on 'drink'. She now knows that there are some drinks for adults – beer, wine, and 'small glass drinks' – and some for children – milkshake, squash and so on.

Human beings automatically amend and alter existing schemas with the arrival of new stimuli. Isn't this exactly what we ask children to do all the time in schools? What would happen if this process were made explicit? What would happen if children had access to tools to help them form and incorporate new stimuli into existing schemas. What would happen if all teachers understood how children form schemas and were able to model this to the learners in their classrooms?

You will see by now that schema formation and development is not something weird but something so fundamental to everything we do that we do not even notice we are doing it.

We continually and automatically update our schemas as we navigate through life.

Schemas mean that we do not need to consider each and every detail at the time of each new encounter. Past experiences have installed in our memories our responses to similar inputs of information. Instantaneous, effective recognition becomes so commonplace we are not even aware that the schema is operating. Our learning is most successful when it leads us to develop unconscious competencies.

If we think of life as a journey, and of an individual's physical and mental presence in the world as a vessel, then it would seem logical to accept that the individual is continually making adjustments to compensate for the changes in the environmental conditions and the actions of other navigators, responding to her own inner feelings, sensations and intuitions.

Schools and classrooms are like busy ports. In the bustle, it is easy to become lost. Travellers who are not sufficiently organised are often stranded. So it is with learners. By making acts of learning visible and inclusive teachers can provide obvious, distinctive signs and meeting points.

'Self-schema' is knowledge of our inner space.

We need to be aware of our own talents and abilities, our strengths and our limitations. We should develop a realistic assessment of what goes on inside us, intellectually and emotionally. If our perceptions of our capabilities are negative, are we likely to approach fresh topics or seemingly complex challenges in a positive mindset? Our state of mind determines the quality of our learning.

Displaying publicly and discussing the individual's contribution to the learning that takes place in our schools is vital to the development of self-esteem. Low self-esteem and anxiety are serious impediments to success in learning. Success emerges from a climate in which there is respect for individuals and for their thoughts and ideas. This entails bringing the inner thoughts into public view. Visual tools, by providing a location for placing and connecting an assembly of thoughts, achieve this. It is rewarding for students to see their ideas linked with those of other group members.

differential visual tool	matrix	lexicon link	page 178

self-esteem	
high	**low**
work displayed	work hidden
teacher reveals thinking	teacher hides thinking
learning signposted	learning unmapped
knowledge overt	knowledge implicit
confidence	anxiety

Clearly, our potential for learning is not predetermined. We are able to adapt and change as we journey through life. Yet it is not the experience itself that shapes our own humanity. It is the constant interaction between our basic capacity for learning and change and the challenges and problems that, as individuals, we are continually asked to resolve.

Schemas operate without us being aware of them.

What does it mean if we comment that someone is 'acting without thinking'? The amount of data that we receive each second is far too great for us to cope with in an analytical way. The effort to make sense of the detail would overwhelm us. At times our thinking is done for us – we run on 'autopilot', scarcely conscious of the connection that exists between our mind and body, so seamless is the join. At other times we are required to focus and it is at this point of interaction that learning may become difficult.

We know what the brain consists of, physically – it is the content that fascinates and drives us. We need to know and understand not just our own minds but also those of others. How often have we said, 'I wish I knew what was going on in her head,' or 'What's on his mind?'

Classrooms provide wonderful opportunities for meetings of minds – but they need to be flexible, open minds. Visual tools encourage and actively promote alternative theories and viewpoints. They lead to more informed decision making. It is the decisions we make about new experiences that mould our schemas. Is there acceptance, rejection or modification?

As teachers, we need to see the links between the individual's schema and the life of the classroom.

Minds are filled with information, with memories, with theories about the world. No two minds are the same. Unique schemas have been constructed. These schemas define the limits of our intellectual growth. Difficulties occur when we cannot respond positively to challenges to our thoughts, when we are unable to take in new information and connect it to the theories and concepts we already possess.

Recent research undertaken by Hay McBer (2000) into school effectiveness stressed the importance of climate in schools where students were achieving well. Among the characteristics that were valued were respect for others

and a belief that individuals matter. Out of mutual respect grow confidence and self-esteem. At the classroom level, effective teachers believed their skills and behaviour were central to the progress they wished for their students. Aspects of 'behaviour' listed in McBer's report include participation, standards, clarity, support, fairness, safety and interest. Teachers who possess a range of visual tools to support their students' progress in all subjects are more likely to create positive, interactive learning experiences. In addition, visual tools offer students strategies for becoming autonomous, creative and purposeful learners.

Progress is achieved by building on what has gone before. So teachers need to be able to create a picture and record of each individual learner. In other words, teachers must be familiar with individuals' schemas. They need to know not just *what* has been learned but – at a deeper level – *how* the individual sets about the task of learning. 'Learning' is the key word.

Visual tools provide a highly effective, ongoing form of assessment. They are critical in the transference of thoughts from the inner space of private brains to the public domain of the classroom. Learning is made visible. The uncertainty about what goes on inside the students' heads is reduced.

Teachers are being encouraged to respect individuals, to value the aspirations and expectations of their students, and to assist them in achieving their potential. We need to see our learners as unique human beings whose present view of the world, and their place in it, has been shaped by their prior learning experiences both inside and outside school. In other words, their schemas need to be made visible.

viewpoints

children's schemas

'Children's schemas can be viewed as part of their motivation for learning, their insatiable drive to move, represent, discuss, question, find out.'

C. Nutbrown (1999)

hidden mental models

'Mental models are very important, very powerful and very individual ... Usually, however, they are not discussed explicitly.'

D. Sherwood (1998)

revealing mental models

'... you are not only mapping the system 'out there', but your own understanding at the same time, you are drawing your own thought processes and will see your own mental models.'

J. O'Connor and I. McDermott (1997)

relying on mental models

'One funny thing about our mental models: we can't operate without them, but we tend not even to notice we have them.'

M. Lissack and J. Roos (1999)

knowledge

'Knowledge is organised into mental packages that are developed to provide clear interpretation and smooth expertise in familiar domains of experience.'

G. Claxton (1990)

behaviour

'Although people do not (always) behave congruently with their espoused theories (what they say), they do behave congruently with their theories-in-use (their mental models).'

C. Argyris (1982)

review

professional understanding

How might a knowledge of schema formation affect your professional understanding of how children learn?

visible schema

How might making schema structure and formation visible affect discussion and argument both in the classroom and in life generally?

self-awareness

How well do you know your schemas – your own mini-theories, assumptions, even prejudices. Map some out and find out!

ROUTE MAP FOR YOUR READING

SECTION 1 — CONTEXT

CHAPTER ONE BACKGROUND
The primary assertion is that we are all *Eye Q* experts. Throughout history, humans have used an assortment of visual tools to reflect and communicate knowledge. Current knowledge creation dynamics are based on this same notion. The 'inside story' of learning is obtained by looking both inside (cognitive psychology) and outside (Accelerated Learning).

CHAPTER TWO THE iDESK MODEL
Most of our activities are not based on a theory of learning. Consequently, there is little sense of meaning or coherence. The iDesk model is holistic. It connects thinking, feeling and doing. Finally, it links these faculties to the environment and the individual. Visual tools impact all areas of the iDesk model, and all components interact with each other. Serious schools need models.

CHAPTER THREE THE KNOWLEDGE AGE
We are living in the knowledge age with a need for more knowledge workers. These new types of workers require new, extended mental skills and knowledge tools. Visual tools are central in creating and communicating knowledge. Schools need to learn from business theory and practice with regard to intellectual capital and the use of visual tools.

SECTION 2 — VISUALS

CHAPTER FOUR VISUAL TOOLS AND COMPUTERS
We are learning that the use of computers can reinforce poor learning habits. The attraction of the screen can degenerate into visual 'candyfloss'. This turns computer users into consumers. Behind the screen lies a knowledge structure. Visual tools make this explicit and turn consumers into explorers of knowledge. Clarity about visual literacy will support this.

CHAPTER FIVE VISUAL LITERACY
In our culture, the visual–verbal polarity may well be more divisive than the sciences–arts gulf. There are historical, philosophical reasons for the low value placed on visuals. Visual literacy, nonetheless, is an established discipline. All visual content exists in the spatial dimension. Space is our first and primary frontier. The spatial metaphor shapes our understanding.

CHAPTER SIX TOOLS TO LEARN
The successes of our civilisation are based on tools. We have created these tools and they, in turn, end up shaping our behaviour. Using new tools causes new learning to take place. Habitual use of tools changes our habits. The most effective use of tools happens when accompanied with theory. Visual tools impact on learning habits. New eras need new tools.

SECTION 3 — MEANING

CHAPTER SEVEN SCHEMAS
We all have schemas. They are personal and unique and are based on how we view the world. In business they are termed mental models. Their organisation represents how we think and shape our behaviour. All students have these mental maps but are unaware of them — as are teachers. Making schemas visible allows students and teachers to see what they are thinking.

CHAPTER EIGHT HOLOGRAPHIC–LINEAR
Every day, every student, in every lesson has to turn linear communication (what she reads or hears) into what is termed her holographic understanding. Schemas are holographic in structure — definitely not linear. The student then has to turn her new, enlarged understanding back into linear format. This process has, until now, been an unknown phenomenon.

CHAPTER NINE CONSTRUCTING KNOWLEDGE
All our students construct knowledge — even the very youngest and the least able. Knowledge cannot be delivered. It has to be created each time by the individual, for knowledge is created not discovered. This view of learning is called constructivism. Understanding this process stimulates teachers to make learning more meaningful and motivating for all students.

SECTION 4 — LANGUAGE

CHAPTER TEN SUPPORT FOR LANGUAGE
It is normally thought that visuals 'compete' with words. With visual tools, this is not true. Visual tools exist in the overlapping area between words and pictures. If you examine language, you realise that images play a big part in stimulating thought and supporting planning. They help the organisation of our language, which normally has to take place in the unseen interior of our heads.

CHAPTER ELEVEN READING
Reading is active. Readers' interrogation of text is shaped by their own schemas. They have to adapt their existing schemas in order to absorb text into meaningful messages. Visual tools can reveal the hidden structure and meaning of a text. Just as computer software can show you what your voice looks like, visual tools can show you what your thinking looks like.

CHAPTER TWELVE WRITING
Writing is difficult. Students' difficulties and fears stem from not knowing what to write. Visual tools make planning explicit, easy and empowering. Through the use of visual tools, students can model the planning that excellent writers do 'in their heads'. Planning in linear fashion is too difficult for most. The schematic nature of visual tools matches the way the brain naturally works.

SECTION 5 — THINKING

CHAPTER THIRTEEN THINKING SKILLS
When we think, we are either thinking of objects (in space) or events (in time). Our thoughts become 'thought–objects'. Just as we manipulate real, physical objects in space, so we move our 'thought–objects' in our inner space. This is thinking. It is, however, invisible and demands much short term memory. Visual tools make thinking visible, easier and obvious.

CHAPTER FOURTEEN QUESTIONS
Questions are more powerful than answers. They directly determine our focus and thinking. Young children are wonderful questioners — young scientists. Schools have conditioned students to demand only questions. This severely limits their thinking and learning. Visual tools are themselves questions. They demand investigation. Their visible nature makes questioners of all students.

CHAPTER FIFTEEN THINKING IN ACTION
There is a link between text, thinking and visual tools. The nature of different types of text (genres) demand different types of thinking. All thinking is the manipulation of 'thought–objects'. Visual tools show students what this looks like. Matching types of visual tools to specific genres and linking them to the National Curriculum thinking skills is a powerful matrix.

SECTION 6 — LEARNING

CHAPTER SIXTEEN ACTIVE LEARNING
You don't have to leave your seat to be actively learning. Active doesn't mean kinaesthetic! Active learning involves becoming engrossed, relating new material to personal prior knowledge, and creating meaning. Active learning needs to be encouraged by teachers. It is what is demanded of business. Visual tools stimulate and challenge active learning from students.

CHAPTER SEVENTEEN STYLES OF LEARNING
Learning style labels can be dangerous. They can limit rather than stimulate expansion. Behind their often surface description lies a common cognitive activity — putting the detail into the big picture. Visual tools meet the needs of all learners, involving them in visual, verbal, analytic and holistic thinking. They also promote the four essential skills of learning.

CHAPTER EIGHTEEN ABILITY RANGE
We have many labels for our pupils — from the gifted and talented to SEN. Behind all these labels there lies the act of meaning making. Visual tools show students what understanding looks like. This gives confidence to them all. It allows the least able to see their intelligence and supports the more able to organise and communicate their sometimes erratic thinking.

SECTION 7 — LEXICON

CHAPTER NINETEEN LEXICON

CATEGORIES OF VISUAL TOOLS
- structural thinking — Structural Visual Tools
- differential thinking — Differential Visual Tools
- representational thinking — Representational Visual Tools
- temporal thinking — Temporal Visual Tools
- causal thinking — Causal Visual Tools
- numerical thinking — Numerical Visual Tools
- organisational thinking — Organisational Visual Tools
- individual thinking — Individual Visual Tools

There are seven types of visual tools related to seven types of thinking. The eighth is a hybrid of all seven. Within each category, there is a variety of visual tools. Visual tools within the categories achieve slightly different results, at different levels of complexity to suit age, ability and the nature of the tasks set. Each visual tool is described, its workings explained and ideas given for introducing it to students. Differences between similar visual tools are clarified. Each visual tool is illustrated both in templated format and as a hand-drawn example in use. The context for each hand-drawn visual tool is a well known story.

CH7 schemas P53

CH8 holographic–linear P61

CH9 constructing knowledge P69

overview

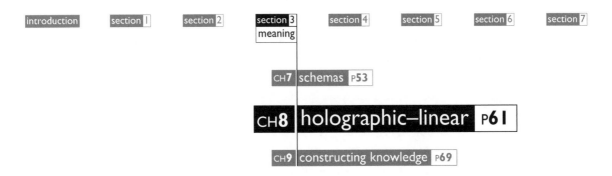

preview

- The holographic nature of our 'thinking' is to humans what 'water' is to fish.

- Inherent in learning are two acts of transformation that we accomplish without knowing it.

- Students' experience a linear world through curriculum design, the written word and spoken language.

- The formation of mental maps when we visit any unfamiliar place reflects and further illustrates the holographic–linear process.

- A linear experience may lead to surface or superficial learning.

- A holographic experience is more likely to result in deeper levels of understanding.

- In using visual tools, the learner is making her spatial and temporal connections visible and is accessing long-term memory.

- Visual tools reveal the meaning buried in linear text.

- Visual tools offer all learners access to a variety of 'pathways' through learning experiences.

- Visual tools support students at all stages of the thinking process – input, elaboration and output.

The holographic nature of our 'thinking' is to humans what 'water' is to fish.

In Japan they have a saying, 'Don't ask a fish about water'. Why would it be pointless to ask a fish about water, even if it could speak? Because a fish has no idea what water is. It is so much part of its life that it doesn't even know it is there. What would need to happen for a fish to understand 'water'? The fish would need to be removed from the water – to be apart from it. The holographic–linear distinction is our equivalent of the fish's water.

Inherent in learning are two acts of transformation that we accomplish without knowing it.

The process of learning requires the learner firstly to transform linear input into holographic understanding, and secondly to transform her holographic understanding back into linear output. As you read this chapter you are doing exactly this. You are receiving linear input, by reading one word at a time. At the end of the chapter, try to explain the holographic–linear distinction to someone else. Your output will be linear – one word at a time. What has happened in between the linear input and the linear output?

Reuven Feuerstein, an eminent and highly influential Israeli psychologist, calls the stage in between input and output the 'elaboration' stage of thinking. How have you been processing the information? How have you been 'elaborating' on what you have heard? Have you processed the information presented to you in the same way as you received it, in a linear way? Obviously not. If you had, you would only ever be able to relate each word to the word immediately preceding it. As you read, you relate each word not only to the immediately preceding one but to all the words that have gone before. You have processed the information *holographically*.

Are you aware of doing this or does it 'just happen?' What if you had access to a range of tools that could help you receive, process or elaborate, and then present information? What if you, and all learners, were supported in learning specifically these acts of transformation?

Students certainly seem to appreciate help in understanding transformation, as Cooper and McIntyre, two educational researchers, have reported:

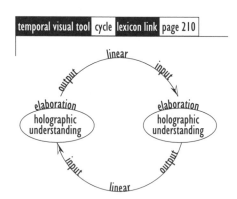

temporal visual tool | cycle | lexicon link | page 210

'The theme of transformation is a powerful one in student accounts. When it occurs it usually involves students forging connections between their past or present experiences and teacher input … the students engage actively in the process; by constructing the context …'

P. Cooper and D. McIntyre (1993)

Once we understand what our 'water' is, so to speak, we can begin to see why visual tools can have a profound impact in helping us understand our world.

Students experience a linear world through curriculum design, the written word and spoken language.

Most students' direct experience of school is of a curriculum that is linear in nature. They go from one subject area to the next, to the next, to the next. There may be a period of several days before they return to a topic under study in any particular subject area. It is as if we are asking them to complete many jigsaw puzzles simultaneously without knowing what any of the box lids look like!

Students listen to language that is presented to them in each lesson in a linear fashion, one word at a time. The actual mechanics of speaking determine that we can only say and listen to one word at a time. When students access written text they read one word at a time. So in all schools, even those where topic or cross-curricular approaches are used, a student's experience of language is linear. Just as you are transforming this linear input into holographic understanding, so students are being asked to do this in every school in every country around the world.

The formation of mental maps when we visit any unfamiliar place reflects and further illustrates the holographic–linear process.

Imagine two people, both on day trips to Rye in Sussex, England. The first person is going to have a very stimulating but linear experience. The second person is going to have the opportunity to have a holographic experience. As you read through the scenarios described below, ask yourself which one most closely mirrors a child's experience of school.

A linear experience may lead to surface or superficial learning.

Imagine you are the first person visiting Rye. You are met off the train. Then you are blindfolded, before being taken to the bottom of Mermaid Street, regarded by some as one of the prettiest streets in England. At the bottom of Mermaid Street, the blindfold is replaced with horses' blinkers. You are then led slowly to the top of the street, perhaps stopping off for a drink in the Mermaid Inn en route. You are told interesting facts and intriguing stories about the features you see. At the top of the street, just before you get to a 'T' junction, your blindfold is put back on. You are taken to the top of the Mint, and the blindfold is replaced with blinkers once more as you visit the site. The same thing happens over and over again until you have visited all of the major landmarks in Rye. You have had a great time.

All your senses were stimulated including taste and smell (Rye has some great restaurants!). At the end of the day you had seen all the main attractions that Rye has to offer. But if someone asked you to find your way to one of the places you had been to, on your own and without guidance, how easy would you find this?

A holographic experience is more likely result in deeper levels of understanding.

Now imagine you are the second visitor to Rye, who is going to have a very different experience of the town. You are met at the train station as before, but this time there are no blindfolds and no blinkers. This time you are going to go up in a helicopter. You are going to hover over the same landmarks seen by the 'linear' visitor, for five minutes each. You will hear the same stories, taste the same snacks, and you too will go to the Mermaid Inn.

Is it the first or the second visit that gives the best overall understanding of how Rye 'fits together'. Which visitor is going to be able to find their way around Rye most effectively, using various routes?

When you visit a theme park, you're usually given a map of the site showing how to reach the attractions. Imagine instead that you were simply given a list of the attractions, perhaps with some written instructions about how to get to one place from another. Both the map and the list give the same information, but which would allow you to make best use of your time at the theme park?

Perhaps you think you don't need a map or a list because you have been to the theme park many times before. If this is the case, you will still be using a map, in fact. It's in your head. It's your 'water'.

In using visual tools, the learner is making her spatial and temporal connections visible and is accessing long-term memory.

We have seen that visual tools reveal to learners the spatial and temporal relationships that are implicit in all tasks.

The 'Rye Case Study' dealt with geographical terrain. In classrooms, learners in all subject areas are being asked to navigate linguistic terrains. You will remember from chapter 7, Schemas, that learners develop their schemas by incorporating new information into existing schemas. This is what learning is. As Frank Smith (1990) tells us, 'memory is organisation'.

structural visual tool | clustering | lexicon link | page 154

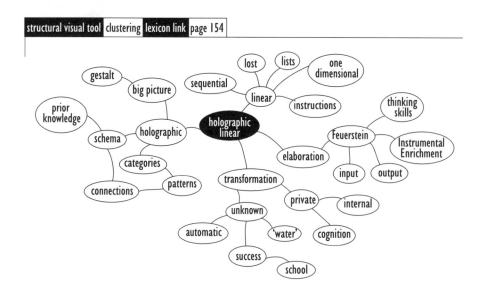

We know that learners transfer information from short-term memory to long-term memory when they have incorporated new learning into existing structures of knowledge and understanding. When they do this they are creating spatial and temporal relationships that go beyond their direct linear experience. For decades, teachers have known instinctively that learners remember things they have understood and they skilfully design ways that learners can demonstrate their understanding. Visual tools reveal what this understanding looks like.

Visual tools reveal the meaning buried in linear text.

In the United Kingdom much emphasis is being placed on teaching children grammar. It is useful here for us to distinguish between surface grammar and deeper semantic grammar.

Surface grammar is concerned with the parts of speech and their relationships to each other. This is being taught explicitly. Semantic grammar is the grammar of meaning – the meaning the reader creates when she reads and understands. This is not being taught specifically in schools, yet it is this level of grammar that would empower both teachers and learners.

Visual tools support learners in accessing the meaning of texts. They make explicit, public and available the spatial and temporal relationships that are only implicit in linear text.

Visual tools offer all learners access to a variety of 'pathways' through learning experiences.

The holographic–linear distinction is the key to understanding why some students experience deeper levels of learning than others.

Many learners do reach deep levels of understanding, which they establish for themselves, in spite of a linear sequential education. For them it is so automatic it is as if it has happened by accident. The learner doesn't know how she has done it. It has simply happened. For other learners, linear experience can often result in superficial levels of learning with limited understanding. They have, perhaps, only been able to make some connections directly related to their experience.

How many students have you taught that have not been able to make connections beyond their immediate experience? It is as if they can only relate one episode of learning to itself and to no other episode. This is what Feuerstein calls 'episodic' learning. They may only access a singular linear pathway. What happens if they fall off this pathway? How many alternative routes do they have available?

We can't do anything about the fact that we can only say or read one word at a time. What we can do is support all learners by revealing to them the spatial relationships embedded in the linguistic explorations and explanations we provide in classrooms. Without access to such relationships, learners are left with a singular, mechanical, linear route. As all teachers know, some learners fall off this route. Some do not get back on.

Visual tools offer a very powerful way of revealing the spatial relationships buried in text-based information, and therefore making these linear–holographic transformations explicit and available to all learners.

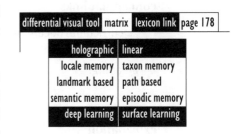

differential visual tool	matrix	lexicon link	page 178

holographic	linear
locale memory	taxon memory
landmark based	path based
semantic memory	episodic memory
deep learning	surface learning

The tools teachers and learners select to use will depend on the nature and purpose of the task. Understanding the linear–holographic distinction is a vital step to seeing why it is necessary to introduce and teach students to use visual tools. Without visual tools the holographic nature of learning may for many students be lost in the linear world of text and dialogue. As Meier, an educational author, points out:

> 'Before the invention of the printing press ... learning was a holographic, gestalt, concrete affair. As the book became the major vehicle for education, learning came to emphasise a mechanical, linear, one-thing-at-a-time process.'
>
> *D. Meier (2000)*

Because visual tools represent the whole and the parts simultaneously the learner is supported in both their linear and holographic thinking. Robinson, another education author, explains:

> 'It is a feature of schematic symbols that we respond to them as a whole. We don't only respond to a poem, or a play, or to music, line by line or note by note. The complete work is more than the sum of its parts.'
>
> *K. Robinson (2001)*

Visual tools support students at all stages of the thinking process – input, elaboration and output.

Visual tools can be used by teachers to help them effectively communicate ideas, explanations and instructions to students. In so doing, they are ensuring that students can *see* connections and associations between the individual details (the linear elements of the idea, instruction or explanation). What Feuerstein calls the 'input' stage of the learning process is thereby transformed from a wholly linear experience into one that is also holographic.

Visual tools provide students with a range of structures to use as they work through the explorations and learning opportunities that have been set for them. The tools transform the private act of thinking (which for many students may occur as a 'hit or miss' affair) into one in which they can publicly build, construct and develop their understanding, either individually or in groups.

Their thoughts are transformed into 'thought-objects' (see section 5, Thinking), which they can manoeuvre in space as their thinking is elaborated. The elaboration stage of thinking is therefore made visible.

The tools themselves become a physical representation of the understanding that students have gained from the learning opportunities provided to them. As a teacher, you need no longer wade through pages of linear text trying to glean the extent of its author's understanding. Students now have a range of holographic structures available that support them in translating their holographic understanding back into linear text. The linear output stage of learning is now also transformed from an experience that previously demanded the learner to draw on hidden holographic structures held in the mind into one in which the structures are visible. So, linear output, whether oral or written, is supported.

Now, try to explain this chapter to someone else!

viewpoints

conceptual links

'... curriculum documents and schemes of work need to concentrate on links between concepts as much as on the concepts themselves, as without appropriate links the concepts lose meaning.'

I. M. Kinchin, D. B. Hay and A. Adams (2000)

explanation

'We teachers – perhaps all human beings – are in the grip of an astonishing delusion. We think that we can take a picture, a structure, a working model of something, constructed in our minds out of long experience and familiarity, and by turning it into a long string of words, transplant it whole into the mind of someone else.'

J. Holt (1983)

kinds of knowledge

'The mind contains many different kinds of knowledge structures, some truer to perception, more metric, more consistent – for example, images. Others may bear structural similarities to some state or process in the world, yet are categorical and more abstract, such as mental models.'

D. Getner and A. L. Stevens (1983)

courtroom graphics

'Such displays are likely to be especially persuasive and memorable in situations where most information communicated consists of spoken words – as in a trial. Courtroom graphics can overcome the linear, non-reversible, one-dimensional sequencing of talk, talk, talk, allowing members of the jury to reason about an array of data at their own pace and in their own manner.'

E. Tufte (1990)

relationships

'When you are able to move issues or ideas around in relationship to each other, it becomes easier to see the thread of what has been written. You are simply escaping the left–right and top–down trap that text imposes on our thinking.'

M. Craig (2000)

thinking

'We do not think in a linear, sequential way, yet every body of information that is given to us is given to us in a linear manner … we are taught to communicate in a way that is actually constricting our ability to think.'

R. S. Wurman (1990)

space

'The best way to understand the difference between the two memory systems as they can be applied to teaching is to understand the difference between using a route (taxon systems) or a map (locale memory) to go somewhere.'

R. N. Caine, and G. Caine (1991)

review

explanations

Think of a book you have read recently. Imagine yourself describing what it is about to someone else. What comes to mind when you think about the book is a holographic understanding (schema) that you have gleaned from the linear input, without knowing it. The language you use to describe it is the linear output occurring from your holographic understanding.

orientation

How could you use the scenario of finding your way around a new house to explain the holographic–linear distinction?

misunderstanding

How does this chapter add to your understanding of why students in your classroom, or school, get 'stuck' or misunderstand something?

ROUTE MAP FOR YOUR READING

SECTION 1 — CONTEXT

CHAPTER ONE — BACKGROUND

The primary assertion is that we are all *Eye Q* experts. Throughout history, humans have used an assortment of visual tools to reflect and communicate knowledge. Current knowledge creation dynamics are based on this same notion. The 'inside story' of learning is obtained by looking both inside (cognitive psychology) and outside (Accelerated Learning).

CHAPTER TWO — THE iDESK MODEL

Most of our activities are not based on a theory of learning. Consequently, there is little sense of meaning or coherence. The iDesk model is holistic. It connects thinking, feeling and doing. Finally, it links these faculties to the environment and the individual. Visual tools impact all areas of the iDesk model, and all components interact with each other. Serious schools need models.

CHAPTER THREE — THE KNOWLEDGE AGE

We are living in the knowledge age with a need for more knowledge workers. These new types of workers require new, extended mental skills and knowledge tools. Visual tools are central in creating and communicating knowledge. Schools need to learn from business theory and practice with regard to intellectual capital and the use of visual tools.

SECTION 2 — VISUALS

CHAPTER FOUR — VISUAL TOOLS AND COMPUTERS

We are learning that the use of computers can reinforce poor learning habits. The attraction of the screen can degenerate into visual 'candyfloss'. This turns computer users into consumers. Behind the screen lies a knowledge structure. Visual tools make this explicit and turn consumers into explorers of knowledge. Clarity about visual literacy will support this.

CHAPTER FIVE — VISUAL LITERACY

In our culture, the visual—verbal polarity may well be more divisive than the sciences—arts gulf. There are historical, philosophical reasons for the low value placed on visuals. Visual literacy, nonetheless, is an established discipline. All visual content exists in the spatial dimension. Space is our first and primary frontier. The spatial metaphor shapes our understanding.

CHAPTER SIX — TOOLS TO LEARN

The successes of our civilisation are based on tools. We have created these tools and they, in turn, end up shaping our behaviour. Using new tools causes new learning to take place. Habitual use of tools changes our habits. The most effective use of tools happens when accompanied with theory. Visual tools impact on learning habits. New eras need new tools.

SECTION 3 — MEANING

CHAPTER SEVEN — SCHEMAS

We all have schemas. They are personal and unique and are based on how we view the world. In business they are termed mental models. Their organisation represents how we think and shape our behaviour. All students have these mental maps but are unaware of them — as are teachers. Making schemas visible allows students and teachers to see what they are thinking.

CHAPTER EIGHT — HOLOGRAPHIC—LINEAR

Every day, every student, in every lesson has to turn linear communication (what she reads or hears) into what is termed her holographic understanding. Schemas are holographic in structure — definitely not linear. The student then has to turn her new, enlarged understanding back into linear format. This process has, until now, been an unknown phenomenon.

CHAPTER NINE — CONSTRUCTING KNOWLEDGE

All our students construct knowledge — even the very youngest and the least able. Knowledge cannot be delivered. It has to be created each time by the individual, for knowledge is created not discovered. This view of learning is called constructivism. Understanding this process stimulates teachers to make learning more meaningful and motivating for all students.

SECTION 4 — LANGUAGE

CHAPTER TEN — SUPPORT FOR LANGUAGE

It is normally thought that visuals 'compete' with words. With visual tools, this is not true. Visual tools exist in the overlapping area between words and pictures. If you examine language, you realise that images play a big part in stimulating thought and supporting planning. They help the organisation of our language, which normally has to take place in the unseen interior of our heads.

CHAPTER ELEVEN — READING

Reading is active. Readers' interrogation of text is shaped by their own schemas. They have to adapt their existing schemas in order to absorb text into meaningful messages. Visual tools can reveal the hidden structure and meaning of a text. Just as computer software can show you what your voice looks like, visual tools can show you what your thinking looks like.

CHAPTER TWELVE — WRITING

Writing is difficult. Students' difficulties and fears stem from not knowing what to write. Visual tools make planning explicit, easy and empowering. Through the use of visual tools, students can model the planning that excellent writers do 'in their heads'. Planning in linear fashion is too difficult for most. The schematic nature of visual tools matches the way the brain naturally works.

SECTION 5 — THINKING

CHAPTER THIRTEEN — THINKING SKILLS

When we think, we are either thinking of objects (in space) or events (in time). Our thoughts become 'thought—objects'. Just as we manipulate real, physical objects in space, so we move our 'thought—objects' in our inner space. This is thinking. It is, however, invisible and demands much short term memory. Visual tools make thinking visible, easier and obvious.

CHAPTER FOURTEEN — QUESTIONS

Questions are more powerful than answers. They directly determine our focus and thinking. Young children are wonderful questioners — young scientists. Schools have conditioned students to demand only questions. This severely limits their thinking and learning. Visual tools are themselves questions. They demand investigation. Their visible nature makes questioners of all students.

CHAPTER FIFTEEN — THINKING IN ACTION

There is a link between text, thinking and visual tools. The nature of different types of text (genres) demand different types of thinking. All thinking is the manipulation of 'thought—objects'. Visual tools show students what this looks like. Matching types of visual tools to specific genres and linking them to the National Curriculum thinking skills is a powerful matrix.

SECTION 6 — LEARNING

CHAPTER SIXTEEN — ACTIVE LEARNING

You don't have to leave your seat to be actively learning. Active doesn't mean kinaesthetic! Active learning involves becoming engrossed, relating new material to personal prior knowledge, and creating meaning. Active learning needs to be encouraged by teachers. It is what is demanded of business. Visual tools stimulate and challenge active learning from students.

CHAPTER SEVENTEEN — STYLES OF LEARNING

Learning style labels can be dangerous. They can limit rather than stimulate expansion. Behind their often surface description lies a common cognitive activity — putting the detail into the big picture. Visual tools meet the needs of all learners, involving them in visual, verbal, analytic and holistic thinking. They also promote the four essential skills of learning.

CHAPTER EIGHTEEN — ABILITY RANGE

We have many labels for our pupils — from the gifted and talented to SEN. Behind all these labels there lies the act of meaning making. Visual tools show students what understanding looks like. This gives confidence to them all. It allows the least able to see their intelligence and supports the more able to organise and communicate their sometimes erratic thinking.

SECTION 7 — LEXICON

CHAPTER NINETEEN — LEXICON

CATEGORIES OF VISUAL TOOLS

- structural thinking — Structural Visual Tools
- differential thinking — Differential Visual Tools
- representational thinking — Representational Visual Tools
- temporal thinking — Temporal Visual Tools
- causal thinking — Causal Visual Tools
- numerical thinking — Numerical Visual Tools
- organisational thinking — Organisational Visual Tools
- individual thinking — Individual Visual Tools

There are seven types of visual tools related to seven types of thinking. The eighth is a hybrid of all seven. Within each category, there is a variety of visual tools. Visual tools within the categories achieve slightly different results, at different levels of complexity to suit age, ability and the nature of the tasks set. Each visual tool is described, its workings explained and ideas given for introducing it to students. Differences between similar visual tools are clarified. Each visual tool is illustrated both in templated format and as a hand-drawn example in use. The context for each hand-drawn visual tool is a well known story.

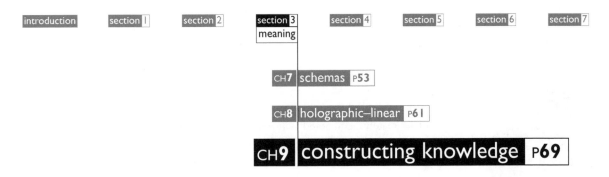

CH7 schemas P53

CH8 holographic—linear P61

CH9 constructing knowledge P69

overview

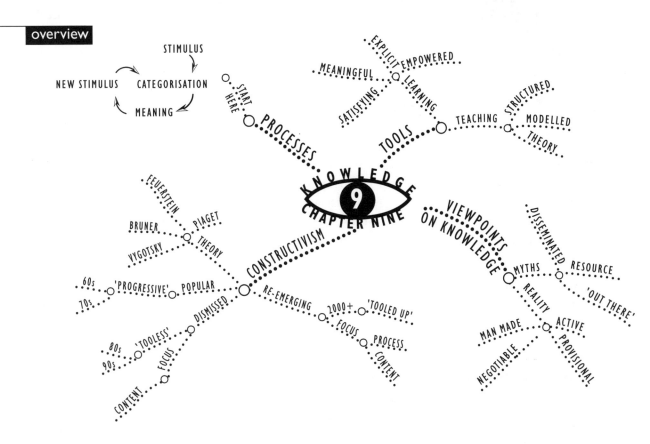

preview

- Students are knowledge workers.

- Making meaning creates knowledge.

- Meaning is built on the act of categorisation.

- Categories are built on hierarchies.

- The map is not the territory.

- Discovery learning, without tools, was bound to fail.

- Schools need more tools now.

- Personal meaning is created internally.

- Subjects are nothing but language.

- Seeing the structure of language is empowering and practical.

Students are knowledge workers.

Classrooms deal in knowledge. It is the commodity through which the educational process occurs. There is no educational context in which this is not the case. Infant and reception classes, no less than sixth forms, navigate their days through terrains of knowledge. It is the very stuff of education.

Therefore, it is all the more surprising, if not shocking, that the teaching profession is not intimately acquainted with conceptions of the nature of knowledge. If our profession is predicated on the existence and transmission of knowledge, then surely we should have coherent, accessible and practical theories of knowledge.

Currently, the UK government is bashfully picking up the agendas put aside since the introduction of the National Curriculum, which include ideas about theories of knowledge. With the inclusion of thinking skills in the National Curriculum, the limitations of a solely content-focused delivery approach to learning have been acknowledged. What must now accompany this favourable trend is a communal investigation into the nature and construction of knowledge itself.

Making meaning creates knowledge.

Perhaps the most powerful way to stimulate an inquiry into the nature of knowledge is to ask whether knowledge is something that is discovered or invented. Do *you* think knowledge exists 'out there', ready to be gathered up? Or must it be created afresh by each individual learner? These questions are at the centre of an approach to knowledge known as constructivism. As its name makes clear, this discipline adopts a position based on the assertion that knowledge is *not* 'out there' to be discovered. Rather, knowledge is made 'in here' – inside the learner.

As new experiences, new data and new interpretations come into being, so existing notions of knowledge are challenged, and sometimes superseded. Joseph Novak (1993) has outlined this process as being one where individuals, from birth to old age and death, construct and reconstruct the meaning of events and objects they observe.

> '[Meaning is] not something we possess, it is something we make.'
>
> *M. Lissack and J. Roos (1999)*

Consequently, knowledge is not a resource, a commodity, that can become scarce (Funes and Johnson, 1998). It is created by the learner, negotiable and provisional in nature.

Humans seek to create meaning from their environment, and do this through the formation of concepts. By this means, the world can be transformed from a series of single events that are disjointed and meaningless, to one where patterns can be perceived across time and place. These patterns give meaning to our experiences. Indeed, the patterns are themselves the meaning.

Meaning is built on the act of categorisation.

In order to create patterns, we have to identify common elements across various events or experiences. This process is one of categorisation. So, we can say that categorisation is the way in which we create meaning (Hyerle, 1996). Steven Pinker, author of *The Language Instinct,* writes elsewhere that:

> 'People think in categories ... The categories underlie much of our vocabulary ... and they underlie much of our reasoning.'
>
> *S. Pinker (1999)*

In noticing a common thread in someone's behaviour, for example, we could attach the meaning 'kind'. The concept 'kind', we can say, 'hosts' a series of behaviours. Instead of observing a behaviour and finding it devoid of meaning, we can see it as being 'kind'. Now, if we create more meanings from observing this person's behaviours, such as 'hard working' and 'honest', for example, we start to build a richer picture of the person. We feel we are getting to know her.

Categories are built on hierarchies.

By now, another process begins. Upon the patterns we have already created, we start to see new patterns being overlaid. The concepts 'kind', 'hard working' and 'honest', can themselves be grouped together to constitute an over-arching pattern we could call 'good citizen'. The observed pattern 'good citizen' has, in a sense, captured within its orbit the subordinate patterns of 'kind', 'hard working' and 'honest'.

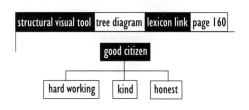

So, the concept of 'good citizen' is one built on other concepts. It is meaning that we have created from our earlier meaning making. Such a process is only possible because of the structure of concepts. Concepts are hierarchical in both nature and structure. Because of such a structure, we are able to build levels of meanings.

The map is not the territory.

When these meanings are formulated, we must not consider them 'fact' or anything other than a provisional construct. Nor should we think of them as being 'fixed' within even a short time span.

The structures of knowledge change depending on the context and purpose of the knowledge. 'Kind', 'hard working' and 'honest' may categorise well for a structure that builds up a picture of 'good citizen', but are inappropriate and inaccurate to describe the dominant characteristics of 'con artist', for example! In this reformulation of concepts, we can say that 'new knowledge' is created.

Discovery learning, without tools, was bound to fail.

With this brief overview of constructivism complete, we can return to the issue of knowledge and classroom practice. David Hyerle, in his wonderful book *Visual Tools for Constructing Knowledge* (1996), elegantly explains how the progressive practices of the 1960s and 1970s were well informed by theory but critically hampered by a lack of tools. Theorists such as Feuerstein, Bruner and Piaget, while different in many ways, could all be said to subsume under the conceptual category of constructivism. They saw concept formation as being the foundation for learning and knowledge creation.

Classroom teachers, advisors, authors and educational journalists spoke the constructivists' language. There was a shared knowledge-base in the educational community about learners' thinking processes. The theory of constructivism was, however, fatally ineffective without any knowledge tools to give to students to use. Without tools to create, manage and evaluate knowledge, students were left to 'fend for themselves':

'The ascendant philosophy of mathematical education in the United States is constructivism, a mixture of Piaget's psychology with counterculture and post-modern ideology. Children must actively construct mathematical knowledge for themselves in a social enterprise driven by disagreements about the meanings of concepts. The teacher provides the materials and the social milieu but does not lecture or guide the discussion.'

S. Pinker (1997)

Schools need more tools now.

Such observations of the disorganised and worst practices of discovery learning prompted governments around the world to take control of education through the instigation of national curricula and a single-minded focus on

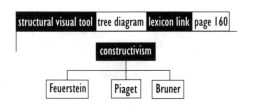

content. Having now accomplished their aims, the UK government is returning to the promotion of the processes of learning. This time, educators must not miss the opportunity to make learning more meaningful and satisfying for students.

Students cannot become independent learners and critical thinkers by exhortation alone. Conferences on thinking skills and pamphlets from government departments will not achieve this either. What will empower students to learn in more sophisticated, meaningful and satisfying ways is giving them the tools to do the job. Such tools need to be theory-based – that is to say they need to be consistent with our understanding of both knowledge creation and cognitive processes. The visual tools in this book are such a set of tools.

Personal meaning is created internally.

All the processes described so far occur privately. They happen within a learner's developing network of understanding. They are personal and knowledge is 'personalised'. The central factor that influences how this 'personalisation' takes place is the learner's prior knowledge – what she already knows. What we already know influences what we will know (Lloyd, 2000). New information has to be integrated into existing, prior structures of personal knowledge. Only in this way can it 'make sense'.

Personal meaning needs to be made public. However much sense something makes to one person, it does not mean that understanding is adopted by others. Personal metaphors, analogies and understandings give meaning to one's life, but are not necessarily the common currency of others' understanding. 'While one person holds a unique map ['meaning'] it is a fragile construction' explains management author Michael B. McCaskey (1991). Consequently, he continues 'A map becomes increasingly 'objective' as more people come to share its view of reality.'

For personal meaning to coincide with public knowledge, there needs to be a process of negotiation. The negotiation process demands that personal meanings are made explicit. Internal constructs need to be made external, the private made public. Through this process, the individual may have to restructure elements of her constructs. She may have to accept that some of her categories do not have the agreement of others. There may follow a process of 're-framing' in which new perspectives are adopted and personal constructs are adapted.

Subjects are nothing but language.

These personal and public processes take place through the medium of language. Knowledge, both personal and public, is built on linguistic labels and categories. Without language we have very little left that we can call knowledge. Philosopher Neil Postman makes this blazingly obvious point:

'If you eliminate the words of a subject you have eliminated the subject.'

N. Postman (1990)

It is not only the language that shapes our thoughts and concepts, but also the structure within which the language operates. They form what philosopher Ludwig Wittgenstein called 'language games' (1953). These games are the rules of our knowledge construction. Just because these linguistic rules and structures shape our meaning making, it does not mean they are obvious to us, however. Language follows a linear, sequential order but its meaning has another altogether different and hidden structure.

Seeing the structure of language is empowering and practical.

The structure of language is hierarchical in nature and multi-dimensional in form. In her book *The Pyramid Principle*, which examines the link between the structure of language and thinking, Barbara Minto writes:

> 'Normal prose is written one-dimensionally, in that it presents one sentence after another, more or less vertically down the page. But that vertical follow-on obscures the fact that the ideas occur at various levels of abstraction. Any idea below the main point will always have both a vertical and a horizontal relationship to the other ideas in the document.'
>
> *B. Minto (1995)*

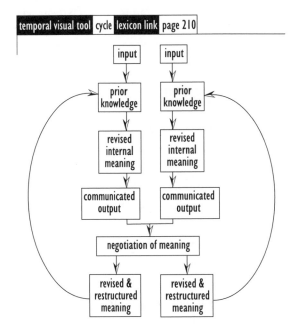

temporal visual tool **cycle** lexicon link **page 210**

Additionally, the structure of language is fluid and reshapes itself in relation to different perspectives.

Finding and creating meaning from linear text requires an ability to integrate a sequential logic into a hierarchical structure. Such an ability involves becoming familiar with the hierarchical categories of concepts of the language being used. Failure to do so leaves the student with what is called 'surface learning', unable to make connections and links that enrich and deepen her meaning making. The greater the ability to scale the hidden linguistic terrains within linear text, the greater will be the construction of knowledge – for they amount to the same thing.

viewpoints

knowing

> 'To map is to know.'
>
> *J. H. Wandersee (1990)*

constructivism

> 'Pupils, in the constructivist view, theorise experience and construct mental structures or schemas for representing it.'
>
> *C. Desforges and P. Lings (1998)*

no theories

> 'We lack sophisticated theories and models of knowledge creation in education simply because such activity has not been seen as a key to educational improvement.'
>
> *D. H. Hargreaves (1999)*

meaning

> 'Meaning is not something we possess, it is something we make. Making sense of things, finding their meaning, is a task of leadership.'
>
> *M. Lissack and J. Roos (1999)*

making public

'All those ideas locked up in our heads which we say are too complicated to be explained are no use at all. Until the idea is made public in some way it cannot be recognised, transmitted, shared, refined or even destroyed.'

M. Funes and N. Johnson (1998)

review

knowledge

To what extent does your school operate in a manner that suggests knowledge is 'out there'?

support

What support does a teacher give students to create personal meaning when she merely disseminates information?

understanding

Check *your* understanding. Explain to someone how meaning making takes place.

subject vocabulary

Write down 50 words related to your subject, and:

- look for relationships between the words and move them into hierarchies

- cross the words out and see how much is left of your subject.

ROUTE MAP FOR YOUR READING

SECTION 1 — CONTEXT

CHAPTER ONE — BACKGROUND

The primary assertion is that we are all *Eye Q* experts. Throughout history, humans have used an assortment of visual tools to reflect and communicate knowledge. Current knowledge creation dynamics are based on this same notion. The 'inside story' of learning is obtained by looking both inside (cognitive psychology) and outside (Accelerated Learning).

CHAPTER TWO — THE iDESK MODEL

Most of our activities are not based on a theory of learning. Consequently, there is little sense of meaning or coherence. The iDesk model is holistic. It connects thinking, feeling and doing. Finally, it links these faculties to the environment and the individual. Visual tools impact all areas of the iDesk model, and all components interact with each other. Serious schools need models.

CHAPTER THREE — THE KNOWLEDGE AGE

We are living in the knowledge age with a need for more knowledge workers. These new types of workers require new, extended mental skills and knowledge tools. Visual tools are central in creating and communicating knowledge. Schools need to learn from business theory and practice with regard to intellectual capital and the use of visual tools.

SECTION 2 — VISUALS

CHAPTER FOUR — VISUAL TOOLS AND COMPUTERS

We are learning that the use of computers can reinforce poor learning habits. The attraction of the screen can degenerate into visual 'candyfloss'. This turns computer users into consumers. Behind the screen lies a knowledge structure. Visual tools make this explicit and turn consumers into explorers of knowledge. Clarity about visual literacy will support this.

CHAPTER FIVE — VISUAL LITERACY

In our culture, the visual—verbal polarity may well be more divisive than the sciences—arts gulf. There are historical, philosophical reasons for the low value placed on visuals. Visual literacy, nonetheless, is an established discipline. All visual content exists in the spatial dimension. Space is our first and primary frontier. The spatial metaphor shapes our understanding.

CHAPTER SIX — TOOLS TO LEARN

The successes of our civilisation are based on tools. We have created these tools and they, in turn, end up shaping our behaviour. Using new tools causes new learning to take place. Habitual use of tools changes our habits. The most effective use of tools happens when accompanied with theory. Visual tools impact on learning habits. New eras need new tools.

SECTION 3 — MEANING

CHAPTER SEVEN — SCHEMAS

We all have schemas. They are personal and unique and are based on how we view the world. In business they are termed mental models. Their organisation represents how we think and shape our behaviour. All students have these mental maps but are unaware of them — as are teachers. Making schemas visible allows students and teachers to see what they are thinking.

CHAPTER EIGHT — HOLOGRAPHIC—LINEAR

Every day, every student, in every lesson has to turn linear communication (what she reads or hears) into what is termed her holographic understanding. Schemas are holographic in structure — definitely not linear. The student then has to turn her new, enlarged understanding back into linear format. This process has, until now, been an unknown phenomenon.

CHAPTER NINE — CONSTRUCTING KNOWLEDGE

All our students construct knowledge — even the very youngest and the least able. Knowledge cannot be delivered. It has to be created each time by the individual, for knowledge is created not discovered. This view of learning is called constructivism. Understanding this process stimulates teachers to make learning more meaningful and motivating for all students.

SECTION 4 — LANGUAGE

CHAPTER TEN — SUPPORT FOR LANGUAGE

It is normally thought that visuals 'compete' with words. With visual tools, this is not true. Visual tools exist in the overlapping area between words and pictures. If you examine language, you realise that images play a big part in stimulating thought and supporting planning. They help the organisation of our language, which normally has to take place in the unseen interior of our heads.

CHAPTER ELEVEN — READING

Reading is active. Readers' interrogation of text is shaped by their own schemas. They have to adapt their existing schemas in order to absorb text into meaningful messages. Visual tools can reveal the hidden structure and meaning of a text. Just as computer software can show you what your voice looks like, visual tools can show you what your thinking looks like.

CHAPTER TWELVE — WRITING

Writing is difficult. Students' difficulties and fears stem from not knowing what to write. Visual tools make planning explicit, easy and empowering. Through the use of visual tools, students can model the planning that excellent writers do 'in their heads'. Planning in linear fashion is too difficult for most. The schematic nature of visual tools matches the way the brain naturally works.

SECTION 5 — THINKING

CHAPTER THIRTEEN — THINKING SKILLS

When we think, we are either thinking of objects (in space) or events (in time). Our thoughts become 'thought—objects'. Just as we manipulate real, physical objects in space, so we move our 'thought—objects' in our inner space. This is thinking. It is, however, invisible and demands much short term memory. Visual tools make thinking visible, easier and obvious.

CHAPTER FOURTEEN — QUESTIONS

Questions are more powerful than answers. They directly determine our focus and thinking. Young children are wonderful questioners — young scientists. Schools have conditioned students to demand only questions. This severely limits their thinking and learning. Visual tools are themselves questions. They demand investigation. Their visible nature makes questioners of all students.

CHAPTER FIFTEEN — THINKING IN ACTION

There is a link between text, thinking and visual tools. The nature of different types of text (genres) demand different types of thinking. All thinking is the manipulation of 'thought—objects'. Visual tools show students what this looks like. Matching types of visual tools to specific genres and linking them to the National Curriculum thinking skills is a powerful matrix.

SECTION 6 — LEARNING

CHAPTER SIXTEEN — ACTIVE LEARNING

You don't have to leave your seat to be actively learning. Active doesn't mean kinaesthetic! Active learning involves becoming engrossed, relating new material to personal prior knowledge, and creating meaning. Active learning needs to be encouraged by teachers. It is what is demanded of business. Visual tools stimulate and challenge active learning from students.

CHAPTER SEVENTEEN — STYLES OF LEARNING

Learning style labels can be dangerous. They can limit rather than stimulate expansion. Behind their often surface description lies a common cognitive activity — putting the detail into the big picture. Visual tools meet the needs of all learners, involving them in visual, verbal, analytic and holistic thinking. They also promote the four essential skills of learning.

CHAPTER EIGHTEEN — ABILITY RANGE

We have many labels for our pupils — from the gifted and talented to SEN. Behind all these labels there lies the act of meaning making. Visual tools show students what understanding looks like. This gives confidence to them all. It allows the least able to see their intelligence and supports the more able to organise and communicate their sometimes erratic thinking.

SECTION 7 — LEXICON

CHAPTER NINETEEN — LEXICON

CATEGORIES OF VISUAL TOOLS

- structural thinking — Structural Visual Tools
- differential thinking — Differential Visual Tools
- representational thinking — Representational Visual Tools
- temporal thinking — Temporal Visual Tools
- causal thinking — Causal Visual Tools
- numerical thinking — Numerical Visual Tools
- organisational thinking — Organisational Visual Tools
- individual thinking — Individual Visual Tools

There are seven types of visual tools related to seven types of thinking. The eighth is a hybrid of all seven. Within each category, there is a variety of visual tools. Visual tools within the categories achieve slightly different results, at different levels of complexity to suit age, ability and the nature of the tasks set. Each visual tool is described, its workings explained and ideas given for introducing it to students. Differences between similar visual tools are clarified. Each visual tool is illustrated both in templated format and as a hand-drawn example in use. The context for each hand-drawn visual tool is a well known story.

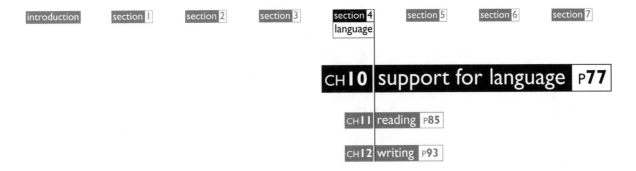

CH**10** support for language P**77**

CH**11** reading P85

CH**12** writing P93

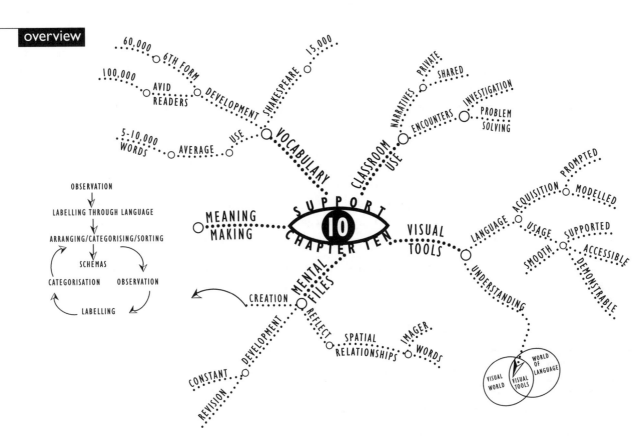

preview

■ The way in which children acquire language is quite remarkable.

■ Vocabulary develops at a tremendous rate but we use only a small fraction of it.

■ Words enable us to make sense of the world around us.

■ Mental filing systems are continually updated and revised.

■ The contents of children's files of understanding are words that reflect the spatial relationships established with the world.

■ For young children, the process of talking to themselves aids activity.

■ We all talk to ourselves.

■ Having to organise your thoughts entirely in your head is very demanding.

■ Visual tools operate in the overlap between pictures and words.

The way in which children acquire language is quite remarkable.

The acquisition of language is a feat of learning surpassing anything a computer can achieve. Yet the infant capable of this miracle is quite unable to take care of itself in any other way. By listening to the sounds emanating from sets of vocal cords and moulded, in countless different ways, the child 'unpicks' the music of words within the first year.

During that time, cognitive scientists tell us, babies move from being potential speakers of any tongue on the planet to decoders of their own native language. From a seemingly endless and seamless string of noise, they identify words and separate them from one another – they develop their own personal lexicon. They manage it effortlessly and in a holographic fashion. How do they do it?

We do not have all the answers. We know that they need to understand what is going on around them and inside them. The words are related to the immediate environment and to their relationship with it. Think for a moment about what happens when you visit a foreign country, unable to speak the language. You make sense of your surroundings, understand what you need and require, but without a shared language you feel lost. That is why it is so comforting when someone speaks your language.

Vocabulary develops at a tremendous rate but we use only a small fraction of it.

From about the age of three, infants add to their expanding lexicon a staggering number of words on a daily basis. Research indicates that new words are stored at a rate of between 16 and 20 a day (Winston, 1998, and Smith,

1992). This means that the lexicon is growing by something in the region of 3,000–4,000 words each year. By the time children enter school they may well have 8,000 words at their disposal.

How are they to make use of them all? Opportunities should lie within the conversations of the classroom, in private or shared narratives and problem solving encounters. Children are bursting with questions in the classroom. They are anxious to find out if their beliefs are true or, at least, understood. They are looking for approval for their thoughts.

By the time students leave school and reach adulthood, they have acquired an impressive vocabulary. Research suggests that students leaving sixth form probably know somewhere in the region of 60,000 words. Avid readers may well be able to draw upon 100,000 words or more. In total, the English language is said to contain in excess of 500,000 words.

However, if we accept current figures, we find that the average person uses only 5,000 to 10,000 words as a working vocabulary (Shakespeare used about 15,000 words in his writings). So only a tiny percentage of the individual's stock of words is utilised. This seems a tragic waste, when the richness of daily life is so much enhanced by the richness of our vocabulary. So, the opportunities for vocabulary enrichment that visual tools bring into our classrooms facilitate richer learning.

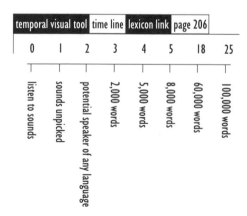

temporal visual tool	time line	lexicon link	page 206

0	1	2	3	4	5	18	25
listen to sounds	sounds unpicked	potential speaker of any language	2,000 words	5,000 words	8,000 words	60,000 words	100,000 words

Words enable us to make sense of the world around us.

As children embark on the learning journey, their eyes fix on the horizon. They take in the strange and unfamiliar shapes of objects they pass or that pass by them. They make use of words to serve as landmarks in their voyage of exploration. They watch as events unfold and find words to describe what they believe is happening.

Those who are observing a child's language development notice a noun here, a verb there, the odd scattering of adjectives and adverbs. In short, the observers witness the beginnings of an organising system for all those files that together create the child's schemas. In mapping the world, the children compose lists of objects and events. The words in these lists begin to appear and be located under separate headings. These young learners are beginning to make their first tentative efforts at creating categories for their findings.

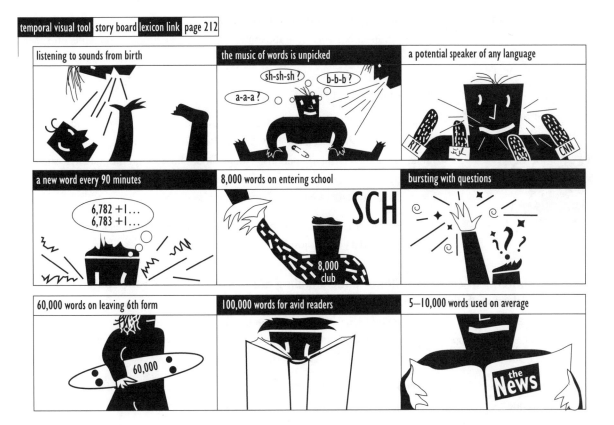

temporal visual tool story board lexicon link page 212

listening to sounds from birth	the music of words is unpicked	a potential speaker of any language
a new word every 90 minutes	8,000 words on entering school	bursting with questions
60,000 words on leaving 6th form	100,000 words for avid readers	5—10,000 words used on average

Before them is arrayed the external world, a universe that is to be encountered through their senses. This outer space comprises living and non-living, moving and non-moving, natural and non-natural objects. Children begin to see similarities and differences. They establish relationships between the items and people on view. They create a network of associations.

Children learn how to create meaning in language through a process of attributing words to spatial relationships. Through observation and categorisation, they bring the visual, auditory and kinaesthetic world into their minds. Concepts are rooted in the images constructed from sensory materials. From these conceptions children construct schemas. They transform their experiences into a memorable storage system. They do all of this effortlessly, without direct instruction for the most part.

Younger children cannot explain everything in words but need to show us, often by using the real objects or by telling us about their own pictorial representations. This bridge between the two worlds, words and images, needs to be maintained at every opportunity.

structural visual tool affinity diagram lexicon link page 157

early language	language use	
listening	interactions	VAK
sounds	self-talk	visits
vocal chords	personal lexicon	internal organisation
first year	memory	10—100,000
potential speakers	landmarks	shorthand
holographic	interpretation	Piaget
opportunities to use	multiple meanings	Vygotsky
questions	categories	

purpose of language	visual tools
experiences	inner space
filing system	abstract—concrete
understanding	visible
adjust schemas	words & pictures
check personal meaning	vocabulary enrichment
	categories
	associations
	network

Mental filing systems are continually updated and revised.

A word in itself has very little meaning. It is a combination of phonemes in speech, of graphemes in writing; it contains morphemes or units of meaning. But when all is said and done, it is just a word. Words have 'suggestibility'. We hear a word and it suggests a context in which it belongs.

Children need a range of social and cultural experiences in order to expand their vocabulary and develop meaning within it. Behind the words there lies in wait a whole range of potential interpretations. Adults and children do not always share these interpretations. So we need to make use of pictorial resources, of lines and signs, to create a shared view of what is being talked about.

This updating process is based on our memories. We need to check what we recall with the incoming data and adjust our schemas accordingly.

The contents of children's files of understanding are words that reflect the spatial relationships established with the world.

Naming, in the early stages of a child's language development, is usually directly linked to immediacy. Physical presence and the opportunity for tactile experiences exist. For example, an infant's attention focuses on a nearby object, say a cup, and it is named. This is concrete experience.

As word usage develops, the cup can quite literally be *brought to mind* simply by the use of the word. In fact, the cup in question may be one of many, not a particular cup as in the early naming. This process applies to all those elements that are contained within schemas.

Included in this are abstract terms like 'sad', 'fair', 'kindness'. Although young children may be unable to offer a definition of these terms they 'know' the concepts and use the vocabulary. They can see sadness and happiness around them; they experience the sense of it. Connections are made between the objects and events in the real world and the feelings that they instil.

Multiple meanings cause problems in understanding when a speaker and listener are not using the same file. For example, terms like 'table' can be used in a range of contexts: in relation to water, as a piece of furniture, as a geometrical shape containing grids and data. Words therefore need to create a link between the real world and the lexicon in the individual's head. If they don't, misconceptions arise.

For young children the process of talking to themselves aids activity.

What Piaget (1960) describes as 'egocentric speech' and Vygotsky (1962) refers to as 'speech for oneself' may be observed when children are engaged in some aspect of problem solving or play. They find the commentaries that

accompany their physical endeavours enable them to work more successfully. They readily correct their own miscalculations or errors. Piaget reached the conclusion that this practice of self-talk disappeared as the child matured.

Vygotsky held a different opinion. For him, children's use of language follows two directions and serves two purposes. At times it is used in a highly personal way, a kind of shorthand, or note form – in essence, a monologue. But in a social way, in conversation, it fulfils Wittgenstein's 'games' notion (page 72). Through dialogue, conventional word-meanings are established and grammatical structures explored and acquired. Idiosyncratic language use then fades; it has served its purpose.

Finally, according to Vygotsky, the process of thinking verbally becomes thought itself. In the end, whenever we need to communicate our thoughts, it is necessary for us to impose some form of organisation on them. It is during this process that we find ourselves further involved in Wittgenstein's games. We learn the rules that are found in the 'forms of life'. We share a common language and become grammarians.

In some cases it is possible for us to articulate a fully formed thought that is understood by our audience. At other times, we revert to thinking aloud; we struggle to compose. What is going on in the mind may be some form of imagery, some act of sensory recall or problem solving that is beyond the limits of our sentences. How often do we hear the expression, 'I know but I just can't put it into words?'

We all talk to ourselves.

Do you talk to yourself? Of course, you do. People are often reluctant to admit to the practice but it is far more common that you might expect. This particular habit is a 'leftover' from our infancy, a residual from a time when self-talk played a crucial role in the evolution of our language and thought processes.

We talk to ourselves, mutter under our breath, reprimand or praise our own actions and efforts. We sometimes do it in the presence of other people, perhaps even directly criticising them in a whispered aside and then denying that we have done so: 'I was just talking to myself'.

Worse still, sitting alone with the radio or television, we may find the programme that is on is challenging our schema. We may then suddenly launch ourselves into an imaginary argument with a person who cannot possibly be aware of our existence. But we need to feel that we can justify our thinking to the world at large. We need to be vocal.

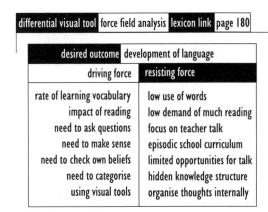

Having to organise your thoughts entirely in your head is very demanding.

When young children interact with the world, they physically interact with real objects. They label the objects with words. Often, they are compelled to show you the object they are naming. Words and objects need to be *literally* related. This relationship continues in a more sophisticated way through pictures. The pictures represent the objects and are given words and relationships through accompanying text and parent talk.

Later, the physical relationship between the pictorially represented world and words becomes less important. Thoughts themselves are treated as objects. The re-arrangement of these thought-objects is done in the virtual space of the mind. This takes an enormous amount of mental energy and requires copious feats of memory. Certainly, those who are termed 'clever' succeed in this, but for the majority it is not an efficient way to think and learn.

An alternative to relying on the exclusive creation of thoughts internally is to make them concrete and visible. Visual tools enable students to arrange their thoughts in a way that they used to arrange objects, when they were small children. This places less demand on short-term memory, thereby freeing up mental energy to focus on the relationships between the thought-objects. This connection-making is what we call thinking.

Visual tools operate in the overlap between pictures and words.

The point was made in chapter 5, Visual literacy, that the polarity of rationality and emotion leads to misunderstanding. Our world is organised when experiences are treated as real objects. By combining visual and verbal modes of thought we develop a more comprehensive viewpoint.

The pictorial world is considered to be different from, if not inferior to, the world of words. Both are assumed to be operating in completely different domains. The truth is, however, that the domains work in tandem. They overlap. It is in this shared area, between words and pictures, that visual tools exist.

This central ground is composed of images and words together. Each visual tool is itself an image and its use unique. The locations of words within the visual tools represent their constructed meaning and form the image. Words alone are never enough to create real understanding; they unlock our access to deeper thoughts. Visual tools play an important role in this process and create a vital support for language, not an alternative.

differential visual tool	force field analysis	lexicon link	page 180

desired outcome	development of language
driving force	resisting force
rate of learning vocabulary	low use of words
impact of reading	low demand of much reading
need to ask questions	focus on teacher talk
need to make sense	episodic school curriculum
need to check own beliefs	limited opportunities for talk
need to categorise	hidden knowledge structure
using visual tools	organise thoughts internally

viewpoints

telling stories

'Drawing a system is like telling a story in pictures.'

J. O'Connor and I. McDermott (1997)

architecture

'These visual symbols support the construction of networks of language.'

D. Hyerle (2000)

language patterns

'The maps provide students with a means to learn the language patterns of science and construct scientific knowledge.'

M-W. A. Elhelou (1997)

two systems

'... if a stimulus is coded in both representational systems (i.e. verbally and visually), it should increase both the recall and understanding of the material.'

C. Eastwood (2000)

links

What links can you see between this chapter and chapters 7 (Schemas) and 9 (Constructing knowledge)?

language development

How might visual tools support the use and development of language in your school or classroom?

ROUTE MAP FOR YOUR READING

SECTION 1 — CONTEXT

CHAPTER ONE BACKGROUND
The primary assertion is that we are all *Eye Q* experts. Throughout history, humans have used an assortment of visual tools to reflect and communicate knowledge. Current knowledge creation dynamics are based on this same notion. The 'inside story' of learning is obtained by looking both inside (cognitive psychology) and outside (Accelerated Learning).

CHAPTER TWO THE iDESK MODEL
Most of our activities are not based on a theory of learning. Consequently, there is little sense of meaning or coherence. The iDesk model is holistic. It connects thinking, feeling and doing. Finally, it links these faculties to the environment and the individual. Visual tools impact all areas of the iDesk model, and all components interact with each other. Serious schools need models.

CHAPTER THREE THE KNOWLEDGE AGE
We are living in the knowledge age with a need for more knowledge workers. These new types of workers require new, extended mental skills and knowledge tools. Visual tools are central in creating and communicating knowledge. Schools need to learn from business theory and practice with regard to intellectual capital and the use of visual tools.

SECTION 2 — VISUALS

CHAPTER FOUR VISUAL TOOLS AND COMPUTERS
We are learning that the use of computers can reinforce poor learning habits. The attraction of the screen can degenerate into visual 'candyfloss'. This turns computer users into consumers. Behind the screen lies a knowledge structure. Visual tools make this explicit and turn consumers into explorers of knowledge. Clarity about visual literacy will support this.

CHAPTER FIVE VISUAL LITERACY
In our culture, the visual—verbal polarity may well be more divisive than the sciences—arts gulf. There are historical, philosophical reasons for the low value placed on visuals. Visual literacy, nonetheless, is an established discipline. All visual content exists in the spatial dimension. Space is our first and primary frontier. The spatial metaphor shapes our understanding.

CHAPTER SIX TOOLS TO LEARN
The successes of our civilisation are based on tools. We have created these tools and they, in turn, end up shaping our behaviour. Using new tools causes new learning to take place. Habitual use of tools changes our habits. The most effective use of tools happens when accompanied with theory. Visual tools impact on learning habits. New eras need new tools.

SECTION 3 — MEANING

CHAPTER SEVEN SCHEMAS
We all have schemas. They are personal and unique and are based on how we view the world. In business they are termed mental models. Their organisation represents how we think and shape our behaviour. All students have these mental maps but are unaware of them — as are teachers. Making schemas visible allows students and teachers to see what they are thinking.

CHAPTER EIGHT HOLOGRAPHIC—LINEAR
Every day, every student, in every lesson has to turn linear communication (what she reads or hears) into what is termed her holographic understanding. Schemas are holographic in structure — definitely not linear. The student then has to turn her new, enlarged understanding back into linear format. This process has, until now, been an unknown phenomenon.

CHAPTER NINE CONSTRUCTING KNOWLEDGE
All our students construct knowledge — even the very youngest and the least able. Knowledge cannot be delivered. It has to be created each time by the individual, for knowledge is created not discovered. This view of learning is called constructivism. Understanding this process stimulates teachers to make learning more meaningful and motivating for all students.

SECTION 4 — LANGUAGE

CHAPTER TEN SUPPORT FOR LANGUAGE
It is normally thought that visuals 'compete' with words. With visual tools, this is not true. Visual tools exist in the overlapping area between words and pictures. If you examine language, you realise that images play a big part in stimulating thought and supporting planning. They help the organisation of our language, which normally has to take place in the unseen interior of our heads.

CHAPTER ELEVEN READING
Reading is active. Readers' interrogation of text is shaped by their own schemas. They have to adapt their existing schemas in order to absorb text into meaningful messages. Visual tools can reveal the hidden structure and meaning of a text. Just as computer software can show you what your voice looks like, visual tools can show you what your thinking looks like.

CHAPTER TWELVE WRITING
Writing is difficult. Students' difficulties and fears stem from not knowing what to write. Visual tools make planning explicit, easy and empowering. Through the use of visual tools, students can model the planning that excellent writers do 'in their heads'. Planning in linear fashion is too difficult for most. The schematic nature of visual tools matches the way the brain naturally works.

SECTION 5 — THINKING

CHAPTER THIRTEEN THINKING SKILLS
When we think, we are either thinking of objects (in space) or events (in time). Our thoughts become 'thought—objects'. Just as we manipulate real, physical objects in space, so we move our 'thought—objects' in our inner space. This is thinking. It is, however, invisible and demands much short term memory. Visual tools make thinking visible, easier and obvious.

CHAPTER FOURTEEN QUESTIONS
Questions are more powerful than answers. They directly determine our focus and thinking. Young children are wonderful questioners — young scientists. Schools have conditioned students to demand only questions. This severely limits their thinking and learning. Visual tools are themselves questions. They demand investigation. Their visible nature makes questioners of all students.

CHAPTER FIFTEEN THINKING IN ACTION
There is a link between text, thinking and visual tools. The nature of different types of text (genres) demand different types of thinking. All thinking is the manipulation of 'thought—objects'. Visual tools show students what this looks like. Matching types of visual tools to specific genres and linking them to the National Curriculum thinking skills is a powerful matrix.

SECTION 6 — LEARNING

CHAPTER SIXTEEN ACTIVE LEARNING
You don't have to leave your seat to be actively learning. Active doesn't mean kinaesthetic! Active learning involves becoming engrossed, relating new material to personal prior knowledge, and creating meaning. Active learning needs to be encouraged by teachers. It is what is demanded of business. Visual tools stimulate and challenge active learning from students.

CHAPTER SEVENTEEN STYLES OF LEARNING
Learning style labels can be dangerous. They can limit rather than stimulate expansion. Behind their often surface description lies a common cognitive activity — putting the detail into the big picture. Visual tools meet the needs of all learners, involving them in visual, verbal, analytic and holistic thinking. They also promote the four essential skills of learning.

CHAPTER EIGHTEEN ABILITY RANGE
We have many labels for our pupils — from the gifted and talented to SEN. Behind all these labels there lies the act of meaning making. Visual tools show students what understanding looks like. This gives confidence to them all. It allows the least able to see their intelligence and supports the more able to organise and communicate their sometimes erratic thinking.

SECTION 7 — LEXICON

CHAPTER NINETEEN LEXICON

CATEGORIES OF VISUAL TOOLS

- structural thinking — Structural Visual Tools
- differential thinking — Differential Visual Tools
- representational thinking — Representational Visual Tools
- temporal thinking — Temporal Visual Tools
- causal thinking — Causal Visual Tools
- numerical thinking — Numerical Visual Tools
- organisational thinking — Organisational Visual Tools
- individual thinking — Individual Visual Tools

There are seven types of visual tools related to seven types of thinking. The eighth is a hybrid of all seven. Within each category, there is a variety of visual tools. Visual tools within the categories achieve slightly different results, at different levels of complexity to suit age, ability and the nature of the tasks set. Each visual tool is described, its workings explained and ideas given for introducing it to students. Differences between similar visual tools are clarified. Each visual tool is illustrated both in templated format and as a hand-drawn example in use. The context for each hand-drawn visual tool is a well known story.

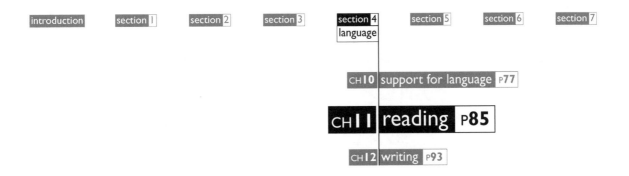

overview

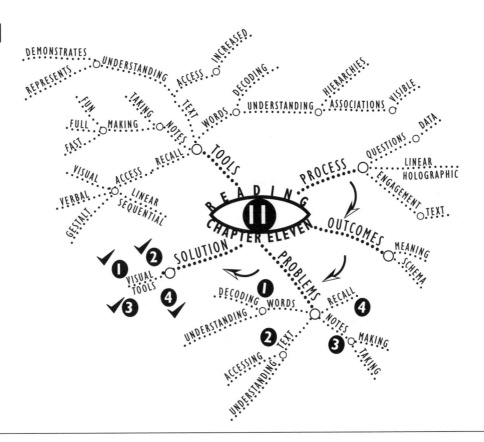

preview

■ Reading is the process of engaging with and interrogating texts.

■ Through the process of reading, readers are adapting or modifying their schemas.

■ Visual tools help readers to 'repack' the meaning of texts within their own schemas, according to the author's original plan.

■ Our perceptions of texts vary according to our beliefs and expectations.

■ Reading is very tricky.

■ Like a musical score, a text communicates the intentions and ideas of its composer and each of us makes it swing according to our own sense of rhythm.

■ There are black marks on the page, there is space between the lines and there is a whole world beyond the text.

■ Knowing how to make sense of the marks leads us to understand how we should bring the reading to life.

■ Teachers need to make sure that students are assimilating the 'right' messages from their reading.

■ We read for pleasure and we read to learn.

■ Just as computer software can show you what your voice looks like, so visual tools can show you what your 'swing' looks like.

Reading is the process of engaging with and interrogating texts.

Language is essential to the way in which we think and to the choice of symbols we use in representing and creating our inner worlds. As our vocabulary expands so does our potential for understanding the meanings communicated by others. We also increase our capacity to say what we mean clearly so that we may be understood.

This understanding of meaning cannot be guaranteed, even when the wording is carefully thought out and put down in writing. In the same way that we can mishear what is said, so we can misread what is written or represented. Any text is an expression of the author's schema. A piece of writing on a page has permanence, but it won't necessarily continue to convey the same meaning wherever and whenever it is read.

Through the process of reading, readers are adapting or modifying their schemas.

Our schemas are unique packets of information, knowledge, feelings and understanding. We have constructed them from our experiences and memories.

In the process of reading our schemas are being challenged by the text. Texts contain units of meaning arranged according to the author's plan. But our filing systems differ. Sometimes the difference is marked. At other times the difference is slight. Our perception of the world is not exactly the same as that of any other person. So we compare our schemas with those of the author and of those around us.

In visually recording and sharing what texts mean to us we reveal our understanding and interpretations. Using visual tools, we can literally see the links between our thoughts and those of other people.

Visual tools help readers to 'repack' the meaning of texts within their own schemas, according to the author's original plan.

Imagine somebody with years of 'packing experience' filling a hamper for you. When you receive it, there is no indication of what might be inside the hamper. So you open it. You eagerly take everything out, inspect the contents, test their weight, submit them to scrutiny, and then put everything back. But you can never put the things back in exactly the same way. You may even have items left over that you do not know what to do with!

You have not made the same use of space as the original packer, or made the same organisational decisions about how the contents sit side by side. Imagine how much easier the task of repacking would be if you had been given a plan, or if you had noted the sequence and arrangement of the objects while removing them. This is where visual tools come in!

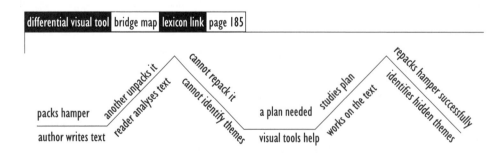

differential visual tool | **bridge map** | **lexicon link** | **page 185**

- packs hamper / author writes text
- another unpacks it / reader analyses text
- cannot repack it / cannot identify themes
- a plan needed / visual tools help
- studies plan / works on the text
- repacks hamper successfully / identifies hidden themes

Our perceptions of texts vary according to our beliefs and expectations.

Visual tools enable us to record the way we 'unpack' a text. If we have some idea of what kind of contents there are, we may be able to visualise how they have been stored. We might even deduce the sequence in which they were packed. We would have expectations about the text that would affect our perception of the meaning conveyed.

No text means the same to any two people, since no text is treated in isolation – each new reading is layered on past readings and prior knowledge. When reading, we often search out those clues, those phrases and statements, that will support our own personal hypotheses. Give a group of people an article on 'Hunting' or 'Laboratory Testing and the Use of Animals', for example, and see what happens. Most people cannot be impartial, factions emerge, and arguments are inevitable. Each person is seeking support for her own views within the text. Of course, it is here that we come face to face with the issues of stereotype and bias.

Critical literacy is, in theory at least, embedded in our ability to de-centre ourselves, to take a step back and see the world as others do. It is important to recognise that others have the right to hold different opinions and have different values, even though we are under no obligation to share them. Making views, opinions and beliefs accessible through visual representations is a powerful way of highlighting similarities and differences – of bringing competing worlds, quite literally, into a better perspective.

Reading is very tricky.

Teachers perceive that their students experience a number of problems as they approach texts:

- difficulties in decoding the words

- problems with vocabulary – everyday and specialist

- difficulties in making sense of the text as a whole

- problems with making notes and being able to represent text

- recalling what they have read.

The world is awash with assumptions about reading: why it is important, how best to teach it, what employers demand, why boys cannot do it, that if you cannot read by the age of seven you will fail in life. It is also very difficult to monitor. We cannot actually hear people reading for most of the time.

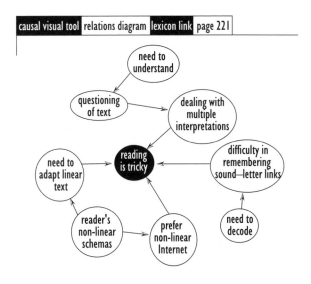

causal visual tool | relations diagram | lexicon link | page 221

Two things are certain, though. First, the ability to 'decode' – to transform the letters of the alphabet into words and sentences – is an essential skill. Second, the nature of communication through reading is continually changing and teachers must take account of the world of communication outside the school context.

The fact that some individuals do not appear to read in the way that we regard as normal (linear) may not be because they are unable to read words on the page. Rather, they choose not to. How often do you hear the complaint that children don't bother to read these days – they spend all their spare time on the Internet?

Each and every one of the problems described above may be addressed through the use of visual tools. Visual tools can show how sounds are related to each other and can be transcribed in a number of different letter combinations. For developing revision notes or preparing drafts for writing assignments there are many tools to utilise and enhance students' thinking skills.

Like a musical score, a text communicates the intentions and ideas of its composer and each of us makes it swing according to our own sense of rhythm.

Every composition, musical or textual, is a personal creation – it is a unique expression of the creator's personality, thoughts and beliefs. There is no such thing as a neutral text. If you listen to readings of texts, no two versions are ever the same either, just as no two recitals of a musical piece are identical.

Purpose and organisation lie at the heart of every publication, from a pay-and-display parking ticket to a prize-winning novel. Some texts are more meaningful than others but perhaps even a sticky square attached to a windscreen may cause a car park warden's heart to skip a beat when its time limit has expired!

Writers, illustrators, designers – all those involved in creating documents and displays – bring their belief systems and views of the world to the symbols and images they present to us. In effect, each time we look at a book, or article, or website, we are seeing somebody else's representation of the world – seeing the working of that person's mind (thoughts) made visible.

Before that image ever appeared in the visual world it had to exist in the imagination of the creator. There will be information, accounts of events, descriptions of objects and places, theories of what might exist in the world of abstract thought for us to encounter – contrasting schemas.

There will be meaning for us to construct and assimilate into our own minds – or, in some cases, reject. We will need to interpret what has been offered. And we will need to use every means at our disposal to perform this task efficiently. Visualisation and the use of visual tools are critical in this process.

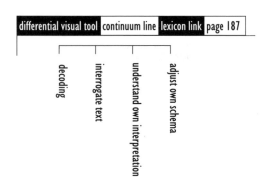

differential visual tool | continuum line | lexicon link | page 187

decoding
interrogate text
understand own interpretation
adjust own schema

There are black marks on the page, there is space between the lines and there is a whole world beyond the text.

Reading can have a physiological effect upon us. It can move us to anger, joy and even to confusion (when we have no real sense of what is going on). Reading can relocate us in the past, propel us into the future, set us down on foreign shores or take our minds and hearts into areas previously unexplored. Just like music.

The words on the page then, those black marks composed of the letters of the alphabet or symbols chosen to take the place of words, must first of all be recognised and linked to our personalised dictionaries.

Knowing how to make sense of the marks leads us to understand how we should bring the reading to life.

The person who created the piece – whether musical or textual – had a plan. In the case of Mozart, whole symphonies and operas may have been played out in his imagination. He had no need to spend laborious hours piecing together separate passages or phrases.

For most of us, though, the element of composition requires a good deal of mental gymnastics, perhaps accompanied by sets of cards that can be shuffled and re-arranged in different ways, or some other technique of

physically organising the intended content. The final draft – which has been edited, negotiated and finally published – sets down the composer's ideas in concrete form. It is then up to the reader of the piece to interpret it.

In order to be able to 'breathe life' into a sheet of printed paper, our previous experiences, our knowledge and understanding, need to match up with those of the composer. We need to be in tune with the composer's thoughts – otherwise the message will certainly not come across, and there may even be cacophony. Nothing will 'swing'. This, of course, is what happens when we read without understanding, without being able to assimilate the message.

Teachers need to make sure that students are assimilating the 'right' messages from their reading.

No reading will mean exactly the same to any two people, but teachers must ensure that when students decipher text in schools they are all 'in tune' with the composer – that they are constructing the intended meaning from the piece. As a class, the entire ensemble must be able to 'swing'.

Each individual is allowed the space and freedom to express a personal reconstruction of the reading, but the teacher – like the conductor of an orchestra – needs to be aware of each and every player, and to spot the 'wrong notes'.

The use of visual tools at the individual level allows students to represent in a concrete way their own experience and deconstruction of the text. Tools are instruments for learning. Each can be assigned a special role and is more useful when working on a special kind of text. Each unit of meaning and the links between them can be identified and represented.

We read for pleasure and we read to learn.

Why do we look at texts? Some forms of text quite literally 'catch our eye' and draw us towards them. They have instant, tantalising appeal. If our desires are satisfied by the text, we may develop a compelling interest in the genre. How many readers do you know who are addicted to specific forms of literature – detective stories, fantasy tales, biographies? Reading for pleasure is an important habit.

Alternatively, text may be presented or selected in a conscious manner, the choice being made by the reader or by someone who believes that the reader needs to investigate and explore it. In such instances, we set out to read with a purpose in mind. This 'set book' type of reading is mainly found in education, linked to objectives. It is in this situation that we need to make notes, to summarise and paraphrase what has been read.

So, there are essentially two main reasons for reading. We read in order to obtain information and facts that will be of use to us, either immediately or in the longer term. We also read to deepen our understanding of the world of feelings, situations and events and to enhance the development of sensibility. Whatever our reason for reading, visual tools can support us in the process.

Just as computer software can show you what your voice looks like, so visual tools can show you what your 'swing' looks like.

In a recording studio, with the benefit of a graphic equaliser, we could display the sound waves generated at every point in an orchestra's performance. This is, in effect, what visual tools can do for a group reading.

By comparing their own versions of a reading with those of others, students may see where they are in harmony and where they place their emphasis. Where there are disagreements, they can refer back to the page and negotiate their reading. As pairs and groups share and discuss what they have observed and detected, the class as a whole achieves amplification.

People often talk about the need to 'sing from the same hymn sheet'. By using visual representation in classroom encounters, we can record the exchanges of ideas that might otherwise vanish into the air and be lost. We can make sure, at the end of the session, that we are indeed 'singing in harmony'. We must try to be sure that every individual's contribution has been heard.

viewpoints

understanding

'Seeing solitary facts in relation to a general principle, then, is the essence of understanding.'

M. L. Bigge and S. S. Shermis (1999)

children's problems

'... children's reading problems are often caused by the form and structure of the text rather than by its content alone.'

P. Pumfrey and A. Stamboltizis (2000)

geometry

'I quickly learned that reading is cumulative and proceeds by geometric progression: each new reading builds upon whatever the reader has read before.'

A. Manguel (1996)

tools

'... the International Reading Association ... state that this approach [visual tools] embodies a significant new set of tools used between reader and text by which meaning is found and created.'

D. Hyerle (1996)

extracting meaning

'... reading is not a matter of decoding words but of extracting meaning from a text.'

R. N. Caine and G. Caine (1991)

experience

How do personal schemas affect the reading experience?

the writer

How do visual tools help the reader 'get into the writer's head'?

expert readers

Do visual tools introduce something new or do they simply reveal what expert readers construct in their heads?

ROUTE MAP FOR YOUR READING

SECTION 1 — CONTEXT

CHAPTER ONE — BACKGROUND
The primary assertion is that we are all *Eye Q* experts. Throughout history, humans have used an assortment of visual tools to reflect and communicate knowledge. Current knowledge creation dynamics are based on this same notion. The 'inside story' of learning is obtained by looking both inside (cognitive psychology) and outside (Accelerated Learning).

CHAPTER TWO — THE iDESK MODEL
Most of our activities are not based on a theory of learning. Consequently, there is little sense of meaning or coherence. The iDesk model is holistic. It connects thinking, feeling and doing. Finally, it links these faculties to the environment and the individual. Visual tools impact all areas of the iDesk model, and all components interact with each other. Serious schools need models.

CHAPTER THREE — THE KNOWLEDGE AGE
We are living in the knowledge age with a need for more knowledge workers. These new types of workers require new, extended mental skills and knowledge tools. Visual tools are central in creating and communicating knowledge. Schools need to learn from business theory and practice with regard to intellectual capital and the use of visual tools.

SECTION 2 — VISUALS

CHAPTER FOUR — VISUAL TOOLS AND COMPUTERS
We are learning that the use of computers can reinforce poor learning habits. The attraction of the screen can degenerate into visual 'candyfloss'. This turns computer users into consumers. Behind the screen lies a knowledge structure. Visual tools make this explicit and turn consumers into explorers of knowledge. Clarity about visual literacy will support this.

CHAPTER FIVE — VISUAL LITERACY
In our culture, the visual–verbal polarity may well be more divisive than the sciences–arts gulf. There are historical, philosophical reasons for the low value placed on visuals. Visual literacy, nonetheless, is an established discipline. All visual content exists in the spatial dimension. Space is our first and primary frontier. The spatial metaphor shapes our understanding.

CHAPTER SIX — TOOLS TO LEARN
The successes of our civilisation are based on tools. We have created these tools and they, in turn, end up shaping our behaviour. Using new tools causes new learning to take place. Habitual use of tools changes our habits. The most effective use of tools happens when accompanied with theory. Visual tools impact on learning habits. New eras need new tools.

SECTION 3 — MEANING

CHAPTER SEVEN — SCHEMAS
We all have schemas. They are personal and unique and are based on how we view the world. In business they are termed mental models. Their organisation represents how we think and shape our behaviour. All students have these mental maps but are unaware of them — as are teachers. Making schemas visible allows students and teachers to see what they are thinking.

CHAPTER EIGHT — HOLOGRAPHIC–LINEAR
Every day, every student, in every lesson has to turn linear communication (what she reads or hears) into what is termed her holographic understanding. Schemas are holographic in structure — definitely not linear. The student then has to turn her new, enlarged understanding back into linear format. This process has, until now, been an unknown phenomenon.

CHAPTER NINE — CONSTRUCTING KNOWLEDGE
All our students construct knowledge — even the very youngest and the least able. Knowledge cannot be delivered. It has to be created each time by the individual, for knowledge is created not discovered. This view of learning is called constructivism. Understanding this process stimulates teachers to make learning more meaningful and motivating for all students.

SECTION 4 — LANGUAGE

CHAPTER TEN — SUPPORT FOR LANGUAGE
It is normally thought that visuals 'compete' with words. With visual tools, this is not true. Visual tools exist in the overlapping area between words and pictures. If you examine language, you realise that images play a big part in stimulating thought and supporting planning. They help the organisation of our language, which normally has to take place in the unseen interior of our heads.

CHAPTER ELEVEN — READING
Reading is active. Readers' interrogation of text is shaped by their own schemas. They have to adapt their existing schemas in order to absorb text into meaningful messages. Visual tools can reveal the hidden structure and meaning of a text. Just as computer software can show you what your voice looks like, visual tools can show you what your thinking looks like.

CHAPTER TWELVE — WRITING
Writing is difficult. Students' difficulties and fears stem from not knowing what to write. Visual tools make planning explicit, easy and empowering. Through the use of visual tools, students can model the planning that excellent writers do 'in their heads'. Planning in linear fashion is too difficult for most. The schematic nature of visual tools matches the way the brain naturally works.

SECTION 5 — THINKING

CHAPTER THIRTEEN — THINKING SKILLS
When we think, we are either thinking of objects (in space) or events (in time). Our thoughts become 'thought–objects'. Just as we manipulate real, physical objects in space, so we move our 'thought–objects' in our inner space. This is thinking. It is, however, invisible and demands much short term memory. Visual tools make thinking visible, easier and obvious.

CHAPTER FOURTEEN — QUESTIONS
Questions are more powerful than answers. They directly determine our focus and thinking. Young children are wonderful questioners — young scientists. Schools have conditioned students to demand only questions. This severely limits their thinking and learning. Visual tools are themselves questions. They demand investigation. Their visible nature makes questioners of all students.

CHAPTER FIFTEEN — THINKING IN ACTION
There is a link between text, thinking and visual tools. The nature of different types of text (genres) demand different types of thinking. All thinking is the manipulation of 'thought–objects'. Visual tools show students what this looks like. Matching types of visual tools to specific genres and linking them to the National Curriculum thinking skills is a powerful matrix.

SECTION 6 — LEARNING

CHAPTER SIXTEEN — ACTIVE LEARNING
You don't have to leave your seat to be actively learning. Active doesn't mean kinaesthetic! Active learning involves becoming engrossed, relating new material to personal prior knowledge, and creating meaning. Active learning needs to be encouraged by teachers. It is what is demanded of business. Visual tools stimulate and challenge active learning from students.

CHAPTER SEVENTEEN — STYLES OF LEARNING
Learning style labels can be dangerous. They can limit rather than stimulate expansion. Behind their often surface description lies a common cognitive activity — putting the detail into the big picture. Visual tools meet the needs of all learners, involving them in visual, verbal, analytic and holistic thinking. They also promote the four essential skills of learning.

CHAPTER EIGHTEEN — ABILITY RANGE
We have many labels for our pupils — from the gifted and talented to SEN. Behind all these labels there lies the act of meaning making. Visual tools show students what understanding looks like. This gives confidence to them all. It allows the least able to see their intelligence and supports the more able to organise and communicate their sometimes erratic thinking.

SECTION 7 — LEXICON

CHAPTER NINETEEN — LEXICON

CATEGORIES OF VISUAL TOOLS

- structural thinking — Structural Visual Tools
- differential thinking — Differential Visual Tools
- representational thinking — Representational Visual Tools
- temporal thinking — Temporal Visual Tools
- causal thinking — Causal Visual Tools
- numerical thinking — Numerical Visual Tools
- organisational thinking — Organisational Visual Tools
- individual thinking — Individual Visual Tools

There are seven types of visual tools related to seven types of thinking. The eighth is a hybrid of all seven. Within each category, there is a variety of visual tools. Visual tools within the categories achieve slightly different results, at different levels of complexity to suit age, ability and the nature of the tasks set. Each visual tool is described, its workings explained and ideas given for introducing it to students. Differences between similar visual tools are clarified. Each visual tool is illustrated both in templated format and as a hand-drawn example in use. The context for each hand-drawn visual tool is a well known story.

overview

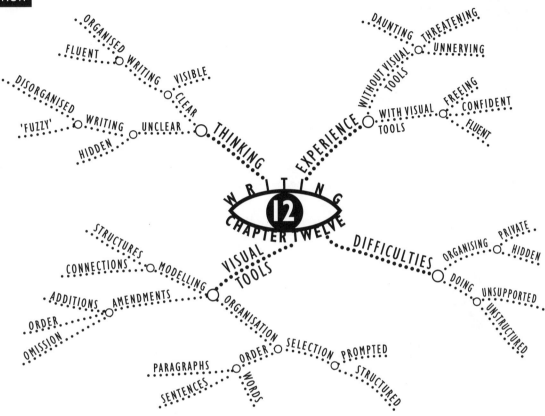

preview

- Writing can be a daunting task for many of us.

- If instead of adopting a linear approach to writing we map our thoughts, the burden is considerably eased.

- Visual tools enable average writers to emulate the excellent.

- Avid readers model authors, either consciously or subconsciously.

- You can write clearly when you think clearly.

- In a sense, a piece of writing is largely a vision or series of jottings that exists in our heads and in our notes.

- Visual tools make writing easier.

Writing can be a daunting task for many of us.

Imagine that instead of the book in front of you there is a vast array of plain white pages. No numbers, no letters, just a sea of white. Imagine then that in two months time a publishing house wants those pages filled with 35,000 words. The total package is to give an account of the theory and practice of education, as realised by a group of three people, communicated in an efficient way to an editor. Daunting prospect, no?

This is the way many of us respond to writing. It is a task facing most of us in our daily lives. Even if our writing is never realised, every one of us has, in our heads, the potential scripts for countless essays, articles, booklets and diaries. In school, writing does become a reality, but the act of committing our thoughts to paper can be unnerving.

If instead of adopting a linear approach to writing we map our thoughts, the burden is considerably eased.

Dialogue is the key to developing imagination, ideas and creative thinking. This dialogue can be internal, or conducted with others. Having a range of visual strategies at our disposal increases the likelihood that dialogue will take place. They also allow us to mark our thoughts on the page and to link them.

Linking ideas is the essence of writing, of creating a text. James Britton (1982) sets out the difficulties that young writers encounter and deftly sums up where the problem lies. He argues that organisation is the critical factor in satisfying the external needs for which a piece of writing is constructed. It is no surprise then that the two words 'purpose' and 'organisation' are so central to the markers of test papers.

Visual tools enable average writers to emulate the excellent.

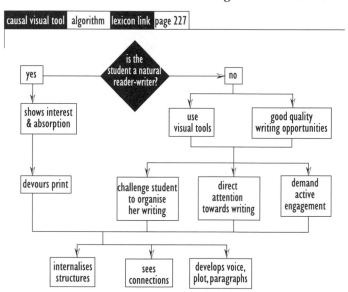

We learn to write in different ways. Some young readers find themselves effortlessly absorbing the styles and patterns of authors they admire. The excellent are not content to devour print – they have aspirations to create and to share their output with their audiences. As though by osmosis, they develop their voice, their plots and paragraphs. They spend time devising characters, events and situations, and by the time they attack the page so much linguistic rehearsal has occurred that the words flow. If you are one of these natural writers, then 'writing goes on in your head even when you are away from your desk and computer' say writing coaches Frank and George Andrews (1996).

These natural reader–writers are gifted with three advantages not enjoyed by the majority of students:

- they show interest and absorption

- they internalise structures of written language

- they are able to see connections.

Our classrooms, then, need to provide opportunities for students to acquire these skills. The way students can achieve this is through adopting an active, direct and challenging approach to texts of all sorts. Visual tools challenge students to organise their writing in a way that fits its purpose. They direct students' attention towards the writing itself. They demand an active engagement with the whole writing process.

By combining a variety of good quality writing opportunities with access to visual tools, teachers can compensate for any lack of desire and fluidity shown by students – the desire to absorb what the author has to offer, and the fluidity to investigate and play with the ideas communicated. When students can see the particular way words are manipulated and employed by good writers, they are able to build up a picture of the craft of writing.

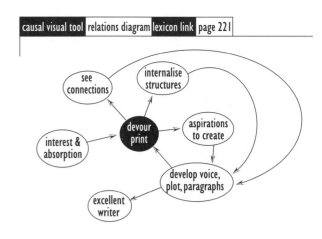

causal visual tool | relations diagram | lexicon link | page 221

Avid readers model authors, either consciously or subconsciously.

Learning how to write involves the teacher as a demonstrator or expert passing on skills and knowledge to students. Teaching writing involves the teacher as writer. Since purpose and organisation are the keys to successful writing, teachers need to model how best to achieve these objectives while actively composing in front of the class. They must talk aloud, sharing their thoughts as they emerge during the process of thinking – what Wim Wenger (1980) calls 'polebridging'. Visual tools allow us to take polebridging to a new level – they illuminate the 'bridge' from plan to product. They show us what our thoughts look like – and their structure.

The teachers' own texts can then be studied and discussed in a more informed way because of this inside knowledge. If required to write up their understanding as linear text, students are supported using visual planning tools.

You can write clearly when you think clearly.

'Clear writing comes from clear thinking.'

F. and G. Andrews (1996)

Writing is complex. It is both shaped by us and, when thoughtfully explored, it shapes us. Additional time spent at the rehearsal or planning stage of writing enables students to approach writing tasks with more confidence. Having visual cues in front of them has a remarkably freeing effect. Knowing where to start and having a clear idea of the route they then wish to follow makes the next stage of writing considerably easier. Composition flows, as does spoken language.

In a sense, a piece of writing is largely a vision or series of jottings that exists in our heads and in our notes.

It is useful to have the 'big picture' before starting a composition. When doing a jigsaw puzzle, it makes things much easier to be able to consult the picture on the box lid. With writing, however, we can not have the completed assembly before us. Even with visual tools, the details of the text are not fixed. We can never be certain exactly what we are going to write until we actually start writing.

Nevertheless, the direction that visual tools give the writer enable her to feel confident. Assured by the structure the tools offer her, she is free to lose herself in the act of writing, allowing the words to stream from mind to page. Visual tools support both the planning and process of writing.

Visual tools make writing easier.

Putting their thoughts into a supporting structure, and having this structure visible, enables students to see what to write, what to emphasise, how to put it into chunks and how to join it together. Freed from the agonies of either not knowing what to write, or trying to hold these notions in the head, students can focus on the act of writing itself. Linear notes made in preparation do help, but still mean the student has to extract the structure from the lines and hold it in her head.

Visual tools, however, make it all so obvious, remain constantly in view and are easily amended. They are effective because they represent the kind of preparation naturally good writers engage in. A preparation that is abstract – that lives in their heads. This is not only too difficult for most students, it is totally unnecessary. Visual tools can help liberate the writer inside all students.

viewpoints

thinking

'Style models, genres, all these things have been important, but they still assume that the thinking is just there.'

M. Jeffries (2000)

non-linear

'Writing is essentially a linear process, requiring us to 'think in a straight line', which for many children does not come naturally. Preliminary planning can help – but non-linear thinkers may feel just as threatened by the traditional 'story plan' or 'essay plan' which also has a linear format ... Children often enjoy representing information in pictorial or diagrammatic form – such as flow chart, time line or grid.'

S. Palmer (2000)

two structures

'The grammar of deep structure is semantic; it's relationships are concerned with meaning.'

F. Smith (1990)

knowledge transfer

'... we believe that the effective transfer of knowledge between groups of individuals depends critically upon the creation of appropriate representational frameworks to facilitate the exteriorisation and ingestion of knowledge in different forms.'

P. Barker and P. Van Schank (2000)

assessment

'Possibly the greatest area of time saving is in this area of assessment. Visual tools provide teachers with a picture of students' thinking – in the same display that students can use for their self-assessment.'

D. Hyerle (1996)

difficulty

Have you ever found the writing process difficult because you weren't sure what to write next? Would you have found a visual plan of what to write helpful?

modelling

What strategies do you use in your classrooms to model the writing process? How can you see visual tools contributing to this?

confidence

In what ways can visual tools create more confident and cogent writers?

ROUTE MAP FOR YOUR READING

SECTION 1 — CONTEXT

CHAPTER ONE — BACKGROUND

The primary assertion is that we are all *Eye Q* experts. Throughout history, humans have used an assortment of visual tools to reflect and communicate knowledge. Current knowledge creation dynamics are based on this same notion. The 'inside story' of learning is obtained by looking both inside (cognitive psychology) and outside (Accelerated Learning).

CHAPTER TWO — THE iDESK MODEL

Most of our activities are not based on a theory of learning. Consequently, there is little sense of meaning or coherence. The iDesk model is holistic. It connects thinking, feeling and doing. Finally, it links these faculties to the environment and the individual. Visual tools impact all areas of the iDesk model, and all components interact with each other. Serious schools need models.

CHAPTER THREE — THE KNOWLEDGE AGE

We are living in the knowledge age with a need for more knowledge workers. These new types of workers require new, extended mental skills and knowledge tools. Visual tools are central in creating and communicating knowledge. Schools need to learn from business theory and practice with regard to intellectual capital and the use of visual tools.

SECTION 2 — VISUALS

CHAPTER FOUR — VISUAL TOOLS AND COMPUTERS

We are learning that the use of computers can reinforce poor learning habits. The attraction of the screen can degenerate into visual 'candyfloss'. This turns computer users into consumers. Behind the screen lies a knowledge structure. Visual tools make this explicit and turn consumers into explorers of knowledge. Clarity about visual literacy will support this.

CHAPTER FIVE — VISUAL LITERACY

In our culture, the visual—verbal polarity may well be more divisive than the sciences—arts gulf. There are historical, philosophical reasons for the low value placed on visuals. Visual literacy, nonetheless, is an established discipline. All visual content exists in the spatial dimension. Space is our first and primary frontier. The spatial metaphor shapes our understanding.

CHAPTER SIX — TOOLS TO LEARN

The successes of our civilisation are based on tools. We have created these tools and they, in turn, end up shaping our behaviour. Using new tools causes new learning to take place. Habitual use of tools changes our habits. The most effective use of tools happens when accompanied with theory. Visual tools impact on learning habits. New eras need new tools.

SECTION 3 — MEANING

CHAPTER SEVEN — SCHEMAS

We all have schemas. They are personal and unique and are based on how we view the world. In business they are termed mental models. Their organisation represents how we think and shape our behaviour. All students have these mental maps but are unaware of them — as are teachers. Making schemas visible allows students and teachers to see what they are thinking.

CHAPTER EIGHT — HOLOGRAPHIC—LINEAR

Every day, every student, in every lesson has to turn linear communication (what she reads or hears) into what is termed her holographic understanding. Schemas are holographic in structure — definitely not linear. The student then has to turn her new, enlarged understanding back into linear format. This process has, until now, been an unknown phenomenon.

CHAPTER NINE — CONSTRUCTING KNOWLEDGE

All our students construct knowledge — even the very youngest and the least able. Knowledge cannot be delivered. It has to be created each time by the individual, for knowledge is created not discovered. This view of learning is called constructivism. Understanding this process stimulates teachers to make learning more meaningful and motivating for all students.

SECTION 4 — LANGUAGE

CHAPTER TEN — SUPPORT FOR LANGUAGE

It is normally thought that visuals 'compete' with words. With visual tools, this is not true. Visual tools exist in the overlapping area between words and pictures. If you examine language, you realise that images play a big part in stimulating thought and supporting planning. They help the organisation of our language, which normally has to take place in the unseen interior of our heads.

CHAPTER ELEVEN — READING

Reading is active. Readers' interrogation of text is shaped by their own schemas. They have to adapt their existing schemas in order to absorb text into meaningful messages. Visual tools can reveal the hidden structure and meaning of a text. Just as computer software can show you what your voice looks like, visual tools can show you what your thinking looks like.

CHAPTER TWELVE — WRITING

Writing is difficult. Students' difficulties and fears stem from not knowing what to write. Visual tools make planning explicit, easy and empowering. Through the use of visual tools, students can model the planning that excellent writers do 'in their heads'. Planning in linear fashion is too difficult for most. The schematic nature of visual tools matches the way the brain naturally works.

SECTION 5 — THINKING

CHAPTER THIRTEEN — THINKING SKILLS

When we think, we are either thinking of objects (in space) or events (in time). Our thoughts become 'thought—objects'. Just as we manipulate real, physical objects in space, so we move our 'thought—objects' in our inner space. This is thinking. It is, however, invisible and demands much short term memory. Visual tools make thinking visible, easier and obvious.

CHAPTER FOURTEEN — QUESTIONS

Questions are more powerful than answers. They directly determine our focus and thinking. Young children are wonderful questioners — young scientists. Schools have conditioned students to demand only questions. This severely limits their thinking and learning. Visual tools are themselves questions. They demand investigation. Their visible nature makes questioners of all students.

CHAPTER FIFTEEN — THINKING IN ACTION

There is a link between text, thinking and visual tools. The nature of different types of text (genres) demand different types of thinking. All thinking is the manipulation of 'thought—objects'. Visual tools show students what this looks like. Matching types of visual tools to specific genres and linking them to the National Curriculum thinking skills is a powerful matrix.

SECTION 6 — LEARNING

CHAPTER SIXTEEN — ACTIVE LEARNING

You don't have to leave your seat to be actively learning. Active doesn't mean kinaesthetic! Active learning involves becoming engrossed, relating new material to personal prior knowledge, and creating meaning. Active learning needs to be encouraged by teachers. It is what is demanded of business. Visual tools stimulate and challenge active learning from students.

CHAPTER SEVENTEEN — STYLES OF LEARNING

Learning style labels can be dangerous. They can limit rather than stimulate expansion. Behind their often surface description lies a common cognitive activity — putting the detail into the big picture. Visual tools meet the needs of all learners, involving them in visual, verbal, analytic and holistic thinking. They also promote the four essential skills of learning.

CHAPTER EIGHTEEN — ABILITY RANGE

We have many labels for our pupils — from the gifted and talented to SEN. Behind all these labels there lies the act of meaning making. Visual tools show students what understanding looks like. This gives confidence to them all. It allows the least able to see their intelligence and supports the more able to organise and communicate their sometimes erratic thinking.

SECTION 7 — LEXICON

CHAPTER NINETEEN — LEXICON

CATEGORIES OF VISUAL TOOLS

- structural thinking — Structural Visual Tools
- differential thinking — Differential Visual Tools
- representational thinking — Representational Visual Tools
- temporal thinking — Temporal Visual Tools
- causal thinking — Causal Visual Tools
- numerical thinking — Numerical Visual Tools
- organisational thinking — Organisational Visual Tools
- individual thinking — Individual Visual Tools

There are seven types of visual tools related to seven types of thinking. The eighth is a hybrid of all seven. Within each category, there is a variety of visual tools. Visual tools within the categories achieve slightly different results, at different levels of complexity to suit age, ability and the nature of the tasks set. Each visual tool is described, its workings explained and ideas given for introducing it to students. Differences between similar visual tools are clarified. Each visual tool is illustrated both in templated format and as a hand-drawn example in use. The context for each hand-drawn visual tool is a well known story.

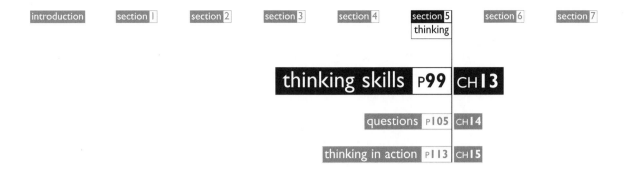

thinking skills P99 CH13

questions P105 CH14

thinking in action P113 CH15

overview

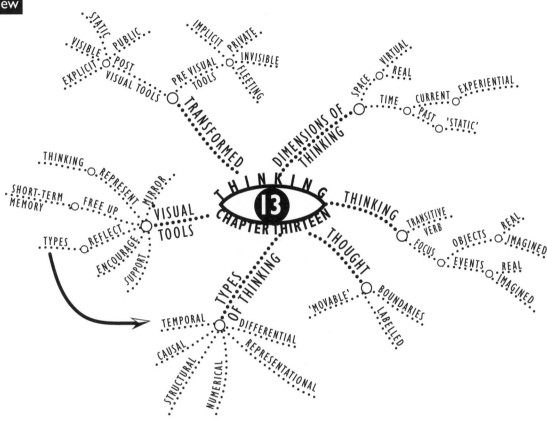

preview

- 'Think' is a transitive verb – you can only think *about* something.

- The thoughts you have can be viewed as 'thought-objects'.

- What we call reasoning is merely the manipulation of these thought-objects.

- When we put thought-objects into particular permutations, we are constructing concepts and schemas.

- Thinking requires energy and skill.

- Visual tools free up short-term memory, enabling the thinker to focus, concentrate and organise.

- Visual tools represent, on paper, the thinking that normally remains hidden from view.

- Visual tools transform thinking that is normally private, invisible, fleeting and implicit into thinking that is public, visible, static and explicit.

- Visual tools can help us become more engaged, enthusiastic and better thinkers.

'Think' is a transitive verb – you can only think *about* something.

You are always thinking of something. There are never moments when you are thinking of nothing. When you think, you have to think about something. Just try and think about nothing! Thinking, you will realise from this experiment, is a transitive verb. Such verbs always have an object – you 'catch' something; you 'eat' something; you 'lift' something; and you 'think' something.

The 'something' that you are thinking about will be either an object or an event. We live in the dimensions of time and space, so events are the 'something' relating to time, and objects are the 'something' relating to space.

> 'Timing is only half of everything. Spacing is the other half.'
>
> T. Siler (1996)

Failure to grasp this notion is the reason why so many children become poor thinkers, according to Reuven Feuerstein (Sharron, 1987).

The thoughts you have can be viewed as 'thought-objects'.

When you think, you can think of either real objects or real events. Or, indeed, you can think of imagined objects or imagined events. In both cases, the things we call thoughts become 'objects' themselves, in a manner of speaking.

Thoughts are not real in the same sense that physical objects are real. They are abstractions of reality. However, when you think of a real object or a real event, the thought you have of it can be said to become itself a kind of virtual, abstract 'thing'. This virtual 'thing' is more usefully termed a 'thought-object' because it shares many of the characteristics of a real object. Real objects have boundaries – there is a definite boundary to a chair, for example. That boundary defines both what the chair is and what it is not. Because of this boundary, the chair can be identified, labelled and manipulated.

So it is with thoughts-as-objects. Thoughts, if viewed as being thought-objects have boundaries. There is a definite boundary to a thought about a chair, for example. That boundary defines the thought about both what the chair is and, also, what it is not. Because of this boundary, the thought about the chair can be identified, labelled and manipulated.

| differential visual tool | double bubble | lexicon link | page 176 |

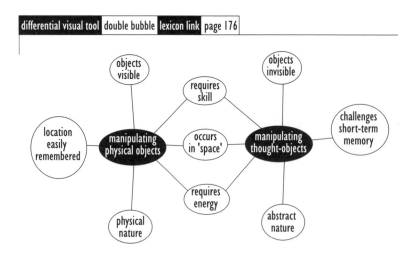

What we call reasoning is merely the manipulation of these thought-objects.

By cutting up and creating boundaries around parts of our perceptions, feelings and impressions, we are able to look at them. This breaking up of our experiences into small 'bits' allows us to have some control over them. We are able to view them as thought-objects, and reason about them. In short, because of this process, we are able think.

The way in which we are able to reason and think about our experiences is by manipulating these thought-objects. We manipulate them in a kind of virtual space because:

'... it is natural for us to conceptualise language metaphorically in terms of space.'

G. Lakoff and M. Johnson (1980)

In the abstract world of the interior of our heads, we approach and deal with thought-objects in the same way in which we approach and deal with physical objects in the physical world. We move them, we place them and we relate them to each other. These actions are what we call thinking. Thinking, therefore, happens through the metaphor of our bodily experiences in the physical world. We become able to understand and deal with our abstractions through the metaphor of our everyday life. As explained in chapter 5, Visual literacy, our language betrays this fundamental way of thinking.

When we put thought-objects into particular permutations, we are constructing concepts and schemas.

Just as we constantly arrange and re-arrange real objects in the physical world, so we constantly arrange and re-arrange thought-objects in our abstract world. Not surprisingly, the different permutations of thought-objects we construct are not random. Patterns emerge. These patterns represent what we call different types of thinking. When we engage in what is termed analytical thinking, for example, then thought-objects are manipulated in particular ways and their permutations have particular characteristics. These special features of thinking can be identified across the span of any taxonomy of thinking.

Thinking requires energy and skill.

Just as manipulating physical objects can demand energy and skill, so too does the manipulation of abstract thought-objects.

Thinking, as we have seen, is the manipulation of 'thought-objects' as if they were real, physical objects. However, unlike physical objects, thought-objects cannot be seen. Therefore, their location, their physical relationships to other thought-objects and their permutations have to be remembered. This places an enormous demand on awareness, attention and short-term memory. You could say that this represents the demands on the thinker's energy.

There is more to thinking than that, however. Exploring, inventing and creating permutations of thought-objects also demand skill. Distinguishing between the two demands – for energy and for skill – is crucial if we are to consider how to liberate more children to become effective and engaged thinkers.

Visual tools free up short-term memory, enabling the thinker to focus, concentrate and organise.

Normally our thinking – our joining together of thought-objects – goes on in our heads. Simultaneously, we have to hold information in our heads (our short-term memory) and try to work out relationships between the discrete pieces – to create meaning. This process is true, irrespective of the type of thinking involved, whether we label it analytical, creative, reflective, or whatever.

Visual tools liberate mental energy from the demands of short-term memory. They free us up to think about how to create, process and demonstrate our thinking.

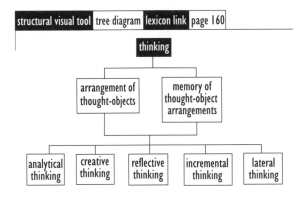

| structural visual tool | tree diagram | lexicon link | page 160 |

thinking
- arrangement of thought-objects
- memory of thought-object arrangements

analytical thinking | creative thinking | reflective thinking | incremental thinking | lateral thinking

Visual tools represent, on paper, the thinking that normally remains hidden from view.

The graphic display of the permutations of thought-objects is the externalisation of the interior world of thinking. Visual tools are not different from our internal thinking, they are not techniques reserved for only particular types of learners, nor are they merely a shorthand for thinking.

When we think, we arrange and re-arrange thought-objects into particular permutations, just as we do with real, physical objects. Just as with real objects, proximity, distance and orientational relationships between our thought-objects have significance and meaning. These meanings are our concepts.

Such meanings, expressed in the spatial arrangement of thought-objects, can be made visible. The physical arrangement of the words within a visual tool directly represents the abstract arrangement of thought-objects in our minds. They are one and the same thing.

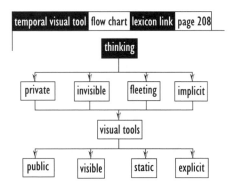

Visual tools transform thinking that is normally private, invisible, fleeting and implicit into thinking that is public, visible, static and explicit.

Using visual tools can significantly alter students' capacity to think effectively. In addition to freeing up mental energy from the demands of short-term memory, visual tools offer the opportunity for students to see what they are thinking. As two of North America's leading exponents of thinking skills explain:

'... diagrams [visual tools] serve as 'mental maps' to depict complex relationships in any subject and at any grade.'

S. Parks and H. Black (1992)

Being able to read their mental maps gives students new opportunities for self-awareness and reflection. Often, students are not really clear what it is they are thinking, and how their thoughts are structured, much less able to reason about and communicate them. Thinking is normally invisible, of course – because it is invisible, we are frequently unaware of it.

In order to be able to notice, analyse, amend and expand their thinking, students need to see what their thinking looks like. They need to be able to 'separate' themselves from the permutations they have constructed with their thought-objects, in order to look at them. Particularly gifted and talented students are able to gain such a perspective on their abstract, cognitive constructions without help. But most students need to be able to actually distance themselves from their interior conceptual fabrications in order to identify and consider them.

Visual tools can help us become more engaged, enthusiastic and better thinkers.

Bartlett, the originator of the term 'schema', pondered on the skill and thrill of manipulating thought-objects into different permutations. He noticed that:

'... as thinking moves towards greater freedom, one thing that happens is that the thinker is less and less concerned with the likelihood of items and more and more with that of packets, or groups of items. He is less detail-ridden, more 'schematic'-minded. If we should ask for the reasons why these lumping schematising developments take place ... My guess is that there are two chief reasons – they are more efficient and they are a lot more fun.'

F. C. Bartlett (1968)

Wouldn't it be marvellous if all our students were engaged thinkers in this way? Such an aspiration is doomed to remain a pipe-dream without the tools to make it happen. However, when students are able to see their thinking – the manipulation of thought-objects – they become engaged in the way Bartlett envisioned. Visual tools make students' thinking visible.

viewpoints

frames of view

'As any photographer knows, the frame of the viewfinder 'organises' the image within it, creating a visual statement where, without the frame, one might see only clutter.'

R. Fisher (1995)

structures

'New concepts become meaningful when they are linked in memory to existing concepts and are organised into a structure.'

C. Lawless, P. Smee and T. O'Shea (1998)

space

'We have primarily focused on maps relating to physical space, but locale memory is not limited to maps in physical space. There are also mental maps of information, which exist as part of an interconnected pattern. That is, they exist in 'mental space'.'

R. N. Caine and G. Caine (1991)

'Researchers have suggested that mental models integrate spatial and verbal information into a single structure.'

R. Lloyd (2000)

review

connections

Spend some time noticing your thoughts. Then jot down your thoughts onto paper.

Notice which thoughts were about objects and which were about events. Can you make any connections between or among these thoughts?

impulsiveness

How many times have you witnessed your students acting impulsively –seemingly without thought? How might the use of visual tools help your students consider and identify alternatives before acting?

visible thinking

Consider how much easier it would be to develop, question and communicate our thinking if its content and structures were made visible.

organisation

In what ways has this chapter changed the organisation of your thoughts about thinking?

ROUTE MAP FOR YOUR READING

SECTION 1 — CONTEXT

CHAPTER ONE — BACKGROUND

The primary assertion is that we are all *Eye Q* experts. Throughout history, humans have used an assortment of visual tools to reflect and communicate knowledge. Current knowledge creation dynamics are based on this same notion. The 'inside story' of learning is obtained by looking both inside (cognitive psychology) and outside (Accelerated Learning).

CHAPTER TWO — THE iDESK MODEL

Most of our activities are not based on a theory of learning. Consequently, there is little sense of meaning or coherence. The iDesk model is holistic. It connects thinking, feeling and doing. Finally, it links these faculties to the environment and the individual. Visual tools impact all areas of the iDesk model, and all components interact with each other. Serious schools need models.

CHAPTER THREE — THE KNOWLEDGE AGE

We are living in the knowledge age with a need for more knowledge workers. These new types of workers require new, extended mental skills and knowledge tools. Visual tools are central in creating and communicating knowledge. Schools need to learn from business theory and practice with regard to intellectual capital and the use of visual tools.

SECTION 2 — VISUALS

CHAPTER FOUR — VISUAL TOOLS AND COMPUTERS

We are learning that the use of computers can reinforce poor learning habits. The attraction of the screen can degenerate into visual 'candyfloss'. This turns computer users into consumers. Behind the screen lies a knowledge structure. Visual tools make this explicit and turn consumers into explorers of knowledge. Clarity about visual literacy will support this.

CHAPTER FIVE — VISUAL LITERACY

In our culture, the visual–verbal polarity may well be more divisive than the sciences–arts gulf. There are historical, philosophical reasons for the low value placed on visuals. Visual literacy, nonetheless, is an established discipline. All visual content exists in the spatial dimension. Space is our first and primary frontier. The spatial metaphor shapes our understanding.

CHAPTER SIX — TOOLS TO LEARN

The successes of our civilisation are based on tools. We have created these tools and they, in turn, end up shaping our behaviour. Using new tools causes new learning to take place. Habitual use of tools changes our habits. The most effective use of tools happens when accompanied with theory. Visual tools impact on learning habits. New eras need new tools.

SECTION 3 — MEANING

CHAPTER SEVEN — SCHEMAS

We all have schemas. They are personal and unique and are based on how we view the world. In business they are termed mental models. Their organisation represents how we think and shape our behaviour. All students have these mental maps but are unaware of them — as are teachers. Making schemas visible allows students and teachers to see what they are thinking.

CHAPTER EIGHT — HOLOGRAPHIC–LINEAR

Every day, every student, in every lesson has to turn linear communication (what she reads or hears) into what is termed her holographic understanding. Schemas are holographic in structure — definitely not linear. The student then has to turn her new, enlarged understanding back into linear format. This process has, until now, been an unknown phenomenon.

CHAPTER NINE — CONSTRUCTING KNOWLEDGE

All our students construct knowledge — even the very youngest and the least able. Knowledge cannot be delivered. It has to be created each time by the individual, for knowledge is created not discovered. This view of learning is called constructivism. Understanding this process stimulates teachers to make learning more meaningful and motivating for all students.

SECTION 4 — LANGUAGE

CHAPTER TEN — SUPPORT FOR LANGUAGE

It is normally thought that visuals 'compete' with words. With visual tools, this is not true. Visual tools exist in the overlapping area between words and pictures. If you examine language, you realise that images play a big part in stimulating thought and supporting planning. They help the organisation of our language, which normally has to take place in the unseen interior of our heads.

CHAPTER ELEVEN — READING

Reading is active. Readers' interrogation of text is shaped by their own schemas. They have to adapt their existing schemas in order to absorb text into meaningful messages. Visual tools can reveal the hidden structure and meaning of a text. Just as computer software can show you what your voice looks like, visual tools can show you what your thinking looks like.

CHAPTER TWELVE — WRITING

Writing is difficult. Students' difficulties and fears stem from not knowing what to write. Visual tools make planning explicit, easy and empowering. Through the use of visual tools, students can model the planning that excellent writers do 'in their heads'. Planning in linear fashion is too difficult for most. The schematic nature of visual tools matches the way the brain naturally works.

SECTION 5 — THINKING

CHAPTER THIRTEEN — THINKING SKILLS

When we think, we are either thinking of objects (in space) or events (in time). Our thoughts become 'thought–objects'. Just as we manipulate real, physical objects in space, so we move our 'thought–objects' in our inner space. This is thinking. It is, however, invisible and demands much short term memory. Visual tools make thinking visible, easier and obvious.

CHAPTER FOURTEEN — QUESTIONS

Questions are more powerful than answers. They directly determine our focus and thinking. Young children are wonderful questioners — young scientists. Schools have conditioned students to demand only questions. This severely limits their thinking and learning. Visual tools are themselves questions. They demand investigation. Their visible nature makes questioners of all students.

CHAPTER FIFTEEN — THINKING IN ACTION

There is a link between text, thinking and visual tools. The nature of different types of text (genres) demand different types of thinking. All thinking is the manipulation of 'thought–objects'. Visual tools show students what this looks like. Matching types of visual tools to specific genres and linking them to the National Curriculum thinking skills is a powerful matrix.

SECTION 6 — LEARNING

CHAPTER SIXTEEN — ACTIVE LEARNING

You don't have to leave your seat to be actively learning. Active doesn't mean kinaesthetic! Active learning involves becoming engrossed, relating new material to personal prior knowledge, and creating meaning. Active learning needs to be encouraged by teachers. It is what is demanded of business. Visual tools stimulate and challenge active learning from students.

CHAPTER SEVENTEEN — STYLES OF LEARNING

Learning style labels can be dangerous. They can limit rather than stimulate expansion. Behind their often surface description lies a common cognitive activity — putting the detail into the big picture. Visual tools meet the needs of all learners, involving them in visual, verbal, analytic and holistic thinking. They also promote the four essential skills of learning.

CHAPTER EIGHTEEN — ABILITY RANGE

We have many labels for our pupils — from the gifted and talented to SEN. Behind all these labels there lies the act of meaning making. Visual tools show students what understanding looks like. This gives confidence to them all. It allows the least able to see their intelligence and supports the more able to organise and communicate their sometimes erratic thinking.

SECTION 7 — LEXICON

CHAPTER NINETEEN — LEXICON

CATEGORIES OF VISUAL TOOLS

- structural thinking — Structural Visual Tools
- differential thinking — Differential Visual Tools
- representational thinking — Representational Visual Tools
- temporal thinking — Temporal Visual Tools
- causal thinking — Causal Visual Tools
- numerical thinking — Numerical Visual Tools
- organisational thinking — Organisational Visual Tools
- individual thinking — Individual Visual Tools

There are seven types of visual tools related to seven types of thinking. The eighth is a hybrid of all seven. Within each category, there is a variety of visual tools. Visual tools within the categories achieve slightly different results, at different levels of complexity to suit age, ability and the nature of the tasks set. Each visual tool is described, its workings explained and ideas given for introducing it to students. Differences between similar visual tools are clarified. Each visual tool is illustrated both in templated format and as a hand-drawn example in use. The context for each hand-drawn visual tool is a well known story.

thinking skills P99 CH13

questions P105 CH14

thinking in action P113 CH15

overview

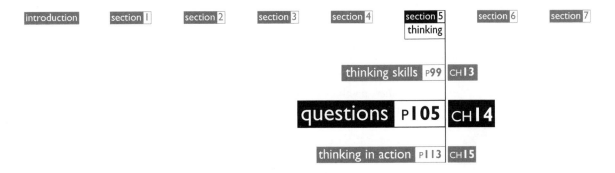

preview

■ We have only to consider the world around us for a few moments to realise the power of questions.

■ We cannot stop asking questions.

■ The young are experts in the ancient art of questioning – they are philosophers in the making.

■ Do you prefer to ask or be asked questions?

■ One of the difficult issues that we all have to deal with is the notion that answers are what really matter.

■ In the climate of the classroom, we bow to answers because that is what we are looking for.

■ How do questions relate to our evaluation of surface and deep meaning?

■ Questions determine our thinking and stretch our vocabulary.

■ The use of visual tools makes questioners of all students.

We have only to consider the world around us for a few moments to realise the power of questions.

Not content with the world as it is, or was, our species has deliberately set about the task of remodelling and reshaping the planet. We began, many thousands of years ago, to ponder, to speculate and to see things differently to other members of the animal kingdom. We began to understand that we had a past and a future.

Our ancestors began to realise that they could change the way things were, not just in the present moment but also for the future. As we began to understand ourselves we started to burn with a desire to know more. We became driven by a need to take control, to shape our destinies. In short, we began to ask questions. We began to think!

Nothing in the world comes question-free. Each and every sensory experience needs to be processed. Sometimes our unconscious can handle the incoming data. Our responses to unidentified questions appear instinctive. Sometimes, however, the burning question is of such magnitude that it can quite literally change the course of our lives.

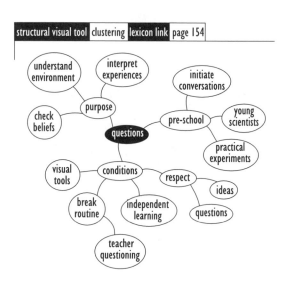

structural visual tool | clustering | lexicon link | page 154

We cannot stop asking questions.

Young children learn through interaction with their parents, carers and siblings. As they respond to sensory input, their schemas are being challenged, expanded, remodelled. It cannot be otherwise.

They need to interpret what they experience and check it against some outside source. There are numerous resources: books, pictures, television programmes, discussions with others, personal experiments. Young scientists are both hypothetical and practical.

At the root of their incessant questioning, silent or voiced, is a need to see if their minds can co-exist with those of others. Their hypotheses need to be tested and for parents and carers the practical experiments are often more frustrating than the wordy exchanges.

The young are experts in the ancient art of questioning – they are philosophers in the making.

What happens when, after years of intuitive exploration in the worlds of art, science and meaning making, children enter school? Studies of language interactions in the home by Wells (1987) tell us that as much as 75% of the interactions that take place are initiated by children. There appears to be a dramatic change in the patterns of engagement when children start school. Instead of being able to initiate conversations and generate questions they become listeners, often for long periods of time.

differential visual tool | matrix | lexicon link | page 178

activity	pre-school	school
ask questions	●	
discuss thinking	●	
initiate conversations	●	
independent learning	●	
listen to others		●
answer questions		●
dependent learning		●

The picture in the classroom is different because most of the questions come from the teacher and the opportunities for a mutually constructed dialogue are greatly reduced. In a sense the purpose of questioning takes on a new dimension – that of preparing for tests. Rather than engaging in a flow of intellectual speculation and exploration of the environment, teachers are responding to the demands of the curriculum and its assessment. These demands continue to dominate throughout the students' schooling.

As noted in chapter 16, Active learning, respect for people's ideas, thoughts, questions and suggestions lies at the heart of effective education. The opportunities for individuals to take responsibility for their own learning and develop independent strategies are not enhanced in classrooms that maintain a culture of dependency.

Do you prefer to ask or be asked questions?

Relationships in the classroom are crucial to successful learning, and the process of questioning is a major factor in determining those relationships. Imagine a classroom filled with people. Within this group are hierarchies based on concepts of intelligence and knowledge. There exists an expectation that teachers will provide answers.

Children are reluctant to raise their hands and to offer suggestions and answers. The majority of the questions are asked by the teacher. Questions are about power and the relationship between the questioner and the questioned; children are very conscious of this fact. How then do we improve and refine our skills in *generating* questions? In what ways can students be encouraged to experience the freedom to contribute to the agenda?

By allowing the individual time and space for personal reflection and the opportunity to ask questions we break the routine of teacher question followed by student answer. Any topic or theme is capable of producing a wide, diverse range of questions. In order to explore any subject fully we need to raise lots of questions. Individual questions are linked to individual levels of understanding. Single answers rarely suffice. Visual tools break routine habits of questioning.

One of the difficult issues that we all have to deal with is the notion that answers are what really matter.

Education systems seem to have been built upon the assumption that the ultimate aim of schooling is for students to give the right answers. But is this really correct? Why are some answers better than others? Certainly we need to pay much greater attention to questions than is presently the case. Asking questions is crucial in the act of learning.

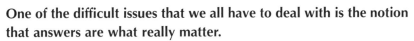

Jostein Gaarder, author of *Sophie's World*, has written a number of interesting books all of which have excellent points for discussion in classrooms. In *Hello? Is anybody there?* (1996), he introduces us to Mika, a young alien who falls to Earth. Mika's behaviour is perplexing for the young boy who spots him in the garden and attempts to communicate with him by asking a string of questions. Mika delivers a string of bows in response.

'Why are you bowing,' I asked.

'Where I come from, we always bow when someone asks an interesting question,' Mika explained. 'And the deeper the question, the deeper we bow.'

This was one of the silliest things I'd ever heard. I couldn't see how a question was anything to bow about.

'So, what do you do when you greet each other,' I asked.

'We try to think of a clever question,' he replied. … 'We try to find something clever to ask so the other person has to bow.'

This answer impressed me so much that I gave the deepest bow I could. When I looked up again, Mika was sucking his thumb. There was a long pause before he took it out.

'Why did you bow?' he asked, sounding rather offended.

'Because you gave such a clever answer to my question,' I replied.

'But an answer is never worth bowing for,' said Mika. 'Even if it sounds clever and correct you still shouldn't bow for it … An answer is always on the stretch of road that's behind you. Only a question can point the way forward.'

His words sounded so wise that I had to stop myself bowing again.

In the climate of the classroom, we bow to answers because that is what we are looking for.

Now, more than ever, a key factor in classroom management is time management. Visual tools can, in the long run, be a most efficient saver of time.

Teachers often feel, understandably, that investigation and discourse – while desirable – aren't really practical if targets are to be reached. There is a belief that, rather than 'waste time' in exploring subjects and topics, it is more economical to give students the answers and to question them sporadically to ensure that they have memorised them.

But answers are far better understood when questions have been thoroughly explored.

How do questions relate to our evaluation of surface and deep learning?

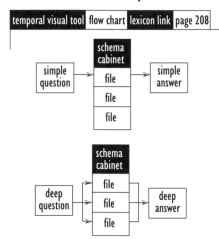

temporal visual tool | flow chart | lexicon link | page 208

Since answers reflect questions, good quality answers can only follow good quality questions. Good quality questions need to be looked at, so they need to be visible.

People often talk of higher and lower order questions. The level of questioning is in direct relation to the level of thinking that is going on and the ways in which the memory is being put to use. In the sense that learning as a process is constructing meaning, it is the meanings that are more important. The higher the order of question, the deeper the level of meaning. When teachers continue to ask superficial, straightforward questions, with simple 'test-like' answers, real learning and meaning is not achieved.

In chapter 7, Schemas, we learned about the 'packages' of information that we all store in 'filing cabinets' in the mind, for future use. In some cases, questions will be directed towards a single file and require simple factual answers.

Sometimes, we will be asked to interpret what is being said and to locate appropriate data. Finally, we may be asked to bring our own views, personal responses and opinions to a discussion. It is this last category of questions that poses the greatest challenge.

Questions determine our thinking and stretch our vocabulary.

Our ability to ask questions depends upon our thinking and the context in which thoughts are being generated. Visual tools play a vital part in enabling us to bring shape to our thinking and increase the chance of higher order questions emerging. We can 'see' where the discussions are leading. Like peeling an onion, we can remove layers to reach a deeper understanding. As layers disappear, so the language of explanation becomes more refined.

As questions arise and are considered, modified and answered, we can follow visually the links and levels of complexity that begin to appear. By making visible the thinking in progress, and by selecting appropriate forms for recording the debate and enquiry, we increase the potential for understanding and retention of the issues investigated. Visual tools and collaborative thinking also provide opportunities for questions from a wider range of viewpoints.

The use of visual tools makes questioners of all students.

Visual tools are very closely related to questions. In choosing which visual tool to use, you will need to engage in a series of questions. When you work with the chosen visual tool, you will find yourself asking questions stemming from the nature of the tool.

For example, the choice of a model map to summarise a passage of text comes about through questions relating to the nature of the text and the relationships of the elements within it. The construction of the model map is dependent on questions relating to the similarities and differences between elements, the characteristics of the chosen groupings and the nature of the relationships between elements across categories.

Using a visual tool to analyse or summarise a piece of writing immediately engages you with the text. It gives you a perspective from which the text is examined. This shaped perception adds momentum to your attention. Questions emerge from this 'enforced' viewing point. Links between the linear text and the form of the visual tool demand an active engagement with the text. Fuelling this engagement is a constant flow of questions.

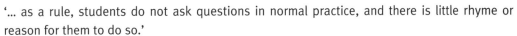

In a book devoted to questions in the classroom, Dillon laments that:

'... as a rule, students do not ask questions in normal practice, and there is little rhyme or reason for them to do so.'

J. T. Dillon (1988)

Visual tools are a compelling 'rhyme and reason' to ask questions. Their use transforms classrooms into communities of enquiry.

viewpoints

complacency

'We often stop being inquisitive as we get older because we learn that it is good to be intelligent and being intelligent is interpreted as already knowing the answers (instead of asking good questions).'

D. Wheton, K. Cameron and M. Woods (1996)

challenge

'One definition of a good question is that it provides an intellectual challenge.'

R. Fisher (1992)

diagrams

'Drawing a causal loop diagram is a very powerful way of asking the question 'Do you see the world in the same way as I do?"

D. Sherwood (1998)

looking ahead

'The best key questions contained a sense of looking ahead, of helping the lesson to move on.'

G. Brown and E. C. Wragg (1993)

ideas

'Ideas are integrating patterns that satisfy the mind when it asks the questions, What does this mean? What is this all about?'

T. Roszak (1986)

review

shaping questions

Look at something, anything. Now think of three questions that you could ask of or about the 'thing' you are looking at. Now glance at a couple of the visual tools in this book (chapter 19, Lexicon). Ask questions about them. You will realise that the tool shapes the questions that you ask.

questioners

Who asks most of the questions in your school or classroom – teachers or students?

quality questions

How do we know what to teach students if they are not asking us questions? Their questions teach us what to teach them and make us look like better teachers. How could you use visual tools in your lessons to help students ask more and better questions?

Consider a piece of work that you will be teaching tomorrow. Which visual tools could you use to help you and your students ask questions about it?

ROUTE MAP FOR YOUR READING

SECTION 1 — CONTEXT

CHAPTER ONE — BACKGROUND
The primary assertion is that we are all *Eye Q* experts. Throughout history, humans have used an assortment of visual tools to reflect and communicate knowledge. Current knowledge creation dynamics are based on this same notion. The 'inside story' of learning is obtained by looking both inside (cognitive psychology) and outside (Accelerated Learning).

CHAPTER TWO — THE iDESK MODEL
Most of our activities are not based on a theory of learning. Consequently, there is little sense of meaning or coherence. The iDesk model is holistic. It connects thinking, feeling and doing. Finally, it links these faculties to the environment and the individual. Visual tools impact all areas of the iDesk model, and all components interact with each other. Serious schools need models.

CHAPTER THREE — THE KNOWLEDGE AGE
We are living in the knowledge age with a need for more knowledge workers. These new types of workers require new, extended mental skills and knowledge tools. Visual tools are central in creating and communicating knowledge. Schools need to learn from business theory and practice with regard to intellectual capital and the use of visual tools.

SECTION 2 — VISUALS

CHAPTER FOUR — VISUAL TOOLS AND COMPUTERS
We are learning that the use of computers can reinforce poor learning habits. The attraction of the screen can degenerate into visual 'candyfloss'. This turns computer users into consumers. Behind the screen lies a knowledge structure. Visual tools make this explicit and turn consumers into explorers of knowledge. Clarity about visual literacy will support this.

CHAPTER FIVE — VISUAL LITERACY
In our culture, the visual—verbal polarity may well be more divisive than the sciences—arts gulf. There are historical, philosophical reasons for the low value placed on visuals. Visual literacy, nonetheless, is an established discipline. All visual content exists in the spatial dimension. Space is our first and primary frontier. The spatial metaphor shapes our understanding.

CHAPTER SIX — TOOLS TO LEARN
The successes of our civilisation are based on tools. We have created these tools and they, in turn, end up shaping our behaviour. Using new tools causes new learning to take place. Habitual use of tools changes our habits. The most effective use of tools happens when accompanied with theory. Visual tools impact on learning habits. New eras need new tools.

SECTION 3 — MEANING

CHAPTER SEVEN — SCHEMAS
We all have schemas. They are personal and unique and are based on how we view the world. In business they are termed mental models. Their organisation represents how we think and shape our behaviour. All students have these mental maps but are unaware of them — as are teachers. Making schemas visible allows students and teachers to see what they are thinking.

CHAPTER EIGHT — HOLOGRAPHIC—LINEAR
Every day, every student, in every lesson has to turn linear communication (what she reads or hears) into what is termed her holographic understanding. Schemas are holographic in structure — definitely not linear. The student then has to turn her new, enlarged understanding back into linear format. This process has, until now, been an unknown phenomenon.

CHAPTER NINE — CONSTRUCTING KNOWLEDGE
All our students construct knowledge — even the very youngest and the least able. Knowledge cannot be delivered. It has to be created each time by the individual, for knowledge is created not discovered. This view of learning is called constructivism. Understanding this process stimulates teachers to make learning more meaningful and motivating for all students.

SECTION 4 — LANGUAGE

CHAPTER TEN — SUPPORT FOR LANGUAGE
It is normally thought that visuals 'compete' with words. With visual tools, this is not true. Visual tools exist in the overlapping area between words and pictures. If you examine language, you realise that images play a big part in stimulating thought and supporting planning. They help the organisation of our language, which normally has to take place in the unseen interior of our heads.

CHAPTER ELEVEN — READING
Reading is active. Readers' interrogation of text is shaped by their own schemas. They have to adapt their existing schemas in order to absorb text into meaningful messages. Visual tools can reveal the hidden structure and meaning of a text. Just as computer software can show you what your voice looks like, visual tools can show you what your thinking looks like.

CHAPTER TWELVE — WRITING
Writing is difficult. Students' difficulties and fears stem from not knowing what to write. Visual tools make planning explicit, easy and empowering. Through the use of visual tools, students can model the planning that excellent writers do 'in their heads'. Planning in linear fashion is too difficult for most. The schematic nature of visual tools matches the way the brain naturally works.

SECTION 5 — THINKING

CHAPTER THIRTEEN — THINKING SKILLS
When we think, we are either thinking of objects (in space) or events (in time). Our thoughts become 'thought—objects'. Just as we manipulate real, physical objects in space, so we move our 'thought—objects' in our inner space. This is thinking. It is, however, invisible and demands much short term memory. Visual tools make thinking visible, easier and obvious.

CHAPTER FOURTEEN — QUESTIONS
Questions are more powerful than answers. They directly determine our focus and thinking. Young children are wonderful questioners — young scientists. Schools have conditioned students to demand only questions. This severely limits their thinking and learning. Visual tools are themselves questions. They demand investigation. Their visible nature makes questioners of all students.

CHAPTER FIFTEEN — THINKING IN ACTION
There is a link between text, thinking and visual tools. The nature of different types of text (genres) demand different types of thinking. All thinking is the manipulation of 'thought—objects'. Visual tools show students what this looks like. Matching types of visual tools to specific genres and linking them to the National Curriculum thinking skills is a powerful matrix.

SECTION 6 — LEARNING

CHAPTER SIXTEEN — ACTIVE LEARNING
You don't have to leave your seat to be actively learning. Active doesn't mean kinaesthetic! Active learning involves becoming engrossed, relating new material to personal prior knowledge, and creating meaning. Active learning needs to be encouraged by teachers. It is what is demanded of business. Visual tools stimulate and challenge active learning from students.

CHAPTER SEVENTEEN — STYLES OF LEARNING
Learning style labels can be dangerous. They can limit rather than stimulate expansion. Behind their often surface description lies a common cognitive activity — putting the detail into the big picture. Visual tools meet the needs of all learners, involving them in visual, verbal, analytic and holistic thinking. They also promote the four essential skills of learning.

CHAPTER EIGHTEEN — ABILITY RANGE
We have many labels for our pupils — from the gifted and talented to SEN. Behind all these labels there lies the act of meaning making. Visual tools show students what understanding looks like. This gives confidence to them all. It allows the least able to see their intelligence and supports the more able to organise and communicate their sometimes erratic thinking.

SECTION 7 — LEXICON

CHAPTER NINETEEN — LEXICON

CATEGORIES OF VISUAL TOOLS

- structural thinking — Structural Visual Tools
- differential thinking — Differential Visual Tools
- representational thinking — Representational Visual Tools
- temporal thinking — Temporal Visual Tools
- causal thinking — Causal Visual Tools
- numerical thinking — Numerical Visual Tools
- organisational thinking — Organisational Visual Tools
- individual thinking — Individual Visual Tools

There are seven types of visual tools related to seven types of thinking. The eighth is a hybrid of all seven. Within each category, there is a variety of visual tools. Visual tools within the categories achieve slightly different results, at different levels of complexity to suit age, ability and the nature of the tasks set. Each visual tool is described, its workings explained and ideas given for introducing it to students. Differences between similar visual tools are clarified. Each visual tool is illustrated both in templated format and as a hand-drawn example in use. The context for each hand-drawn visual tool is a well known story.

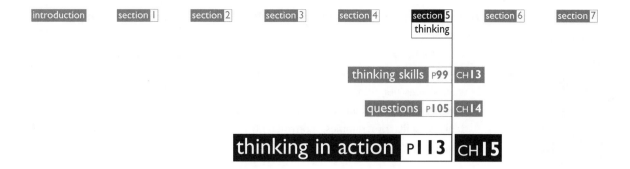

overview

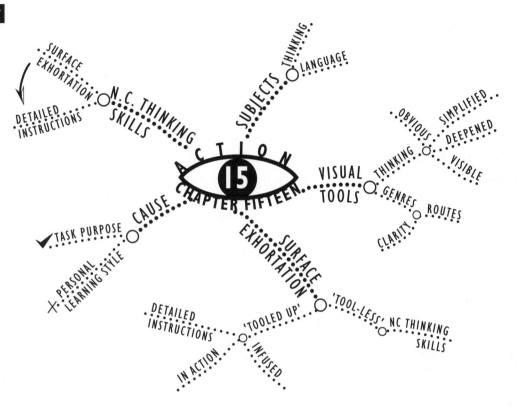

preview

- Your thinking is determined by the purpose and nature of the task, and not by your own personal learning style or preference.

- The nature of the task is determined by genre.

- Particular visual tools encourage, develop, shape, represent and reflect the different types of thinking related to subject and genre.

- Beneath the surface descriptions of types of thinking lie structural features present in them all.

- All subjects involve thinking.

- Knowing what thinking really is transforms the teaching of National Curriculum thinking skills from surface exhortation to detailed and practical instruction.

- When applied to literacy, and genres in particular, visual tools offer clarity and routes to success.

Your thinking is determined by the purpose and nature of the task, and not by your own personal learning style or preference.

We have become so enamoured by analyses of thinking and learning styles that we assume they are the essential factors determining how we think. When we examine what shapes our thinking, however, it soon becomes evident that it is content, not personal learning preference, that counts. John McPeck, a philosopher and critic of thinking skills programmes, convincingly explains in his book *Teaching Critical Thinking* (1990) that subjects shape thinking.

McPeck reminds us that if we are always thinking about something, it is very probable that this 'something' will be language based. In the context of school, the 'something' will be a curriculum subject. All subjects have specific organising principles for their vocabulary. Within the vocabulary some words will be more senior in hierarchies of concepts. These conceptual structures, called 'language triangles' by some (Caviglioli and Harris, 2000), represent the thinking of the subject.

The technical name for 'language triangles' is hyponymic hierarchies. According to *The Cambridge Encyclopedia of the English Language* (Crystal, 1995), the hyponym is the most important linguistic sense relation, and 'is the core relationship within a dictionary'. Hyponymic hierarchies are best illustrated 'in the form of a tree diagram, where the more general term is placed at the top, and the more specific terms are placed underneath'. In the example shown, 'flower' is the hyponym and the particular flower types are the hypernyms. The ways in which words inter-link within such a hierarchy of meaning represent the major ways of thinking peculiar to the subject under consideration.

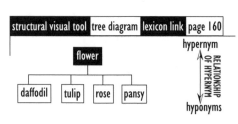

So when we think of a subject, the linguistic structure of it determines how we think. For example, geography has particular organising concepts and so when we think of geography these structures will literally shape our thinking. That is so whatever label we apply to our own personal style.

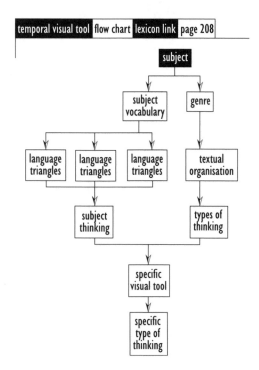

The nature of the task is determined by genre.

Subject content can be written about in a variety of ways. These varieties are called genres. Genres have their own ways of organising the information. They have distinctive frameworks. As you will readily appreciate, the nature of the genre in which subject content is delivered will automatically further determine how we think about it.

There is general agreement that students deal with six types of non-fiction genres at school as described at the top of page 115.

Particular visual tools encourage, develop, shape, represent and reflect the different types of thinking related to subject and genre.

If the organising principles that shape the vocabulary of subjects determine our thinking, then genres add to this shaping process. The type of thinking (holistic, creative, reflective, and so on) depends on the subject and genre through which that subject content is delivered.

Thinking is the arranging and re-arranging of 'thought-objects', so it must be possible to link types of thinking – types of arrangements – with an appropriate selection of visual tools that allow you to manipulate ideas visually in the same way.

Genres	Features
1 Recounts	■ a scene-setting opening, which orientates the reader ■ an account of events ■ a closing, summary statement
2 Reports	■ an opening based on a categorical assertion ■ the actual description or report of what something is like
3 Instructions	■ an outcome to be achieved – the goal of the activity ■ a list of materials to be used ■ the actual sequence of activities to be followed
4 Explanations	■ an introduction to the topic ■ an explanation set out in a series of logical steps ■ a summary statement of the major points
5 Persuasions	■ an opening assertion or proposition ■ an extended argument, made point by point, backing the assertion ■ a summary statement restating the opening assertion
6 Discussions	■ an introduction to the issue at hand ■ a preview of the major arguments related to the issue ■ the arguments with supporting evidence *for* the issue ■ the arguments with supporting evidence *against* the issue ■ a summary conclusion, possibly with a recommendation

Table 1, on page 118, may be used to guide your choice of visual tool when dealing with different types of texts. The table is organised around questions associated with particular text genres.

Table 2, on page 119, shows specifically which visual tools are appropriate to use with particular types of genres. The key explains the relationship the visual tool has to the genre.

Beneath the surface descriptions of types of thinking lie structural features present in them all.

You will be familiar with such terms as hypothetical thinking, analytical thinking, problem solving, creative thinking, organisational thinking and so on. There is no end to the multitude of taxonomies. All these types of thinking have one thing in common. They all deal with either objects or events (the dimensions of space and time).

The table below considers four different types of thinking. Notice the prevalence of the physical 'thoughts-as-objects' metaphor in the language used.

Types of thinking	Question	Considerations
Holistic thinking – seeing the 'big picture', getting an overview	How can I see how it all fits together?	I want to see how it all fits together. I want to be able to see and identify relationships.
Systems thinking – understanding how parts affect each other and the whole	How can I see or work out how the parts of this task affect each other?	I can see now how things influence each other.
Lateral thinking – thinking of alternatives and opportunities	How else could I approach this task?	I can see a range of ways in which I can do this now.
Reflective thinking – looking for insights	How can I learn from what I have already done?	I can see now that doing it this way had this effect. Next time I can …

All subjects involve thinking.

Some may consider that certain subjects demand more thinking than others. As Howard Gardner (1983) has been saying for nearly twenty years, we can profitably think of intelligence as if there were seven (or eight or nine) distinct types:

- logico–mathematical

- linguistic

- interpersonal

- intrapersonal

- musical

- kinaesthetic

- visuo-spatial

- naturalistic

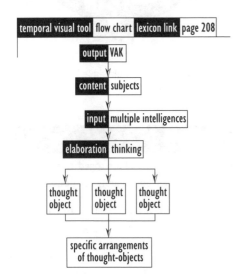

These multiple intelligences span the breadth of the school curriculum. So all subjects involve intelligence. All intelligence involves thinking. Therefore, all subjects must involve thinking.

Underneath the particular culture, practices and procedures of a subject lie the mechanics of thinking. The subject vocabulary will determine the focus and shape of the students' thinking. But the actual mechanics of thinking is the same. It involves the assembling and arranging of thoughts as if they were thought-objects. That is what all students do when they engage in thinking with all their subjects. It is as important for all teachers to grasp this fact as it is for car mechanics to understand how engines work.

Knowing what thinking really is transforms the teaching of National Curriculum thinking skills from surface exhortation to detailed and practical instruction.

The current emphasis on thinking skills in the National Curriculum is certainly to be welcomed. It could be argued that it represents a return to the true agenda of education.

However, the fact that the names of different types of thinking are now more familiar to us all does not in itself mean that there is a real understanding of what thinking is among teachers in general. Scratch the surface and there is perhaps little detailed knowledge of thinking processes themselves.

Thinking skills are on the official platform for the first time. We must not waste this opportunity to make a profound difference to students' learning. We must apply thinking to thinking skills. To make progress, teachers must understand how thinking is formed, how language shapes thinking, and how thinking uses the physical metaphor in order to manipulate and inter-relate thoughts. Most taxonomies are descriptions of thinking, not explanations of it.

Table 3, on page 120, considers the thinking involved in each of the National Curriculum thinking skills.

Table 4, on page 121, shows which category of visual tools is most likely to be useful in stimulating, illustrating, developing, recording or communicating the particular component skills that make up the five National Curriculum thinking skills.

When applied to literacy, and genres in particular, visual tools offer clarity and routes to success.

When teachers and students grasp (note the physical metaphor used) the essential nature of thinking, they are empowered to see (now a visual metaphor) its application in any subject they choose. They arrive at a deeper understanding of why certain strategies for thinking and learning work. It all seems to fall into place (ending with a spatial metaphor).

Subjects are communicated, to a large extent, through text. As discussed above, texts have particular features that can be categorised into genres. However, genres are not absolute classifications in which the characteristics of membership are unambiguous. In practice, there are rarely such distinct delineations. Texts are flexible, often containing features of several genres.

For these reasons, the information and advice contained in the tables in this chapter should not be considered absolute. Rather, the tables provide guidance for you to use in making decisions regarding the choice of visual tool.

Visual tools can be expertly matched to the task and the genre. Their choice can directly represent the type of thinking required to succeed at a task. The structure of the visual tool models and shapes the sort of thinking appropriate to the genre. They help students get into the frame of thinking that lies behind the surface features of the text. Habitual use of visual tools makes students more sensitive to the demands and functions of different genres. By succeeding in this way, students become aware and confident in the use of different kinds of thinking. They become more mature, flexible and resourceful thinkers.

viewpoints

action

'Thinking is thus not something that lies 'behind' or 'under' individual action, it is an integral part of human practices.'

R. Saljo (1998)

representing knowledge

'Upon completion of the research, the children create a second individual web summarising the information they have obtained as a way to monitor their own learning and write their reports.'

L. C. Moll and K. F. Whitmore (1998)

knowledge

'Knowledge is not passively received and absorbed but actively built up by the individual.'

J. Watson (2000)

meaning making

'All learners, pupils and teachers, are in the business of making sense of the world around them. They can do this only by interpreting it in terms of what they already know. However unambiguous a fact or lesson or concept may seem, it can be understood only in terms of a personal interpretation by the learner.'

G. Claxton (1990)

adults

'Meaningful learning for adults is often more to do with seeing the world differently, or reframing it, than it is about learning new facts.'

G. Boak and D. Thompson (1998)

review

genres

What things are your students going to be thinking about tomorrow or during the course of the next week?

Which text genres will your students be working with?

Use the tables on pages 118 to 121, and chapter 19, Lexicon, to find out which visual tools could help you with your teaching and the students with their learning.

views

In what ways does this chapter change your views on thinking skills?

literacy

Can you now (if you hadn't before) see how thinking and literacy are inextricably linked? We are all teachers of thinking and literacy.

Table 1

Genres	Appropriate types of visual tools					
	STRUCTURAL	DIFFERENTIAL	REPRESENTATIONAL	TEMPORAL	CAUSAL	NUMERICAL
RECOUNTS			How are things changed as a result of the action?	What happened, when and in what order?	Why did things happen as they did?	
REPORTS	How do the concepts relate to one another?	What are the features and how do they compare?	Where did the events occur?	When did the events occur, and in what sequence?		
INSTRUCTIONS			How do things change during the process?	When are things supposed to happen?	How do things happen and why?	
EXPLANATIONS	How are the main points related to each other?		What do things look like?	When did things happen and in what sequence?	Why did things inter-relate in the way they did?	
PERSUASIONS	How are the reasons organised?	What are the main differences between certain factors?			How is the argument reasoned?	
DISCUSSIONS	How do the concepts relate to one another?	How are differences emphasised?			How is the logic of the argument constructed?	

Table 2

	VISUAL TOOL	RECOUNT	INSTRUCTION	REPORT	EXPLANATION	PERSUASION	DISCUSSION
SVT	TARGET MAP	P	P	P	P	P	P
	SINGLE BUBBLE	P	P	P	P	P	P
	CLUSTERING	P/T	P/T	T	P/T	T	T
	AFFINITY DIAGRAM	P	P	P/T	P	T	T
	TREE DIAGRAM	P/T	P	T	T	T	T
	MODEL MAP	P/T	P	T	T	T*	T
	CONCEPT MAP	P/T	P	T/E	T*	P/T	T
	VEE MAP			E	E	T/E	A
DVT	VENN DIAGRAM	P		P	P	P	T
	DOUBLE BUBBLE MAP	P		P	P	P	T
	MATRIX			P/T	P/A	A	A
	FORCE FIELD ANALYSIS			E	E	A	T
	SWOT DIAGRAM			E	E	T	T
	BRIDGE MAP			A	E	A	A
	CONTINUUM LINE	P		A	A	A	A
	PRIORITIES GRID			A/E	A/E	A	A
	RANKING CHART			A	A/E	P/A	A
RVT	PICTURE	A	A	A	A	A	A
	CROSS SECTION		A	A	A	A	
	DIAGRAM		A	A	A/T	A	
	PLAN		A	A	A	A	
TVT	TIME LINE	T*	P/T	A/T	A	P/A	A
	FLOW CHART	T*	T	A/T	T	P/A	A
	CYCLE	T		T	T	T	A
	STORY BOARD	T*	P/T*	T	P/A	P/A	
	GANTT CHART		P/T	A	A		
CVT	FISHBONE DIAGRAM	P/T	P	E	T	T	A
	RELATIONS DIAGRAM	P	P	E	T	T	A
	CRITICAL PATH ANALYSIS		P/T	E	T	T	
	ALGORITHM	P	P/T	E	T	T	T
	SYSTEMS DIAGRAM	E	E	E	T	E	
	FLOWSCAPE		E	E	P/T	P	
NVT	PIE CHART			A	A	A	A
	BAR CHART			A	A	A	A
	COLUMN CHART			A	A	A	A
	LINE CHART			A	A	A	A
	DOT CHART			A	A	A	A
OVT	WRITING FRAMES	T	T	T	T	T	T
	COMPARE & CONTRAST ORGANISER	P		A	P	P/T	T
	INTERACTION OUTLINES		P		T	A	A
	PROBLEM—SOLUTION FRAME	P/T	P	E	T	T	A
	ARCH DIAGRAM	A	P	T/E	T	T	A
	PMI			A	T	T	T

KEY

P
PREPARATORY VISUAL TOOL
• useful in getting you ready for using the main task visual tool

T
TASK VISUAL TOOL
• fulfils the core task for the genre

T*
TASK PLUS VISUAL TOOL
• always fulfils the core task
• no other visual tool is needed

A
ACCESSORY VISUAL TOOL
• supports the task visual tool
• illustrates the main task

E
EXTENSION VISUAL TOOL
• adds another dimension
• goes beyond what is required

P/T or any other combination
• the visual tool could be either of the two, depending on the nature of the assignment and question

Table 3

N.C. THINKING SKILLS		THOUGHTS	QUESTIONS	SELF-COMMANDS
INFORMATION PROCESSING	sort	gather everything and split up into heaps	how do I want them split up?	put them into groups
	classify	split heaps into smaller heaps	what order do these go in? what happens if I put them in a different order?	put them in order
	sequence	pick things up and put them one after the other	what order to they go in? what happens if I put them in a different order?	put them in order
	compare & contrast	pick up and separate, and glance from one to the other	how are they similar and how are they different?	spot differences and similarities
	analyse part–whole relationship	get the whole thing, take bits out and put together again	what is the whole? what are the parts? how do they fit?	take it apart and put it together again
	locate & collect relevant information	put things together that I need, discard things I don't need	what do I need? what makes it relevant?	separate the relevant from the irrelevant
REASONING	give reasons for opinions & actions	show somebody my collection	why did I do it like that?	explain myself
	draw inferences & deductions	look at someone else's collections and arrangements	what could this mean? why was it done like this?	work out the underlying meanings
	use precise language	describe my collection to someone else without showing it	what are the key words? what do they mean?	find the key words, check that I understand
	explain own thinking	show someone how my collection is put together	am I clear about my thinking? what will my points be?	make obvious and sequence the underlying meaning
	make judgements & decisions	show different arrangements, and my preferred one	can I support my view?	explain myself
ENQUIRY	ask relevant questions	try new arrangements and check for fit	what questions should I ask?	ask a range of questions
	pose & define problems	which things are on the wrong pile?	what doesn't work? what is wrong? what isn't the way it should be?	be clear what the problem is
	plan what to do & how to research	look at other people's arrangements and try out my own	what could I find out? how far do I have to look?	find out what I need to know
	predict outcomes & anticipate	put one thing after the other and see where I end up	what would happen if…? what is likely to happen if that happens?	put myself into the future and look backwards to now
	test conclusions & improve ideas	disassemble arrangement and put it together again	would it still work if I changed this? how can I prove this?	provide the evidence
CREATIVITY	generate & extend ideas	put things together in ways I haven't tried before	how else could I do this? if a genius did this, what would she do?	think differently
	suggest hypotheses	vary the arrangement	what would happen if…?	imagine alternatives and think them through
	apply imagination	put things together in ways someone else might	what would happen if…?	invent
	look for innovative outcomes	put things together in ways that nobody has ever done	how else could this be finished?	think differently
EVALUATION	evaluate information	see if things are all in the right place	what is this telling me? is it telling me as much as it could do?	judge
	judge value of what read, heard, did	look at the existing arrangements alongside others	how useful is this to me?	judge and decide
	develop criteria for judging value	identify the patterns in the existing arrangement	how do I know this is correct? what is the best way to judge this?	support my arguments
	have confidence in judgements	picture the arrangement in my head	is this correct? how do I know this?	collect evidence, reasons and support my view

Table 4

N.C. THINKING SKILLS		STRUCTURAL VISUAL TOOLS	DIFFERENTIAL VISUAL TOOLS	REPRESENTATIONAL VISUAL TOOLS	TEMPORAL VISUAL TOOLS	CAUSAL VISUAL TOOLS	NUMERICAL VISUAL TOOLS
INFORMATION PROCESSING	sort	✓	✓			✓	✓
	classify	✓					
	sequence				✓	✓	
	compare & contrast	✓	✓				✓
	analyse part–whole relationship	✓		✓	✓	✓	✓
	locate & collect relevant information	✓	✓	✓	✓	✓	✓
REASONING	give reasons for opinions & actions	✓			✓	✓	✓
	draw inferences & deductions	✓	✓	✓	✓	✓	✓
	use precise language	✓	✓		✓	✓	✓
	explain own thinking	✓	✓	✓	✓	✓	✓
	make judgements & decisions	✓	✓	✓	✓	✓	✓
ENQUIRY	ask relevant questions	✓	✓	✓	✓	✓	✓
	pose & define problems	✓			✓	✓	
	plan what to do & how to research	✓			✓	✓	
	predict outcomes & anticipate	✓			✓	✓	✓
	test conclusions & improve ideas	✓	✓			✓	✓
CREATIVITY	generate & extend ideas	✓				✓	
	suggest hypotheses	✓		✓		✓	
	apply imagination	✓		✓		✓	
	look for innovative outcomes	✓		✓			
EVALUATION	evaluate information	✓	✓	✓		✓	✓
	judge value of what read, heard, did	✓	✓			✓	
	develop criteria for judging value	✓	✓			✓	✓
	have confidence in judgements	✓	✓	✓	✓	✓	✓

ROUTE MAP FOR YOUR READING

SECTION 1 — CONTEXT

CHAPTER ONE BACKGROUND
The primary assertion is that we are all *Eye Q* experts. Throughout history, humans have used an assortment of visual tools to reflect and communicate knowledge. Current knowledge creation dynamics are based on this same notion. The 'inside story' of learning is obtained by looking both inside (cognitive psychology) and outside (Accelerated Learning).

CHAPTER TWO THE iDESK MODEL
Most of our activities are not based on a theory of learning. Consequently, there is little sense of meaning or coherence. The iDesk model is holistic. It connects thinking, feeling and doing. Finally, it links these faculties to the environment and the individual. Visual tools impact all areas of the iDesk model, and all components interact with each other. Serious schools need models.

CHAPTER THREE THE KNOWLEDGE AGE
We are living in the knowledge age with a need for more knowledge workers. These new types of workers require new, extended mental skills and knowledge tools. Visual tools are central in creating and communicating knowledge. Schools need to learn from business theory and practice with regard to intellectual capital and the use of visual tools.

SECTION 2 — VISUALS

CHAPTER FOUR VISUAL TOOLS AND COMPUTERS
We are learning that the use of computers can reinforce poor learning habits. The attraction of the screen can degenerate into visual 'candyfloss'. This turns computer users into consumers. Behind the screen lies a knowledge structure. Visual tools make this explicit and turn consumers into explorers of knowledge. Clarity about visual literacy will support this.

CHAPTER FIVE VISUAL LITERACY
In our culture, the visual–verbal polarity may well be more divisive than the sciences–arts gulf. There are historical, philosophical reasons for the low value placed on visuals. Visual literacy, nonetheless, is an established discipline. All visual content exists in the spatial dimension. Space is our first and primary frontier. The spatial metaphor shapes our understanding.

CHAPTER SIX TOOLS TO LEARN
The successes of our civilisation are based on tools. We have created these tools and they, in turn, end up shaping our behaviour. Using new tools causes new learning to take place. Habitual use of tools changes our habits. The most effective use of tools happens when accompanied with theory. Visual tools impact on learning habits. New eras need new tools.

SECTION 3 — MEANING

CHAPTER SEVEN SCHEMAS
We all have schemas. They are personal and unique and are based on how we view the world. In business they are termed mental models. Their organisation represents how we think and shape our behaviour. All students have these mental maps but are unaware of them — as are teachers. Making schemas visible allows students and teachers to see what they are thinking.

CHAPTER EIGHT HOLOGRAPHIC—LINEAR
Every day, every student, in every lesson has to turn linear communication (what she reads or hears) into what is termed her holographic understanding. Schemas are holographic in structure — definitely not linear. The student then has to turn her new, enlarged understanding back into linear format. This process has, until now, been an unknown phenomenon.

CHAPTER NINE CONSTRUCTING KNOWLEDGE
All our students construct knowledge — even the very youngest and the least able. Knowledge cannot be delivered. It has to be created each time by the individual, for knowledge is created not discovered. This view of learning is called constructivism. Understanding this process stimulates teachers to make learning more meaningful and motivating for all students.

SECTION 4 — LANGUAGE

CHAPTER TEN SUPPORT FOR LANGUAGE
It is normally thought that visuals 'compete' with words. With visual tools, this is not true. Visual tools exist in the overlapping area between words and pictures. If you examine language, you realise that images play a big part in stimulating thought and supporting planning. They help the organisation of our language, which normally has to take place in the unseen interior of our heads.

CHAPTER ELEVEN READING
Reading is active. Readers' interrogation of text is shaped by their own schemas. They have to adapt their existing schemas in order to absorb text into meaningful messages. Visual tools can reveal the hidden structure and meaning of a text. Just as computer software can show you what your voice looks like, visual tools can show you what your thinking looks like.

CHAPTER TWELVE WRITING
Writing is difficult. Students' difficulties and fears stem from not knowing what to write. Visual tools make planning explicit, easy and empowering. Through the use of visual tools, students can model the planning that excellent writers do 'in their heads'. Planning in linear fashion is too difficult for most. The schematic nature of visual tools matches the way the brain naturally works.

SECTION 5 — THINKING

CHAPTER THIRTEEN THINKING SKILLS
When we think, we are either thinking of objects (in space) or events (in time). Our thoughts become 'thought—objects'. Just as we manipulate real, physical objects in space, so we move our 'thought—objects' in our inner space. This is thinking. It is, however, invisible and demands much short term memory. Visual tools make thinking visible, easier and obvious.

CHAPTER FOURTEEN QUESTIONS
Questions are more powerful than answers. They directly determine our focus and thinking. Young children are wonderful questioners — young scientists. Schools have conditioned students to demand only questions. This severely limits their thinking and learning. Visual tools are themselves questions. They demand investigation. Their visible nature makes questioners of all students.

CHAPTER FIFTEEN THINKING IN ACTION
There is a link between text, thinking and visual tools. The nature of different types of text (genres) demand different types of thinking. All thinking is the manipulation of 'thought—objects'. Visual tools show students what this looks like. Matching types of visual tools to specific genres and linking them to the National Curriculum thinking skills is a powerful matrix.

SECTION 6 — LEARNING

CHAPTER SIXTEEN ACTIVE LEARNING
You don't have to leave your seat to be actively learning. Active doesn't mean kinaesthetic! Active learning involves becoming engrossed, relating new material to personal prior knowledge, and creating meaning. Active learning needs to be encouraged by teachers. It is what is demanded of business. Visual tools stimulate and challenge active learning from students.

CHAPTER SEVENTEEN STYLES OF LEARNING
Learning style labels can be dangerous. They can limit rather than stimulate expansion. Behind their often surface description lies a common cognitive activity — putting the detail into the big picture. Visual tools meet the needs of all learners, involving them in visual, verbal, analytic and holistic thinking. They also promote the four essential skills of learning.

CHAPTER EIGHTEEN ABILITY RANGE
We have many labels for our pupils — from the gifted and talented to SEN. Behind all these labels there lies the act of meaning making. Visual tools show students what understanding looks like. This gives confidence to them all. It allows the least able to see their intelligence and supports the more able to organise and communicate their sometimes erratic thinking.

SECTION 7 — LEXICON

CHAPTER NINETEEN LEXICON

CATEGORIES OF VISUAL TOOLS

- structural thinking — Structural Visual Tools
- differential thinking — Differential Visual Tools
- representational thinking — Representational Visual Tools
- temporal thinking — Temporal Visual Tools
- causal thinking — Causal Visual Tools
- numerical thinking — Numerical Visual Tools
- organisational thinking — Organisational Visual Tools
- individual thinking — Individual Visual Tools

There are seven types of visual tools related to seven types of thinking. The eighth is a hybrid of all seven. Within each category, there is a variety of visual tools. Visual tools within the categories achieve slightly different results, at different levels of complexity to suit age, ability and the nature of the tasks set. Each visual tool is described, its workings explained and ideas given for introducing it to students. Differences between similar visual tools are clarified. Each visual tool is illustrated both in templated format and as a hand-drawn example in use. The context for each hand-drawn visual tool is a well known story.

active learning P123 CH16

styles of learning P131 CH17

ability range P137 CH18

overview

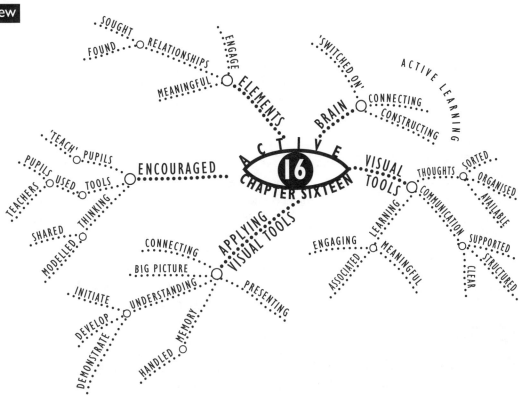

preview

- Active learning keeps students in their seats.

- Good teaching and good learning are inextricably linked.

- You learn from the company you keep – living, dead or distant.

- People are continually learning outside school.

- Real learning appears to involve three main elements – involvement, prior knowledge and meaning.

- Active learning can only take place in lessons that actively encourage it.

- Exploring the world is a risky business, even from the comfort of an armchair.

- Classrooms can play an important part in developing the citizens of the future.

- Visual tools help to create texts as well as to interpret them.

- Lessons should be active from the start.

- Throughout the lesson, lights should be going on inside people's heads.

- In a stress-free, risk-taking, respectful environment people are more willing to share their thoughts.

Active learning keeps students in their seats.

'Active learning' does not mean that the students have to be up and running around the classroom. They can be really active while stuck firmly in their seats. Neither do they have to be undertaking what we call 'practical activities' in order to be actively involved.

It is the connection between learning and making meaning that makes learning *active* – students are constructing with mental building blocks. When their brains are switched on, active learning will fire up their imaginations.

Good teaching and good learning are inextricably linked.

In theory, it should be impossible to look at teaching without also looking at learning, and vice versa. If we are able to identify the characteristics of good teaching, then we can identify what we mean by quality learning.

Learning is a continuous process. Just as it is impossible not to think about anything, it is impossible not to be learning all the time. When learning is productive, you are adding to your store of knowledge and skills. When it is not, you are adding to your awareness of yourself as a learner – you find that you are bored, that your mind wants to be elsewhere.

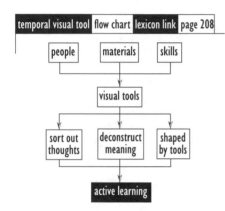

temporal visual tool | flow chart | lexicon link | page 208

people — materials — skills → visual tools → sort out thoughts — deconstruct meaning — shaped by tools → active learning

You learn from the company you keep – living, dead or distant.

In the classroom, we have teachers/guides/mentors surrounded by learners/apprentices/novices. We also have the material/content/stuff of the session. The people in the room share a range of skills that need to be applied to the material in order for learning to happen.

Combining all three together successfully is the secret: people, skills and materials. How can the interactions of people, using their skills on the material they are looking at, create a real learning situation? Visual tools enable students to sort out their thoughts and to organise them for closer inspection. They facilitate immediate sharing and discussion of ideas.

Creating a positive climate in which learning can take place is one thing. But there has to be more than that. People learn from the company they keep – from the people and materials around them. So teachers' acts, and the materials and ideas that teachers introduce, affect students' minds. Students' minds need to be active so that they can react to this input. The result of all this action in the classroom is enhanced learning, or progress. How might teachers act to invoke good reactions in their students?

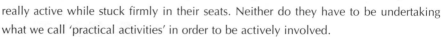

People are continually learning outside school.

Chapter 7, Schemas, suggests that children are like scientists. The learning that takes place is not simply random, and the processes that children experience equip them for life. Long before school life begins there are hypotheses, theories and questions, questions, questions.

At school the agenda for learning shifts. Teachers and schools accept the responsibility for enquiry. Gradually, children's talking becomes internalised and is transformed into thinking. They become quieter and are less likely to initiate discussions. Yet if you see them in their own environment, out of class, they are often animated and passionate about what is going on. It's this passion teachers need to capture in the classroom. We need to get their heads buzzing.

Students learn a great deal in the extra-curricular hours – most of it is relevant to their lives and shapes the people they become. What kinds of contexts exist? What are the features of the learning that takes place?

Real learning appears to involve three main elements – involvement, prior knowledge and meaning.

In the first place, when people really learn, they allow themselves to become lost, engrossed, caught up in their activities. They are motivated by a desire to engage with whatever it is that they wish to learn, especially if they perceive that there will be 'something in it for them' – that the learning will be useful. They may become so involved that they lose track of time. They are, in effect, learning missiles, guided by their own targeting mechanism. They know what they are seeking and they tend to know when they have found it.

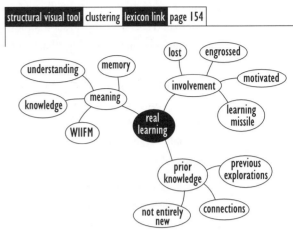

structural visual tool | clustering | lexicon link | page 154

Secondly, learners need to be able to relate this new engagement or learning episode to previous explorations and undertakings. It is unlikely that anything they decide to tackle will be completely new. There will be a connection with prior knowledge.

Finally, the learning episode has to be meaningful, it has to add to the learner's 'treasure house' of understanding and knowledge. It needs to be stored somewhere in the vaults of memory where it is unlikely to gather dust or disintegrate. Probably, the learner has already decided that this is something of which she is going to make good use ('something in it for her').

Active learning can only take place in lessons that actively encourage it.

'Learning is not a spectator sport', someone once remarked – how true! It is, rather, an interactive, collaborative, 'no-holds-barred' assault on the world of meaning. Think of times, in your own life, when you have watched someone demonstrate a skill and been anxious to have a go yourself. Joining in is natural and having to wait for your turn can be off-putting.

While the teacher is the ultimate arbitrator of the overall lesson structure, the wise teacher makes use of every drop of intellectual perspiration the students can muster. We all learn through teaching. Real professional development involves more than attendance at courses and the use of pre-packaged lessons. We need to feel confident enough to share our thinking and our organisational skills with our students. Providing clear examples of visual tools and their applications is an important part of good teaching – and learning.

Good students make good teachers. We are most successful as teachers when we find that the lessons flow effortlessly – when the students are 'teaching themselves'. Empowering students by offering a range of alternative strategies and methods for representing their thoughts provides a more inclusive atmosphere, in which students are fully involved in their own learning and teachers are granted more chance to observe and assess what is happening. Active learning frees teachers.

Exploring the world is a risky business, even from the comfort of an armchair.

We need to be able to move outside our 'comfort zones' – to take risks and try out new ideas. Only then can we really experience freedom of thought, savour the power of decisions, delight in the reassurance of wisdom. If you feel restricted and confined are you likely to give of your best?

Thresholds for teachers vary from subject to subject, from topic to topic. What is deemed to be appropriate behaviour in one lesson may be unacceptable at another time. But underpinning all successful learning enterprises there is a recognisable pattern – students have been permitted to take risks, to answer questions and question answers. They set out to solve problems and define new challenges. This may sound idealistic but if our lives are to be fulfilling, successful and exciting then we need to recognise the crucial part these elements play in our roles as life-long learners.

The world of work is changing rapidly and as teachers we need to change as well. Without a real shift towards active, autonomous learning, the school-leavers of future years may be unable to make decisions or respond to questions and challenges. Imagine a lifestyle devoid of real interest and the potential for change, a world of boredom and social apathy. In short, unless we can show them how to be independent learners, our students may find themselves unable to play an active role in the twenty-first century.

Classrooms can play an important part in developing the citizens of the future.

As teachers, our task is to equip students with skills for their futures. Children are highly motivated human beings, engaged in a process of imparting meaning to their daily lives. Each and every lesson should be designed to allow individuals to gain further insights into themselves and their worlds. Active learning encourages active and proactive attitudes to life.

We have all experienced sessions where engagement has been intense, where time has flown, where everyone has been lost in thought. There is an air of disappointment when the lesson ends. Czikszentmihalyi (1990) calls this 'flow' – a state that he links to the experience of 'mindful challenge'. Of course, it is unreasonable to expect every lesson to be like this, but unless the conditions are right then we have little chance of achieving more than a superficial level of learning.

Visual tools are already common in the business world. Now let us exploit their potential in classrooms, and help students both to learn in school and to prepare for the world of work. By expanding the range of strategies for organising and communicating ideas and thoughts, a visual tool box equips learners for life.

Visual tools help to create texts as well as to interpret them.

The word 'text' has a much wider meaning than print on a page. We normally use the word to mean a piece of writing that is to be studied, but let us look at the word in a wider sense.

Texts may be created orally (certainly Jesus and Socrates used this approach). They may manifest themselves as monologues. They may be created through a process of mutual construction in which speakers listen, attend to, develop and modify the offerings of others.

The discourse will establish a shape – some sort of order or pattern in the ideas and questions that are drawn up and explored. Undoubtedly, one of the most galling problems with oral engagements is that much that has been said may be lost forever. Great ideas can disappear. We have all had these experiences – if only we could remember just what was said. By capturing ideas and comments in a visual format we can keep sight of them.

The resulting text should be an agreed version of the enquiry or investigation that has taken place. Facts will remain facts and truth will still be truth. But in cases where no single answer is necessary opinions and views will have been considered and evaluated. When ideas and the thinking behind them are visible to the group it is much easier to reach conclusions. Visual tools allow discussions not only to be recorded, but also to be developed constructively, as every participant can see where the arguments are leading.

Lessons should be active from the start.

Let's look at the beginning of the lesson, the introductory element. There is a theme to be considered and an objective or outcome in mind. The teacher probably has an internal synopsis of how the lesson might progress, as a result of prior rehearsal and visualising (we might call this 'planning').

Of course, previous lessons will have an influence on the expectations for this one. Researching the topic in advance will highlight potential avenues for exploration and points to be covered. (Often, when some 'new' area is to be taught for the first time, teachers are only one step ahead of students!) Above all there must be a willingness to adopt a collaborative approach, to draw upon the expertise of the students as well as the teacher, to listen, reflect and learn.

By inviting students to map out their initial thoughts in some form, the teacher can make the lesson active from the outset. Everyone is involved. And if students can use this or other maps to see where they are heading during this lesson and beyond, they will be able to look for links with memories of past experiences. They will come up with connections the teacher may not have even considered.

Throughout the lesson, lights should be going on inside people's heads.

If only we could create some kind of cap that lights up whenever the wearer has a bright idea! Each time a student had a thought, or talked to herself inside her head, telltale patches of intermittent light would let us know. They might be the kinds of thoughts we'd rather she didn't share, but we could at least ask. Instead, we must settle for an alternative way of allowing students' lights to shine – of rescuing them from beneath bushels!

We can do this by asking students to create – individually at first – some form of visual representation of the workings of their minds. Words, images, lines and webs could be used to set their thoughts out on paper. We would not look for 'correctness' and accuracy of syntax, spelling or grammar in such graphic displays, as we do when assessing linear text. Instead, at this stage, we could focus our attention on the clues and keys that unlock meaning. We could get the 'big picture' of students' understanding from the outset.

In a stress-free, risk-taking, respectful environment people are more willing to share their thoughts.

By using a range of tools for exploring, recording and expressing the shapes of ideas, we encourage diversity of thought. By illustrating patterns of thinking, we enable all those taking part to compare their personal hypotheses with those of others. We provide opportunities for learners to create flexibility and openness in their own minds as they evaluate what is happening around them.

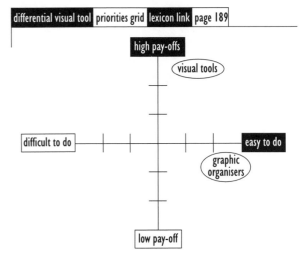

differential visual tool | priorities grid | lexicon link | page 189

high pay-offs

visual tools

difficult to do ———————— easy to do

graphic organisers

low pay-off

The notion of failure is modified when several different 'answers' to a query are seen as equally valid. The belief that mistakes are detrimental to intellectual growth is challenged. We create a respectful, stress-free climate in which diversity of thought and style is promoted and viewed in a positive light.

Instead of restricting and pressurising teachers, communities of active learners – using visual tools to support their collective and individual thinking – act in a supportive way. In fact, everyone involved is able to grasp a clearer, more personal understanding of what autonomous, motivated learning is. Using visible thinking is a powerful way to assist the development of responsibility and independence.

viewpoints

graphic representation

'The development of such constructed and reconstructed knowledge can be represented graphically using concept maps. Teaching that helps this reconstruction process will lead to meaningful learning.'

I. M. Kinchin, D. B. Hay and A. Adams (2000)

talking

'... new thinking, in children, nearly always accompanies talking with someone.'

M. Lake (1990)

visuals

'Visual methods are visible, flexible, inclusive, interactive, and add value.'

T. Hodgson and F. Tait (2000)

memory

'Where the information being learned has a framework or structure that can be used to organise both the learning and the retrieval, then memory is often considerably improved.'

M. W. Eysenck (ed) (1994)

active

'... students learn best by actively making sense of new knowledge – making meaning from it and mapping it in to their existing knowledge map/schema.'

C. V. Gipps (1994)

classrooms

'The use of visual tools creates a shift in classroom dynamics from passive to active and inter-active learning for all to see.'

D. Hyerle (1996)

review

active learning

Choose the most accurate ending to the following statement.

Active learning is:

- getting pupils us out of their seats

- ensuring that they have something to do with their hands

- the connection between learning and meaning making.

connect, interpret, build

Think of a lesson you have taught recently, or are about to teach. How might you use visual tools to:

- help students connect to what you are teaching them?

- help students interpret and make explicit the meaning that is implicit within the linear texts and dialogue you use and engage in?

- help students build and represent their understanding to you, and to each other?

view

In what ways does this chapter change your views on active learning?

Without a way of knowing what is going on inside students' heads, you can have no idea whether or not they are actively learning. How might the use of visual tools change all of this?

ROUTE MAP FOR YOUR READING

SECTION 1 — CONTEXT

CHAPTER ONE — BACKGROUND
The primary assertion is that we are all *Eye Q* experts. Throughout history, humans have used an assortment of visual tools to reflect and communicate knowledge. Current knowledge creation dynamics are based on this same notion. The 'inside story' of learning is obtained by looking both inside (cognitive psychology) and outside (Accelerated Learning).

CHAPTER TWO — THE iDESK MODEL
Most of our activities are not based on a theory of learning. Consequently, there is little sense of meaning or coherence. The iDesk model is holistic. It connects thinking, feeling and doing. Finally, it links these faculties to the environment and the individual. Visual tools impact all areas of the iDesk model, and all components interact with each other. Serious schools need models.

CHAPTER THREE — THE KNOWLEDGE AGE
We are living in the knowledge age with a need for more knowledge workers. These new types of workers require new, extended mental skills and knowledge tools. Visual tools are central in creating and communicating knowledge. Schools need to learn from business theory and practice with regard to intellectual capital and the use of visual tools.

SECTION 2 — VISUALS

CHAPTER FOUR — VISUAL TOOLS AND COMPUTERS
We are learning that the use of computers can reinforce poor learning habits. The attraction of the screen can degenerate into visual 'candyfloss'. This turns computer users into consumers. Behind the screen lies a knowledge structure. Visual tools make this explicit and turn consumers into explorers of knowledge. Clarity about visual literacy will support this.

CHAPTER FIVE — VISUAL LITERACY
In our culture, the visual—verbal polarity may well be more divisive than the sciences—arts gulf. There are historical, philosophical reasons for the low value placed on visuals. Visual literacy, nonetheless, is an established discipline. All visual content exists in the spatial dimension. Space is our first and primary frontier. The spatial metaphor shapes our understanding.

CHAPTER SIX — TOOLS TO LEARN
The successes of our civilisation are based on tools. We have created these tools and they, in turn, end up shaping our behaviour. Using new tools causes new learning to take place. Habitual use of tools changes our habits. The most effective use of tools happens when accompanied with theory. Visual tools impact on learning habits. New eras need new tools.

SECTION 3 — MEANING

CHAPTER SEVEN — SCHEMAS
We all have schemas. They are personal and unique and are based on how we view the world. In business they are termed mental models. Their organisation represents how we think and shape our behaviour. All students have these mental maps but are unaware of them — as are teachers. Making schemas visible allows students and teachers to see what they are thinking.

CHAPTER EIGHT — HOLOGRAPHIC—LINEAR
Every day, every student, in every lesson has to turn linear communication (what she reads or hears) into what is termed her holographic understanding. Schemas are holographic in structure — definitely not linear. The student then has to turn her new, enlarged understanding back into linear format. This process has, until now, been an unknown phenomenon.

CHAPTER NINE — CONSTRUCTING KNOWLEDGE
All our students construct knowledge — even the very youngest and the least able. Knowledge cannot be delivered. It has to be created each time by the individual, for knowledge is created not discovered. This view of learning is called constructivism. Understanding this process stimulates teachers to make learning more meaningful and motivating for all students.

SECTION 4 — LANGUAGE

CHAPTER TEN — SUPPORT FOR LANGUAGE
It is normally thought that visuals 'compete' with words. With visual tools, this is not true. Visual tools exist in the overlapping area between words and pictures. If you examine language, you realise that images play a big part in stimulating thought and supporting planning. They help the organisation of our language, which normally has to take place in the unseen interior of our heads.

CHAPTER ELEVEN — READING
Reading is active. Readers' interrogation of text is shaped by their own schemas. They have to adapt their existing schemas in order to absorb text into meaningful messages. Visual tools can reveal the hidden structure and meaning of a text. Just as computer software can show you what your voice looks like, visual tools can show you what your thinking looks like.

CHAPTER TWELVE — WRITING
Writing is difficult. Students' difficulties and fears stem from not knowing what to write. Visual tools make planning explicit, easy and empowering. Through the use of visual tools, students can model the planning that excellent writers do 'in their heads'. Planning in linear fashion is too difficult for most. The schematic nature of visual tools matches the way the brain naturally works.

SECTION 5 — THINKING

CHAPTER THIRTEEN — THINKING SKILLS
When we think, we are either thinking of objects (in space) or events (in time). Our thoughts become 'thought—objects'. Just as we manipulate real, physical objects in space, so we move our 'thought—objects' in our inner space. This is thinking. It is, however, invisible and demands much short term memory. Visual tools make thinking visible, easier and obvious.

CHAPTER FOURTEEN — QUESTIONS
Questions are more powerful than answers. They directly determine our focus and thinking. Young children are wonderful questioners — young scientists. Schools have conditioned students to demand only questions. This severely limits their thinking and learning. Visual tools are themselves questions. They demand investigation. Their visible nature makes questioners of all students.

CHAPTER FIFTEEN — THINKING IN ACTION
There is a link between text, thinking and visual tools. The nature of different types of text (genres) demand different types of thinking. All thinking is the manipulation of 'thought—objects'. Visual tools show students what this looks like. Matching types of visual tools to specific genres and linking them to the National Curriculum thinking skills is a powerful matrix.

SECTION 6 — LEARNING

CHAPTER SIXTEEN — ACTIVE LEARNING
You don't have to leave your seat to be actively learning. Active doesn't mean kinaesthetic! Active learning involves becoming engrossed, relating new material to personal prior knowledge, and creating meaning. Active learning needs to be encouraged by teachers. It is what is demanded of business. Visual tools stimulate and challenge active learning from students.

CHAPTER SEVENTEEN — STYLES OF LEARNING
Learning style labels can be dangerous. They can limit rather than stimulate expansion. Behind their often surface description lies a common cognitive activity — putting the detail into the big picture. Visual tools meet the needs of all learners, involving them in visual, verbal, analytic and holistic thinking. They also promote the four essential skills of learning.

CHAPTER EIGHTEEN — ABILITY RANGE
We have many labels for our pupils — from the gifted and talented to SEN. Behind all these labels there lies the act of meaning making. Visual tools show students what understanding looks like. This gives confidence to them all. It allows the least able to see their intelligence and supports the more able to organise and communicate their sometimes erratic thinking.

SECTION 7 — LEXICON

CHAPTER NINETEEN — LEXICON

CATEGORIES OF VISUAL TOOLS

- structural thinking — Structural Visual Tools
- differential thinking — Differential Visual Tools
- representational thinking — Representational Visual Tools
- temporal thinking — Temporal Visual Tools
- causal thinking — Causal Visual Tools
- numerical thinking — Numerical Visual Tools
- organisational thinking — Organisational Visual Tools
- individual thinking — Individual Visual Tools

There are seven types of visual tools related to seven types of thinking. The eighth is a hybrid of all seven. Within each category, there is a variety of visual tools. Visual tools within the categories achieve slightly different results, at different levels of complexity to suit age, ability and the nature of the tasks set. Each visual tool is described, its workings explained and ideas given for introducing it to students. Differences between similar visual tools are clarified. Each visual tool is illustrated both in templated format and as a hand-drawn example in use. The context for each hand-drawn visual tool is a well known story.

overview

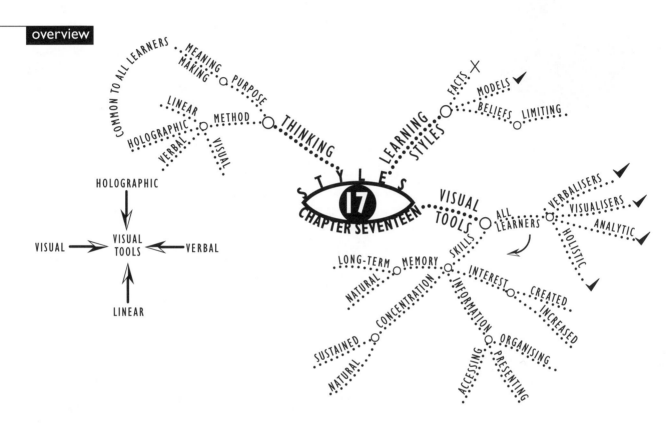

preview

- Learning styles are only models of reality and do not define us.

- Visual tools take us beneath the superficial understanding of learning that learning style investigations can give us.

- The use of visual tools supports students in putting together parts to make the whole.

- All learners are constantly being asked to access internal verbal and visual modalities simultaneously.

- Visual tools support *all* cognitive styles and *all* learning style models.

- Visual tools support the development and use of four essential learning skills that apply to all learners.

- Visual tools support learners in *creating interest* in the topic being studied.

- Visual tools help learners to *sustain concentration* and *organise information*.

- Visual tools *shape* the learner's *memory*.

- Visual tools support all learners in achieving their central task – to form schemas.

Learning styles are only models of reality and do not define us.

By identifying a student's learning preferences, we run the risk of simply replacing one label with another. So instead of them being 'average' or 'clever' or 'weak' they become something else. The label we come up with depends on the questions we ask. You can be a 'visual, auditory or kinaesthetic learner' if you follow the Bandler-Grindler model, or 'Left or Right Limbic' and 'Left or Right Cerebral' if you use Herrmann's processing model.

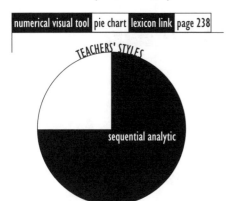

numerical visual tool | pie chart | lexicon link | page 238

Other models use different criteria to produce different labels. Are you an 'abstract random' or 'abstract sequential', 'concrete random' or 'concrete sequential' learner? Do you prefer physical, psychological, sociological, emotional or environmental learning contexts?

Finding out that you are a 'psychological, right limbic, visual abstract sequential learner' can be an exciting experience. It can also be a tedious form-filling exercise (depending on your preferences!). But, does it make any difference?

Visual tools take us beneath the superficial understanding of learning that learning style investigations can give us.

There are four points to be made here.

1 Finding out that you prefer learning in a certain way or you 'learn best when …', does not mean that you *cannot* learn in any other way.

2 The identification of preferences is only useful if it causes the teacher and learner to modify their teaching and learning to support a wider range of learning preferences. According to Eric Jensen, an established authority on learning styles:

75% of teachers are sequential, analytic presenters;

70% of all their students do *not* learn best in this way.

3 Relating to learning styles as a rigid reality can transform a viewpoint into an insidiously limiting belief system. As Gary Woditsch, an eminent author on thinking skills, points out:

'Why ossify existing propensities? Why not change them and make them flexible? Liberating students from predisposed learning modes strikes us as at least as promising as reinforcing those modes.'

G. A. Woditsch (1991)

4 Visual tools mirror the internal thinking processes in which all human beings engage. Visual tools support all learners because we are all meaning makers (chapter 9, Constructing knowledge).

The use of visual tools supports students in putting together parts to make the whole.

Much has been written about hemispheric learning – how the left and right halves of the brain operate – and some educators relate to these notions as if they are facts. But Robert Ornstein (1991), who won the Nobel Prize for his discovery of left–right brain differences, has pleaded with the ubiquitous popularisers of his findings to stop. They argue that, for example, the right hemisphere is responsible for holistic 'big picture' thinking and most visual functions, while the left hemisphere tackles linear sequential detail and language development – but their simplifications are simply inaccurate.

From the teacher's perspective, the most important thing is to acknowledge that there is a 'big picture' – a whole – and that there are parts that make up this whole. This may seem obvious but we can sometimes forget it as we take learners through their linear

journey in the classroom. We cannot expect students to be able to put the whole together, one jigsaw piece at a time, without having recourse to the 'big picture' on the box lid (chapter 8, Holographic–linear).

All learners are constantly being asked to access internal verbal and visual modalities simultaneously.

Our modalities are our senses. We receive external information via our five senses. In schools, for the most part, it is the visual, auditory and kinaesthetic (touch) modalities that are accessed. Put simply, teachers provide students with learning opportunities that involve listening, looking and doing.

We process the information received via our external modalities by using our internal modalities. When we visualise (or imagine) something, we are using our visual internal modality. When we 'talk to ourselves' we are using our internal auditory (verbal) modality. When we 'feel' things inside we are using our internal kinaesthetic modality.

When we engage actively in learning, we are (unknowingly) trying to identify the visual structures that are implicit in written and spoken language. Similarly, when communicating our internal visual models, we rely heavily (if we don't use visual tools) on our verbal skills. So, as explained in chapter 13, Thinking skills, when we think we are accessing our visual and verbal modalities simultaneously.

Visual tools support *all* cognitive styles and *all* learning style models.

In 1998, two educational psychologists – Riding and Rayner – carried out a major study of learning style preferences. They examined the different words people used to describe functions and analysed the constructs

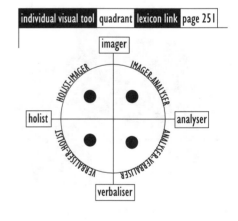

they employed. They then synthesised this knowledge. The result was a two dimensional map of cognitive styles that encompassed the distinctions used in the other inventories. The two dimensions are 'holist–analyser' and 'verbaliser–imager'. These findings are not surprising, given what we know about the nature of thinking.

Consider any of the visual tools (chapter 19, Lexicon). They *all* support the development of understanding of whole–part relationships since both the 'whole' and the 'parts' are visible simultaneously. So we can say that visual tools support those at either extreme of the 'holist–analyser' spectrum.

All visual tools also support verbal–visual relationships. The tools themselves are clearly visual, so they suit those with a preference for the 'imager' cognitive style.

They also clearly support the 'verbaliser', since not only are key words present but the spatial relationships between them are visible. All learners are asked to process and communicate information that is, by its very nature, both visual and verbal. As described in chapter 16, *Active learning*, visual tools can be used to direct, elaborate, represent and record people's thinking, dialogue, discourse – talking!

Visual tools support the development and use of four essential learning skills that apply to all learners.

The use of visual tools encourages the development of four essential good learning habits – the abilities to:

1 create interest

2 sustain concentration

3 organise information

4 shape memory.

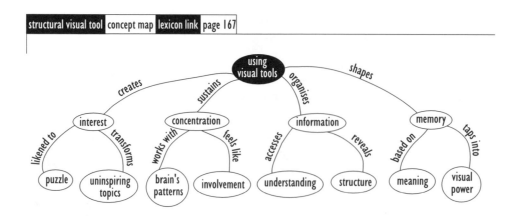

structural visual tool | concept map | lexicon link | page 167

Visual tools support learners in *creating interest* in the topic being studied.

When visual tools are used, the learner is intensely involved in organising information. When this process is taken out of the learner's head and put on to paper, the task becomes a puzzle. She is getting to the core of the information, considering and revealing its structure and purpose, investigating how it 'clicks' and how it is held together.

Even the most uninspiring of topics can be transformed into subjects of curiosity when using visual tools. The dullest of lengthy and bureaucratic meetings can be transformed from a potentially gruelling experience into something of value. Visual tools enable the learner to place information into a range of frameworks. Once this process is begun, interest soon follows.

Visual tools help learners to *sustain concentration* and *organise information.*

We all find it very hard to sustain our focus – especially when faced with a blank sheet of paper and trying to formulate 'the beginning'. The trouble is that a lifetime of exposure to linear, sequential text has shaped our belief

that we must always conform to this format. But as described in chapter 8, Holographic–linear, learning is dependent on images and holographic thinking – not on streams of words.

Teachers and students spend a great deal of effort tearing themselves away from areas of interest and forcing themselves to focus on the 'next thing' on a linear agenda. They do this rather than making the most of their natural inclination to experiment and see connections. Visual tools support this natural cycle of concentration. In fact, it doesn't even feel like concentration – it feels like involvement and interest.

Visual tools support learners in organising information in ways that reflect the intention and purpose of the task in hand. Their very structure gets to the heart of information management. The questions they represent and the processes they reflect get to the very essence of understanding.

Visual tools *shape* the learner's *memory*.

Visual tools provide immediate and accurate feedback on how well the learner is dealing with the information. The tools themselves ensure that students are acutely aware that they are the authors of the 'story' the tool is representing.

Memory can be easily shaped and improved using memory strategies. For the most part, these relate to short-term retention of content, and can be grouped under the heading 'rote learning'. Rote learning does have some part to play in education but by far the greater part is played by 'meaningful learning'. Visual tools help students to create meaning *and* they can act as the perfect summary of the meaning that has been made.

Visual tools offer visual hooks for recall. All the recall aids so beloved by memory experts can be found in, for example, model maps – string images, colour, associations, variety of size, contrast and texture – but they are placed within an organised network of *meaning*. And for something to stay in a student's *long-term* memory, it must be meaningful to that student.

Visual tools support all learners in achieving their central task – to form schemas.

Irrespective of their internal and external preferences, in order to achieve deep learning, learners must create meaning. Meaning is created through the construction of schemas (chapter 7).

Have you ever been unable to attempt a task because you did not have the correct tool? You would feel more helpless still if you didn't even know what tool you needed. Tools shape our ability to tackle tasks. Visual tools shape our schema-making. They help form and develop good learning habits. They help create model learners.

viewpoints

over-generalisations

'... we shared the concern of many educators that learning-styles research is inconclusive and may lead to the reinforcement of over-generalizations and stereotypes.'

S. C. Trent, E. Pernell Junior, A. Mungai and R. Chimedza (1998)

hemispheres

'Even left-brained verbal thought can be enhanced with right-brained visual structure. Even right-brained art can be enhanced by strong verbal description.'

D. M. Moore and F. M. Dwyer (1994)

laterality

'... speculation about specialization quickly outran the facts, so that mythologies of laterality have become established before the evidence could be properly evaluated. The most popular accounts of hemisphere specialization are exaggerated and erroneous.'

M. Craig (2000)

visual learners

' ... many, if not most, of our students are strong visual learners.'

D. Hyerle (2000)

meaningful learning

'... the more we approach meaningful, challenging, and relevant learning in the classroom, the more likely that children of all types will learn well.'

R. N. Caine and G. Caine (1991)

review

big picture

The lessons that you may be teaching tomorrow will be made up of parts that together constitute a whole. Which visual tools could you utilise to support your students in piecing it all together?

visual–verbal overlap

See if you can look at something without thinking about it, without adding any language to what you are looking at. Now read something or listen to a conversation or a radio programme without visualising. How did you get on? Can you now (if you didn't before) see that visual tools reflect the fact that our auditory and visual worlds overlap.

impact

What impact could visual tools have on your learners given that all of them engage in thinking that involves accessing the detail and the big picture, the auditory and the visual?

ROUTE MAP FOR YOUR READING

SECTION 1 — CONTEXT

CHAPTER ONE BACKGROUND
The primary assertion is that we are all *Eye Q* experts. Throughout history, humans have used an assortment of visual tools to reflect and communicate knowledge. Current knowledge creation dynamics are based on this same notion. The 'inside story' of learning is obtained by looking both inside (cognitive psychology) and outside (Accelerated Learning).

CHAPTER TWO THE iDESK MODEL
Most of our activities are not based on a theory of learning. Consequently, there is little sense of meaning or coherence. The iDesk model is holistic. It connects thinking, feeling and doing. Finally, it links these faculties to the environment and the individual. Visual tools impact all areas of the iDesk model, and all components interact with each other. Serious schools need models.

CHAPTER THREE THE KNOWLEDGE AGE
We are living in the knowledge age with a need for more knowledge workers. These new types of workers require new, extended mental skills and knowledge tools. Visual tools are central in creating and communicating knowledge. Schools need to learn from business theory and practice with regard to intellectual capital and the use of visual tools.

SECTION 2 — VISUALS

CHAPTER FOUR VISUAL TOOLS AND COMPUTERS
We are learning that the use of computers can reinforce poor learning habits. The attraction of the screen can degenerate into visual 'candyfloss'. This turns computer users into consumers. Behind the screen lies a knowledge structure. Visual tools make this explicit and turn consumers into explorers of knowledge. Clarity about visual literacy will support this.

CHAPTER FIVE VISUAL LITERACY
In our culture, the visual–verbal polarity may well be more divisive than the sciences–arts gulf. There are historical, philosophical reasons for the low value placed on visuals. Visual literacy, nonetheless, is an established discipline. All visual content exists in the spatial dimension. Space is our first and primary frontier. The spatial metaphor shapes our understanding.

CHAPTER SIX TOOLS TO LEARN
The successes of our civilisation are based on tools. We have created these tools and they, in turn, end up shaping our behaviour. Using new tools causes new learning to take place. Habitual use of tools changes our habits. The most effective use of tools happens when accompanied with theory. Visual tools impact on learning habits. New eras need new tools.

SECTION 3 — MEANING

CHAPTER SEVEN SCHEMAS
We all have schemas. They are personal and unique and are based on how we view the world. In business they are termed mental models. Their organisation represents how we think and shape our behaviour. All students have these mental maps but are unaware of them — as are teachers. Making schemas visible allows students and teachers to see what they are thinking.

CHAPTER EIGHT HOLOGRAPHIC–LINEAR
Every day, every student, in every lesson has to turn linear communication (what she reads or hears) into what is termed her holographic understanding. Schemas are holographic in structure — definitely not linear. The student then has to turn her new, enlarged understanding back into linear format. This process has, until now, been an unknown phenomenon.

CHAPTER NINE CONSTRUCTING KNOWLEDGE
All our students construct knowledge — even the very youngest and the least able. Knowledge cannot be delivered. It has to be created each time by the individual, for knowledge is created not discovered. This view of learning is called constructivism. Understanding this process stimulates teachers to make learning more meaningful and motivating for all students.

SECTION 4 — LANGUAGE

CHAPTER TEN SUPPORT FOR LANGUAGE
It is normally thought that visuals 'compete' with words. With visual tools, this is not true. Visual tools exist in the overlapping area between words and pictures. If you examine language, you realise that images play a big part in stimulating thought and supporting planning. They help the organisation of our language, which normally has to take place in the unseen interior of our heads.

CHAPTER ELEVEN READING
Reading is active. Readers' interrogation of text is shaped by their own schemas. They have to adapt their existing schemas in order to absorb text into meaningful messages. Visual tools can reveal the hidden structure and meaning of a text. Just as computer software can show you what your voice looks like, visual tools can show you what your thinking looks like.

CHAPTER TWELVE WRITING
Writing is difficult. Students' difficulties and fears stem from not knowing what to write. Visual tools make planning explicit, easy and empowering. Through the use of visual tools, students can model the planning that excellent writers do 'in their heads'. Planning in linear fashion is too difficult for most. The schematic nature of visual tools matches the way the brain naturally works.

SECTION 5 — THINKING

CHAPTER THIRTEEN THINKING SKILLS
When we think, we are either thinking of objects (in space) or events (in time). Our thoughts become 'thought–objects'. Just as we manipulate real, physical objects in space, so we move our 'thought–objects' in our inner space. This is thinking. It is, however, invisible and demands much short term memory. Visual tools make thinking visible, easier and obvious.

CHAPTER FOURTEEN QUESTIONS
Questions are more powerful than answers. They directly determine our focus and thinking. Young children are wonderful questioners — young scientists. Schools have conditioned students to demand only questions. This severely limits their thinking and learning. Visual tools are themselves questions. They demand investigation. Their visible nature makes questioners of all students.

CHAPTER FIFTEEN THINKING IN ACTION
There is a link between text, thinking and visual tools. The nature of different types of text (genres) demand different types of thinking. All thinking is the manipulation of 'thought–objects'. Visual tools show students what this looks like. Matching types of visual tools to specific genres and linking them to the National Curriculum thinking skills is a powerful matrix.

SECTION 6 — LEARNING

CHAPTER SIXTEEN ACTIVE LEARNING
You don't have to leave your seat to be actively learning. Active doesn't mean kinaesthetic! Active learning involves becoming engrossed, relating new material to personal prior knowledge, and creating meaning. Active learning needs to be encouraged by teachers. It is what is demanded of business. Visual tools stimulate and challenge active learning from students.

CHAPTER SEVENTEEN STYLES OF LEARNING
Learning style labels can be dangerous. They can limit rather than stimulate expansion. Behind their often surface description lies a common cognitive activity — putting the detail into the big picture. Visual tools meet the needs of all learners, involving them in visual, verbal, analytic and holistic thinking. They also promote the four essential skills of learning.

CHAPTER EIGHTEEN ABILITY RANGE
We have many labels for our pupils — from the gifted and talented to SEN. Behind all these labels there lies the act of meaning making. Visual tools show students what understanding looks like. This gives confidence to them all. It allows the least able to see their intelligence and supports the more able to organise and communicate their sometimes erratic thinking.

SECTION 7 — LEXICON

CHAPTER NINETEEN LEXICON

CATEGORIES OF VISUAL TOOLS

- structural thinking — Structural Visual Tools
- differential thinking — Differential Visual Tools
- representational thinking — Representational Visual Tools
- temporal thinking — Temporal Visual Tools
- causal thinking — Causal Visual Tools
- numerical thinking — Numerical Visual Tools
- organisational thinking — Organisational Visual Tools
- individual thinking — Individual Visual Tools

There are seven types of visual tools related to seven types of thinking. The eighth is a hybrid of all seven. Within each category, there is a variety of visual tools. Visual tools within the categories achieve slightly different results, at different levels of complexity to suit age, ability and the nature of the tasks set. Each visual tool is described, its workings explained and ideas given for introducing it to students. Differences between similar visual tools are clarified. Each visual tool is illustrated both in templated format and as a hand-drawn example in use. The context for each hand-drawn visual tool is a well known story.

overview

preview

■ Visual tools are very useful for students with special educational needs.

■ There is still a myth of 'special tools for special learners'.

■ Visual tools are very useful for gifted and talented students.

■ Visual tools reveal to students what understanding looks like and how to achieve it.

■ Visual tools support students in constructive meaning.

■ Visual tools encourage an interactive, collaborative approach to learning.

■ Visual tools can provide the missing link between understanding and explanation.

■ Visual tools support learners at the point where real learning takes place – when they don't know what to do.

■ Visual tools shape our dispositions to learning.

■ An underlying theory of learning is needed if we are to make best use of visual tools.

Visual tools are very useful for students with special educational needs.

Students with special educational needs are often the victims of the tyranny of linear text. Success is often denied them because of a technical difficulty with reading or writing. Listening to teachers talking also presents problems – their words disappear into thin air. It is a phenomenon that has been termed 'one-pass learning' (Davitt, 1990) – catch it perfectly first time or miss it. Visual tools turn fleeting messages into static, graspable records.

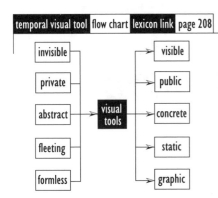

Visual tools turn abstract ideas into concrete images that can be manipulated. Ideas can become 'things' with which to play. Just as building blocks can be physically arranged into patterns and structures, so too can 'thought-objects'.

Students with SEN often find it hard to see what their teachers mean. Visual tools can make teachers' invisible thoughts visible. When students can *literally* 'see what teachers mean', they have a powerful access to understanding.

There is still a myth of 'special tools for special learners'.

Any effective teaching and learning strategy is relevant to all learners irrespective of age or ability. Many educational commentators, practitioners and researchers now conclude that there is no need for specialist techniques and that good educational practice is good for all students at all levels of ability. Mel Ainscow (1994), a one-time special needs guru, sums up when he says:

> 'I have to say that during my career I have spent considerable time and energy attempting to find special ways of teaching that will help special children to learn successfully … My conclusion now is that no such specialised techniques are worthy of consideration.'

M. Ainscow (1994)

Practitioners argue that SEN schools and departments reflect not the needs of students but a lack of learning theory held by the profession.

Visual tools apply equally well to gifted and talented students.

Many gifted and talented students are innovative and creative. However, their thinking can often be disorganised and difficult to communicate. Visual tools support students in untangling their arguments into clearer and reasoned patterns.

The discipline of using visual tools can be transferred across subjects. These tools are not subject specific. The content of the subject language and the nature of the task will shape the thinking – visual tools reflect this interaction. A range of tools from which to choose is all students need.

Visual tools reveal to students what understanding looks like and how to achieve it.

Gifted and talented students very often do not know what it is they do when they understand. Like the rest of us, they simply enjoy the experience of understanding. Yet when they come across something they do not understand the results can be very interesting.

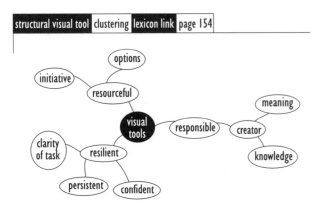

Many gifted and talented students lack persistence and resilience. Because they have never had to persist at anything, their resilience 'muscle' may have barely been used. When something comes along that they perceive as being beyond them, they can display less resilience than many students with SEN who, conversely, have well-developed persistence and resilience 'muscles'. This may be a sweeping generalisation, but it does describe a recognised tendency among gifted and talented students.

Visual tools support learners in constructing meaning.

Perhaps you know of colleagues who have become demoralised at their failure to teach learners who experience difficulties. Perhaps you have heard them seek refuge in the belief that there is simply an inherited lack of ability that is preventing the child from learning. Perhaps it is time to put our hands up and accept that this failure is not a personal one but a professional one.

Without a cohesive theory of how learning occurs, teachers may try different strategies almost blindly. As Gauvain puts it:

> '… with no underlying theory, we may not always appreciate the limitations of a tool, or even its counter-productiveness if used inappropriately. In our rush to solve practical problems, we may grab at ready-made solutions that neither address the fundamental causes of a problem, nor stretch our thinking in important new directions'.
>
> *M. Gauvain (1995)*

Visual tools support a theory of learning known as constructivism. Without an understanding of how they relate to this underlying theory, visual tools risk becoming just another 'fad' used to solve an immediate problem.

Visual tools encourage an interactive, collaborative approach to learning.

The inclusion of the word 'social' in social constructivism reflects the importance of the use and development of language as part of the meaning making process. The word 'social' stresses the essentially interactive nature of learning and the importance of language within it.

Interestingly, both SEN and gifted and talented students can experience difficulties expressing their understanding clearly to others. The former have problems with linear text, and therefore – without visual tools such as model or concept mapping – do not have access to a tool that supports their communication. The latter have difficulties because their schemas are sometimes so complex that they cannot translate them into linear text or spoken words. When the listener can see what the speaker is talking about, she can say things like 'I can see what you mean …', or 'I agree with what you are saying up to a point, but this bit…' As Galloway and co-workers argue, social constructivism:

> 'encourages greater motivational involvement by enabling students to make more sense out of what they are doing.'
>
> *D. Galloway, C. Rogers, D. Armstrong and E. Leo (1998)*

Visual tools can provide the missing link between understanding and explanation.

There is a general acceptance that if you haven't understood something you can't explain it. However, if you can't explain something it does not necessarily mean that 'something' has not been understood. How many of us have ever felt unable to communicate in linear verbal or written form something that we do actually understand? How many students (of all abilities) have occasions in classrooms when this is the case? How many times are we, as teachers, left having to assume that a student has *not* understood something simply because she is unable to articulate her understanding?

Visual tools not only represent a way of demonstrating understanding, but – more significantly – they help you understand in the first place. Most significant is the fact that they can support us *all* in communicating in a linear fashion by providing us with a model of our thoughts to follow. The verbal act of explanation and its linear written

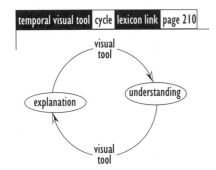

temporal visual tool | cycle | lexicon link | page 210

expression both reflect and develop existing levels of understanding. When listener and explainer can see the structure of what is being talked or written about, reflection, clarification and mediation are supported. This applies to all learners across the ability range.

Visual tools support learners at the point where real learning takes place – when they don't know what to do.

All of us, irrespective of our ability, like to understand and to experience 'knowing'. What would happen if all learners understood what it is they *do* when they understand? What would it be like if all learners knew what it is they are *not* doing when they do *not* understand? Visual tools, in particular model mapping and concept mapping, make this knowledge formation process explicit, available and accessible to the learner.

All children go through a phase when they happily accept the fact that they do not know. (In fact, they don't even know that they don't know!) We have all experienced 'not knowing'. It just happens at different levels for each of us. Visual tools enable us to see, literally, and understand how we learn! Knowing how they learn is as valuable to gifted and talented students as it is to SEN students.

Visual tools can shape our dispositions to learning.

By habitually using visual tools and experiencing success at perceiving patterns within texts, students gain *confidence*. They realise that they have a set of tools available to them that work. Just as a trained and experienced plumber does not become anxious and suffer from negative self-belief if faced with a problematic central heating

system, so students can look at 'problematic' texts with confidence and reasoned curiosity. The plumber's confidence is based on the effectiveness of her tools. Students can easily gain similar confidence based on the effectiveness of their visual tool kit.

Regular use of visual tools promotes *responsibility*. Used in this specific sense, 'responsibility' means the learner's fundamental belief that meaning and learning can only be created by the learner herself. Through experience with visual tools, students become very clear that they are the creators of the networks of meaning. They can literally see it before them in the form of a completed visual tool.

Students become more *resourceful*. Because of the huge range of visual tools available, students can try out a variety of tools until they find the best one for the job. They are not helpless, as is often the case for people without tools.

Finally, the experience of understanding the mechanics of success means that even when students don't know quite what to do at first, they *persist*. Their past successes with visual tools make it clear to them the cognitive work that needs to take place. It is simply a case of finding the correct tool.

An underlying theory is needed if we are to make best use of visual tools.

Without a theory about how learning happens, we may not always understand the limitations of particular learning tools. In our rush to solve pressing and practical problems, we may grab at 'ready-made solutions' that address the symptoms, but not the cause, of the problem.

In some schools there may not be a perceived need for the use of constructivist methods. Examination results may suggest that direct transmission works and why fix what isn't broken? This could be called the NIMBY (Not In My Back Yard) reaction. The school's exam result may be fine, but use of direct transmission methods alone is unlikely to promote in students the habits of reflection and co-operation demanded by businesses (and higher education establishments) as they go out into the twenty-first century world.

We are all meaning makers. We all want to understand. Some of us find it easier to do than others. We would all benefit from understanding how we create meaning for ourselves. We would all benefit from having access to some tools that show us how we understand and help us do it.

cognition

'The packets that organise information and make sense of experience are 'schemas', the building blocks of cognition.'

D. Goleman (1985)

responsibility

'... students are ultimately responsible for transforming such linear text into multirelational holistic concepts.'

D. Hyerle (1996)

deep structure

'A deep approach to study involves getting behind the words, and looking for underlying meaning.'

D. McCabe (1999)

modelling thinking

'The teacher initially leads the group, actively models the desired comprehension strategies and makes them overt, explicit and concrete.'

C. McGuiness (1999)

collaboration

'The diagram serves as a focus of attention to which everyone in the team can relate and use to decide whether or not the diagram adequately captures their own views.'

D. Sherwood (1998)

display

'Maps are tools for displaying intellectual processes.'

A. L. Costa (1996)

review

constructivism

What is constructivism?

    a a type of music   **b** a theory of learning

    c a political movement   **d** a way of making things

ability range

In what ways do visual tools support the least able?

In what ways do visual tools support the most able?

Significant

What is the most significant thing that all learners, irrespective of ability, have in common?

    a they all have to learn the National Curriculum   **b** they all have to attend school

    c they are all meaning makers   **d** they all have to listen to teachers

Visual tools make meaning making explicit.

ROUTE MAP FOR YOUR READING

SECTION 1 — CONTEXT

CHAPTER ONE BACKGROUND

The primary assertion is that we are all *Eye Q* experts. Throughout history, humans have used an assortment of visual tools to reflect and communicate knowledge. Current knowledge creation dynamics are based on this same notion. The 'inside story' of learning is obtained by looking both inside (cognitive psychology) and outside (Accelerated Learning).

CHAPTER TWO THE iDESK MODEL

Most of our activities are not based on a theory of learning. Consequently, there is little sense of meaning or coherence. The iDesk model is holistic. It connects thinking, feeling and doing. Finally, it links these faculties to the environment and the individual. Visual tools impact all areas of the iDesk model, and all components interact with each other. Serious schools need models.

CHAPTER THREE THE KNOWLEDGE AGE

We are living in the knowledge age with a need for more knowledge workers. These new types of workers require new, extended mental skills and knowledge tools. Visual tools are central in creating and communicating knowledge. Schools need to learn from business theory and practice with regard to intellectual capital and the use of visual tools.

SECTION 2 — VISUALS

CHAPTER FOUR VISUAL TOOLS AND COMPUTERS

We are learning that the use of computers can reinforce poor learning habits. The attraction of the screen can degenerate into visual 'candyfloss'. This turns computer users into consumers. Behind the screen lies a knowledge structure. Visual tools make this explicit and turn consumers into explorers of knowledge. Clarity about visual literacy will support this.

CHAPTER FIVE VISUAL LITERACY

In our culture, the visual–verbal polarity may well be more divisive than the sciences–arts gulf. There are historical, philosophical reasons for the low value placed on visuals. Visual literacy, nonetheless, is an established discipline. All visual content exists in the spatial dimension. Space is our first and primary frontier. The spatial metaphor shapes our understanding.

CHAPTER SIX TOOLS TO LEARN

The successes of our civilisation are based on tools. We have created these tools and they, in turn, end up shaping our behaviour. Using new tools causes new learning to take place. Habitual use of tools changes our habits. The most effective use of tools happens when accompanied with theory. Visual tools impact on learning habits. New eras need new tools.

SECTION 3 — MEANING

CHAPTER SEVEN SCHEMAS

We all have schemas. They are personal and unique and are based on how we view the world. In business they are termed mental models. Their organisation represents how we think and shape our behaviour. All students have these mental maps but are unaware of them — as are teachers. Making schemas visible allows students and teachers to see what they are thinking.

CHAPTER EIGHT HOLOGRAPHIC—LINEAR

Every day, every student, in every lesson has to turn linear communication (what she reads or hears) into what is termed her holographic understanding. Schemas are holographic in structure — definitely not linear. The student then has to turn her new, enlarged understanding back into linear format. This process has, until now, been an unknown phenomenon.

CHAPTER NINE CONSTRUCTING KNOWLEDGE

All our students construct knowledge — even the very youngest and the least able. Knowledge cannot be delivered. It has to be created each time by the individual, for knowledge is created not discovered. This view of learning is called constructivism. Understanding this process stimulates teachers to make learning more meaningful and motivating for all students.

SECTION 4 — LANGUAGE

CHAPTER TEN SUPPORT FOR LANGUAGE

It is normally thought that visuals 'compete' with words. With visual tools, this is not true. Visual tools exist in the overlapping area between words and pictures. If you examine language, you realise that images play a big part in stimulating thought and supporting planning. They help the organisation of our language, which normally has to take place in the unseen interior of our heads.

CHAPTER ELEVEN READING

Reading is active. Readers' interrogation of text is shaped by their own schemas. They have to adapt their existing schemas in order to absorb text into meaningful messages. Visual tools can reveal the hidden structure and meaning of a text. Just as computer software can show you what your voice looks like, visual tools can show you what your thinking looks like.

CHAPTER TWELVE WRITING

Writing is difficult. Students' difficulties and fears stem from not knowing what to write. Visual tools make planning explicit, easy and empowering. Through the use of visual tools, students can model the planning that excellent writers do 'in their heads'. Planning in linear fashion is too difficult for most. The schematic nature of visual tools matches the way the brain naturally works.

SECTION 5 — THINKING

CHAPTER THIRTEEN THINKING SKILLS

When we think, we are either thinking of objects (in space) or events (in time). Our thoughts become 'thought—objects'. Just as we manipulate real, physical objects in space, so we move our 'thought—objects' in our inner space. This is thinking. It is, however, invisible and demands much short term memory. Visual tools make thinking visible, easier and obvious.

CHAPTER FOURTEEN QUESTIONS

Questions are more powerful than answers. They directly determine our focus and thinking. Young children are wonderful questioners — young scientists. Schools have conditioned students to demand only questions. This severely limits their thinking and learning. Visual tools are themselves questions. They demand investigation. Their visible nature makes questioners of all students.

CHAPTER FIFTEEN THINKING IN ACTION

There is a link between text, thinking and visual tools. The nature of different types of text (genres) demand different types of thinking. All thinking is the manipulation of 'thought—objects'. Visual tools show students what this looks like. Matching types of visual tools to specific genres and linking them to the National Curriculum thinking skills is a powerful matrix.

SECTION 6 — LEARNING

CHAPTER SIXTEEN ACTIVE LEARNING

You don't have to leave your seat to be actively learning. Active doesn't mean kinaesthetic! Active learning involves becoming engrossed, relating new material to personal prior knowledge, and creating meaning. Active learning needs to be encouraged by teachers. It is what is demanded of business. Visual tools stimulate and challenge active learning from students.

CHAPTER SEVENTEEN STYLES OF LEARNING

Learning style labels can be dangerous. They can limit rather than stimulate expansion. Behind their often surface description lies a common cognitive activity — putting the detail into the big picture. Visual tools meet the needs of all learners, involving them in visual, verbal, analytic and holistic thinking. They also promote the four essential skills of learning.

CHAPTER EIGHTEEN ABILITY RANGE

We have many labels for our pupils — from the gifted and talented to SEN. Behind all these labels there lies the act of meaning making. Visual tools show students what understanding looks like. This gives confidence to them all. It allows the least able to see their intelligence and supports the more able to organise and communicate their sometimes erratic thinking.

SECTION 7 — LEXICON

CHAPTER NINETEEN LEXICON

CATEGORIES OF VISUAL TOOLS

- structural thinking — Structural Visual Tools
- differential thinking — Differential Visual Tools
- representational thinking — Representational Visual Tools
- temporal thinking — Temporal Visual Tools
- causal thinking — Causal Visual Tools
- numerical thinking — Numerical Visual Tools
- organisational thinking — Organisational Visual Tools
- individual thinking — Individual Visual Tools

There are seven types of visual tools related to seven types of thinking. The eighth is a hybrid of all seven. Within each category, there is a variety of visual tools. Visual tools within the categories achieve slightly different results, at different levels of complexity to suit age, ability and the nature of the tasks set. Each visual tool is described, its workings explained and ideas given for introducing it to students. Differences between similar visual tools are clarified. Each visual tool is illustrated both in templated format and as a hand-drawn example in use. The context for each hand-drawn visual tool is a well known story.

overview

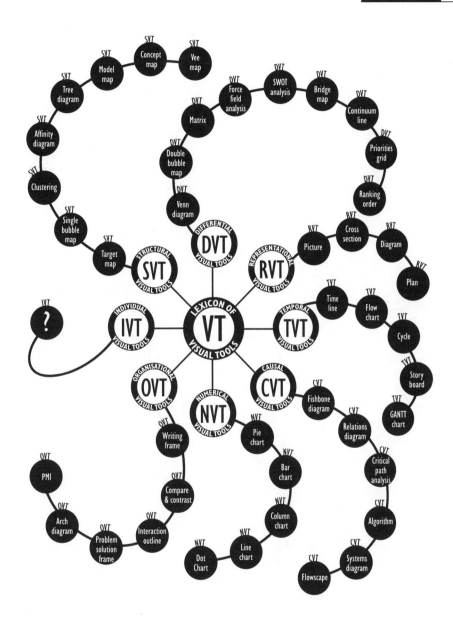

Insight into lexicon

preview

- The categories into which the visual tools are placed in the lexicon do not have absolute boundaries.

- Categorisation differs from classification.

- Genres and thinking skills are categorisations, not classifications.

- Each visual tool is illustrated in two ways.

- Adapt the visual tools for your use – they are not graphic organiser 'worksheets'.

- There are unlimited variations, adaptations and extensions of the visual tools.

The categories into which the visual tools are placed in the lexicon do not have absolute boundaries.

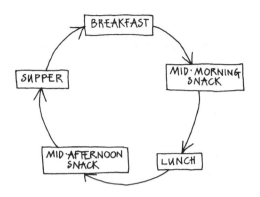

In the lexicon of visual tools that follows, the tools have been grouped into categories according to their features and functions. However, for some uses, you could argue that a particular visual tool would fit better in another category.

For example, the cycle sits within the Temporal Visual Tools category because it's used to show how one event follows after another in time. But in some cases a cycle can represent a chain of *causes* – in which case it would be better placed within the Causal Visual Tools category.

Let's look at this example in more detail so that the principles that lie behind the construction of the categories become more evident. On the left, you will see a cycle depicting a normal sequence of meals during the course of a day. The events repeat themselves, and so the last meal (supper) can be said to precede the following day's first meal (breakfast). Viewed in this way, the meals are placed within a cycle. The cycle represents the temporal sequence of meals.

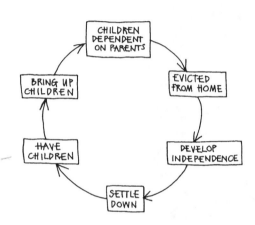

By contrast, the cycle below represents not only a temporal but also a causal sequence of events. Based upon the story of the Three Little Pigs (as are all the examples in the lexicon), this cycle illustrates both the temporal and causal links involved in the development of a dependent child into an independent parent, who later fosters dependency in her own children.

While the Three Little Pigs cycle is both causal and temporal in nature, other cycles may not contain both aspects. Cycles always represent a temporal sequence but not always a causal one. That is why the cycle is placed in the Temporal Visual Tools category of the lexicon.

Categorisation differs from classification.

Understanding the seemingly esoteric distinction between categorisation and classification is crucial to avoid confusion.

Classification is the grouping of items into discrete sets based on a list of specific characteristics. These characteristics, or qualities, are clearly defined. Correspondingly, an element's membership or non-membership of a given set is unambiguous. Examples include the classifications of living species, of rocks, and of chemicals.

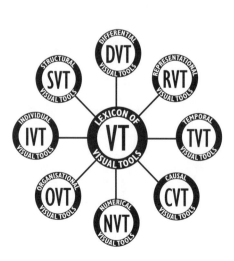

Categorisation, in contrast, is by no means as precise. It is more 'fuzzy around the edges'. The philosopher Ludwig Wittgenstein described the basis of categorisation as being 'family resemblances' rather than clearly defined criteria. Psychologists and linguists have, subsequently, based their own understandings of human thought on the distinction between categorisation and classification. Indeed, Steven Pinker (1999) says that humans think overwhelmingly in categories.

The visual tools represented in the lexicon that follows are organised according to 'family resemblances'. While the resemblances that bind the categories are strong, they do not have the absolute distinctions that are the hallmark of classifications. Therefore, there will be some blurring around the edges – there will be some items that could go in more than one category. The cycle is one such example.

Genres and thinking skills are categorisations, not classifications.

To imagine that the differences between genres, or between types of thinking skills, are clearly defined and absolute is to court trouble and confusion. One of the difficulties in applying thinking skills programmes in classrooms is based entirely on this false assumption. Thinking in the 'real' world, as opposed to the clinically 'clean' world of thinking skills programmes, involves using different types of thinking at the same time. You might say that real-life thinking is 'fast and dirty'. Graduates of thinking skills programmes need to learn how to merge and adapt their clean and distinct thinking processes for use in a world that demands more mixed and multi-processed thinking.

There are dangers in trying to classify, rather than categorise, texts into different genres, for example. While some texts can be purely of one genre, most will be hybrids. The task is to identify – using the many features of the text – which genre it 'looks like' most.

So, be warned against taking any of the categories of thinking skills, genres or visual tools literally. When you select a visual tool to use with a particular genre or thinking skill, remember that the distinctions can be blurred – you may find that a tool from a different category, or a hybrid of different types of visual tool, would be most appropriate for the job.

In order to choose the right tool for the job, it helps to be able to remember broadly what each category of visual tool is best suited for. To this end, each category in the lexicon that follows is illustrated using a 'viewing aid', which could be used to remind students about the general nature of that type of tool.

Structural visual tools are like swimming goggles, because they allow you to see beneath the surface.

Differential visual tools are like binoculars, because they allow two separate viewpoints to be merged into one.

Representational visual tools are like normal glasses, because they give a realistic view of appearance.

Temporal visual tools are like a telescope, because they give a view from far across time.

Causal visual tools are like a microscope, because they allow you to see the inner workings in a way not otherwise available.

Numerical visual tools are like a monocle, because they give you a singular view.

Organisational visual tools are like sunglasses, because they give you a cool view when the topic to be studied can look hazy, even blinding.

Individual visual tools are like opera glasses, because they give a creative viewpoint.

Each visual tool is illustrated into two ways.

For each visual tool described in the lexicon, there is a 'template' version showing the constituent parts with no real content matter. Alongside this is a hand-drawn example of the visual tool 'in action'. These hand-drawn examples all focus on content from the same source – the story of the Three Little Pigs. The reasons for this are three-fold:

1 For the lexicon to be useful, the visual tools had to be illustrated using 'real-life' examples. But if you happen to be unfamiliar with the 'real-life' content chosen, you can't fully understand the workings of the visual tool. The story of the Three Little Pigs was chosen for its universal familiarity – there can be few readers who do not know the characters, setting and plot of this simple nursery tale.

2 To keep things simple, all the visuals tools had to be illustrated using the same content source. The Three Little Pigs were up to the job (although, sadly, the sample size was a little small for the Pigs' data to be usefully applied in the Numerical Visual Tools category!).

3 Lastly, and perhaps most importantly, the content had to be as simple as possible, in order to make sure the nature of the visual tools themselves was obvious. Again, the story of the Three Little Pigs was most appropriate.

Adapt the visual tools for your use – they are not graphic organiser 'worksheets'.

In the USA, graphic organisers are often used as worksheets, which can be very limiting and devoid of real thinking. As the various boxes and arrows on the sheet are predetermined by the teacher or publisher, this leaves very little room for the student to investigate and extend her thinking. David Hyerle in his inspirational book *Visual Tools for Constructing Knowledge* (1996) eloquently explains how graphic organiser templates are perfect for uniform training that does not require much thought other than the search for 'the answer'. Thinking, by contrast, requires tools that can be adapted and extended to suit the nature of the content and the task in hand.

The visual tools in the lexicon below, therefore, are there for you to adapt. The examples given to illustrate the different visual tools can be taken to be what Hyerle calls 'graphic primitives'. They represent the core design around which you can extend your thinking.

There are unlimited variations, adaptations and extensions of the visual tools.

The last category of visual tools in the lexicon is called Individual Visual Tools. This category is included to validate the many different visual representations of thinking that exist in books and that come from children themselves. Most business books now contain visual illustrations of concepts. They differ in their effectiveness. They are, however, individual responses to particular conceptual and communication demands.

Just as for any piece of writing, your aim in using a visual tool should always be towards the audience. While some visual tools may represent your own thinking, or have been a useful tool in generating and sustaining your thinking, you should not assume that their meaning will communicate well to others. So when using visual tools, consider whether they are to be used 'in private' to support your own thinking, or whether they are also to be used for direct communication to another.

Finally, it would be limiting to consider that the lexicon categories, or their content, were the final chapter in the story of visual tools. They are more like the first chapter!

overview

visual tools							
structural	**1** target map	P150	**4** affinity diagram	P157	**7** concept map	P167
	2 single bubble map	P152	**5** tree diagram	P160	**8** Vee map	P170
	3 clustering	P154	**6** model map	P163		
differential	**1** Venn diagram	P174	**4** force field analysis	P180	**7** continuum line	P187
	2 double bubble map	P176	**5** SWOT analysis	P183	**8** priorities grid	P189
	3 matrix	P178	**6** bridge map	P185	**9** ranking order	P192
representational	**1** picture	P196	**4** plan	P202		
	2 cross section	P198				
	3 diagram	P200				
temporal	**1** time line	P206	**4** story board	P212		
	2 flow chart	P208	**5** GANTT chart	P214		
	3 cycle	P210				
causal	**1** fishbone diagram	P218	**4** algorithm	P227		
	2 relations diagram	P221	**5** systems diagram	P230		
	3 critical path analysis	P224	**6** flowscape	P234		
numerical	**1** pie chart	P238	**4** line chart	P241		
	2 bar chart	P239	**5** dot chart	P242		
	3 column chart	P240				
organisational	**1** writing frame	P244	**4** problem–solution frame	P247		
	2 compare & contrast organiser	P245	**5** arch diagram	P248		
	3 interaction outline	P246	**6** PMI	P249		
individual	individually constructed tools for one-off use in a specific context	P252–256				

DIMENSION		VISUAL TOOL
SPACE	**SVT**	TARGET MAP
		SINGLE BUBBLE MAP
		CLUSTERING
		AFFINITY DIAGRAM
		TREE DIAGRAM
		MODEL MAP
		CONCEPT MAP
		VEE MAP
	DVT	VENN DIAGRAM
		DOUBLE BUBBLE MAP
		MATRIX
		FORCE FIELD ANALYSIS
		SWOT ANALYSIS
		BRIDGE MAP
		CONTINUUM LINE
		PRIORITIES GRID
		RANKING ORDER
	RVT	PICTURE
		CROSS SECTION
		DIAGRAM
		PLAN
TIME	**TVT**	TIME LINE
		FLOW CHART
		CYCLE
		GANTT CHART
		STORY BOARD
	CVT	FISHBONE DIAGRAM
		RELATIONS DIAGRAM
		CRITICAL PATH ANALYSIS
		ALGORITHM
		SYSTEMS DIAGRAM
		FLOWSCAPE
SPACE TIME	**NVT**	PIE CHART
		BAR CHART
		COLUMN CHART
		LINE CHART
		DOT CHART
	OVT	WRITING FRAME
		COMPARE & CONTRAST ORGANISER
		INTERACTION OUTLINE
		PROBLEM—SOLUTION FRAME
		ARCH DIAGRAM
		PMI

structural visual tools SVT

purpose

The main purposes of the visual tools in this category are to:

- start thinking about a topic
- reveal the structure of the content
- organise the content
- create hierarchies within the content
- see the relationships between the whole and the parts.

1 target map SVT

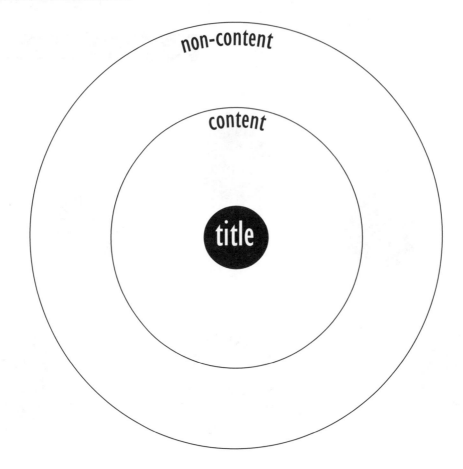

what it is

A target map is a simple way of identifying (targeting) what is part of the topic under study and what is not.

why it has this name

It is called a target map because a motif of a target is used graphically to identify the content of the topic.

other names

Target maps are also known as:

- circle maps
- single set diagrams.

how to make it

To make a target map, follow these steps.

1 Write the title of the topic under study in the centre 'bull's eye' circle.

2 Identify items that constitute parts of the topic and write them down in the next closest circle to the bull's eye.

3 Isolate the invalid content by writing it down in the outer circle.

benefits

Target maps get you off to a good clear start. Students start with a feeling of confidence from the clarity of having the boundary of the topic agreed and made visible. The major key words are identified early on in the topic and this forms a useful way of pre-processing the material.

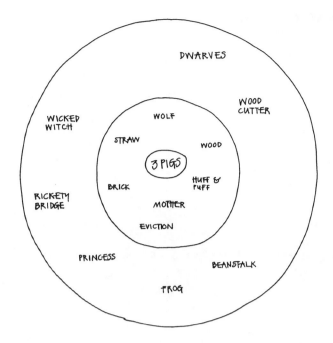

when to use it

Use a target map when you want to:

- start a topic

- review a topic that may have become over-complicated or confused

- keep a class discussion on task by identifying what may not be relevant.

prompt questions

- What are we going to study?

- How can we find out what is involved here?

- How can we agree what is relevant to our discussion?

how to introduce it to students

You can:

- write the title of the topic under study in the centre bull's eye circle

- ask students to think about and propose ideas connected with the topic

- write them all down on the target map, deciding whether they go in the content circle or the outer non-content circle

- use any group strategy to come to this point – for example, 'think, pair, share' and so on.

closely related visual tools

You will find that single bubble maps most closely relate to target maps.

	Similarities	Differences
single bubble maps	Both formats identify and describe the scope of the content.	Single bubble maps do not identify the non-relevant material.
		Single bubble maps separate each element of the content graphically into a small linked circle, while target maps place them together in the content circle.

2 single bubble map SVT

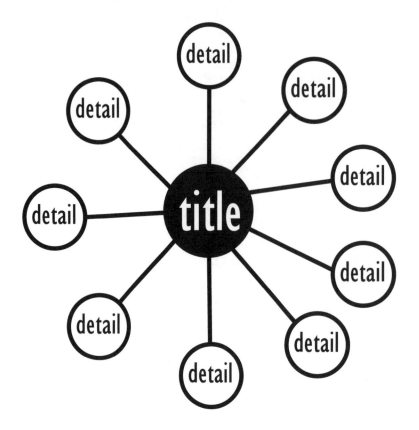

what it is

A bubble map is a way of identifying and describing the constituent parts or features of a topic under study.

why it has this name

It is called a single bubble map because of its shape. There is a single bubble (topic) from which the identified features radiate.

other names

Bubble maps are also known as:

- splay diagrams
- spider diagrams
- webbing
- conceptual webs.

how to make it

To make a bubble map, follow these steps.

1 Write the title of the topic in the centre bubble.

2 As you think of features and characteristics of that topic, write them down around the centre bubble.

3 Put each of these features into a small circle and link it to the centre bubble.

4 Arrange this process so that the features radiate equally around the centre bubble.

benefits

Single bubble maps enable you to:

- identify the characteristics of any topic on one page
- prepare to use a double bubble map for comparison between two topics (page 176).

when to use it

Use a bubble map when you want to:

- start a project
- identify the key features of a topic before studying it
- compare with bubble maps of other topics.

prompt questions

- What do we already know about this topic?
- How can we record what we have learned about this topic?

how to introduce it to students

You can:

- get individuals to draw the title in a central circle and start noting down their prior knowledge about the topic using the above process
- pair up individual students to compare their bubble maps and to construct a new bubble map that incorporates both sets of prior knowledge
- put pairs of students into groups of six or eight and repeat the above process
- incorporate group bubble maps within a whole-class discussion and bubble map construction.

closely related visual tools

You will find that target maps and clustering most closely relate to bubble maps.

	Similarities	Differences
target maps	Both identify the first level of knowledge about the characteristics or features of a topic.	Target maps make the distinction between the valid content and irrelevant material, while bubble maps concentrate solely on the content.
clustering	Both have radiant links to properties of the central topic. Both use a similar graphic format to illustrate these links.	Bubble maps limit the links to one level from the centre, while clustering develops the links further.

3 clustering SVT

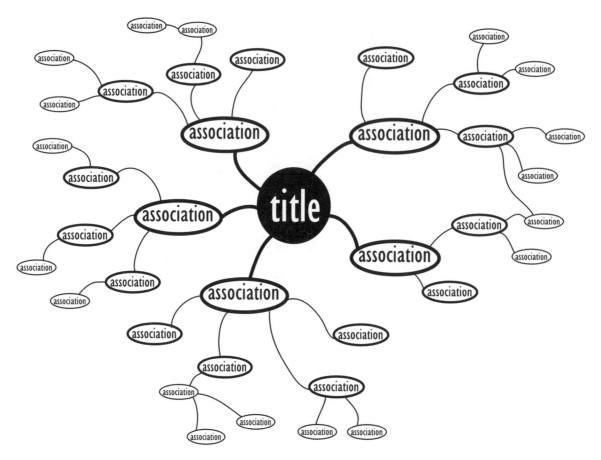

what it is

Clustering is a graphic format that allows you to make and see the links between elements that are part of, and radiate from, the central topic.

why it has this name

Clustering was developed by Gabrielle Rico as a strategy to prompt and develop ideas during the planning stage of writing. It is, therefore, primarily a visual tool to explore the relationships between the constituent parts of any topic under focus, and related issues.

other names

Clustering diagrams are also known as:

- spider webs
- webbing
- concept webs
- splay diagrams
- explosion charts
- web diagrams
- central idea graphs
- brainstorm maps
- spider diagrams
- mubbles.

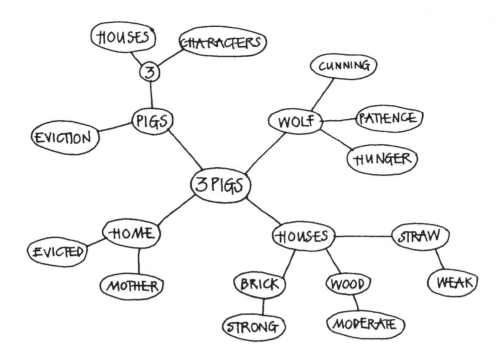

how to make it

To make a clustering diagram, follow these steps.

1 Write the idea under focus in a circle, centrally on your paper.

2 As soon as a related idea comes to you, write it down, circle it and draw a link to the central idea.

3 Continue this process.

4 When you get an idea that is prompted by, and is directly related to, any of these first ideas, link the new idea to the first idea rather than to the centre. In this way, the first wave of ideas, most closely related to the central idea, becomes the centre of a splay of linked ideas or concepts.

5 Continue both processes until you have no further ideas to add.

6 Redraw the clustering diagram if it gets too complicated or messy, by moving related concepts closer to each other, avoiding the need for excessively long and convoluted links.

benefits

Clustering is very useful because it allows a complex network of related ideas and concepts to be recorded easily and simply. It also serves, often within the same recording process, as a stimulus for further conceptual explorations. As an initial record of, and prompt for, ideas about a subject, it is unsurpassed. The avoidance of the need to categorise rigorously allows a free association of ideas.

when to use it

Use clustering when you want to:

■ record the relationships and associations of your prior knowledge of a topic

■ stimulate the generation of ideas for any piece of writing

■ explore the inter-relationships and associations of a topic.

prompt questions

■ What do we already know about this topic?

■ How does this topic relate to other topics?

■ How can I generate ideas for my piece of writing?

■ How could we develop this idea?

how to introduce it to students

You can:

- start with a class bubble map (page 152)
- give each group of students an identified factor or element
- ask each group to use that factor as a central stimulus for a new bubble map, using sticky notes for the newly identified characteristics
- gather the groups' bubble maps together and, as a whole-class activity, integrate the separate bubble maps into one clustering diagram by negotiating and moving the sticky notes into links
- explore and develop these links further
- explain that this process is called clustering.

closely related visual tools

You will find that bubble maps and concept maps most closely relate to clustering.

	Similarities	Differences
bubble maps	Both have related characteristics or elements radiating outwards from the central idea in similar graphic format.	Bubble maps limit the radiant links to one outer level, whereas clustering develops each in turn as it becomes the centre of further radiant links.
concept maps	Both represent graphically the conceptual links between related ideas or characteristics.	Clustering does not organise the links into a hierarchy and nor does it require the nature of the links to be described as propositional statements, which are features of concept maps.

4 affinity diagram SVT

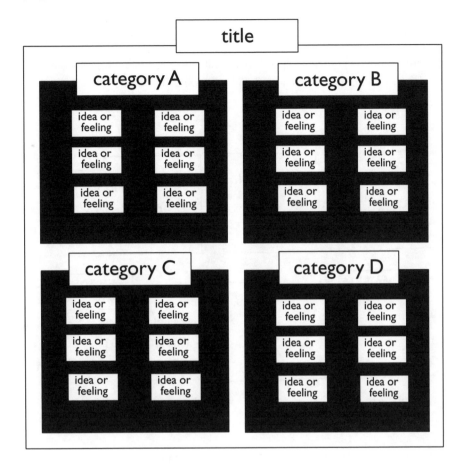

what it is

An affinity diagram is a way of organising views, ideas and responses to any topic or issue. The organisation is achieved through grouping together (categorising) the content.

why it has this name

The term 'affinity diagram' refers to the grouping together of similar views, ideas or responses. By being categorised together, items can be said to have an affinity to other items within the same group.

other names

Affinity diagrams are also known as:

- the 'JK method', after their developer Jiro Kawakita
- the nominal group technique.

how to make it

To make an affinity diagram, follow these steps.

1   Identify all the ideas, concerns and feelings you have about a particular topic or issue.

2   Write down all the perceptions separately onto sticky notes.

3   Sort all the sticky notes into groups based on perceived similarity (affinity).

4   Repeat the process until clear groupings emerge.

5   Eject any strange or inappropriately categorised items and return them to be re-sorted.

6   Isolate any items that fail to be successfully re-sorted and put them to one side.

7   Draw the affinity diagram based on the groupings of sticky notes.

8   Decide on titles for each group of items.

9   If required, break down the groups into sub-groups using the same sorting processes as before.

10 Note the need, if presenting the completed affinity diagram to others, to start with phrases like: 'I/we feel ...', 'my/our impressions are ...', 'it seems to me/us that ...'

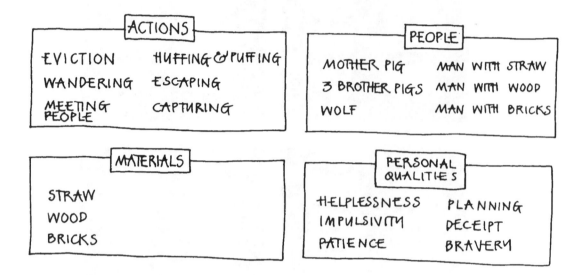

benefits

Affinity diagrams allow groups of individuals to become aware of their own and others' feelings and thoughts about issues. In coming to agreement about these perceptions through the group process of categorising, individuals honour and respect others' responses. Such an exercise can reveal hidden but powerful perceptions shaping people's behaviour.

when to use it

Use an affinity diagram when you want to:

■ achieve some agreement from a group regarding their perceptions about any potentially controversial topic

■ reveal unarticulated views among the group regarding any issue

■ identify themes among people's perceptions

■ achieve a baseline of views before engaging on a project, for later comparison.

prompt questions

■ What do we feel about this issue?

■ How can we identify the themes behind our responses?

■ How much agreement can we achieve regarding this issue?

how to introduce it to students

There are many strategies you can use to introduce affinity diagrams:

■ Start a class discussion on a controversial issue and have a colleague note the different viewpoints onto a whiteboard. Then arrange for groups of students to put the views into categories for later comparison and discussion with other groups.

■ Give groups of students an affinity diagram completed by another class and ask them to re-organise the categories, and justify their decisions.

- Use the outcomes of a circle time discussion about a real conflict and use an affinity diagram to illustrate that others' viewpoints can be accommodated.

- Consider the viewpoints and ideas of other historical periods and construct an affinity diagram from the perspectives of participants in historical events.

closely related visual tools

You will find that model maps most closely relate to affinity diagrams.

	Similarities	Differences
model maps	The categorisation process is similar to the early grouping together of content into the main branches within model maps.	The categorisation in affinity diagrams does not develop into the hierarchy of a model map. The graphic representation of categories differs.

5 tree diagram SVT

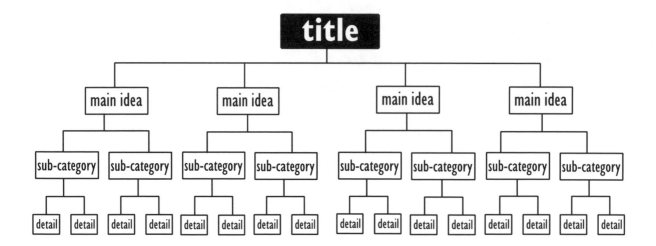

what it is

A tree diagram is a way of representing the hierarchical structure of knowledge. The knowledge can range from concepts, to actions, to family relationships to organisational networks.

why it has this name

The graphic structure of the expanding branches reflects the branching of trees.

other names

Tree diagrams are also known as:

- brace maps
- family trees
- branching diagrams
- structured overviews
- central idea graphs
- tree maps.

how to make it

To make a tree diagram, follow these steps.

1 List all elements of the topic under study.

2 As for an affinity diagram, place the elements in groups.

3 Decide on a hierarchy within each group.

4 Draw out this organisation with the main ideas at the top, descending in order of abstraction.

5 As an alternative, start from the top and 'decode' each element into its constituent parts, and carry this process on for each lower element.

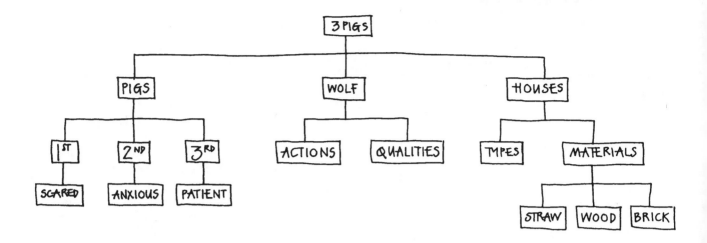

benefits

Tree diagrams offer a familiar graphic format in which to show the knowledge structure of any topic, action or relationship. The branching system most clearly indicates the way in which lower boxes are 'part of' the higher box from which they stem. This graphic format is equally suitable for illustrating the sub-division of actions within an analysis of an event or process.

when to use it

Use a tree diagram when you want to:

- show the structure of an organisation
- reveal the hierarchy of ideas within a topic
- analyse the sub-division of actions and tasks within a process or project.

prompt questions

- How is this organisation structured?
- How do the parts of this topic relate to each other?
- How can we organise the tasks within a project?

how to introduce it to students

You can:

- firstly, introduce and then work with the familiar family tree structure
- plan a class project, listing all tasks to be accomplished
- group the tasks into separate categories, using an affinity diagram
- organise the contents of each category of task into the important and the less important
- complete this process until all tasks have a 'place'
- draw out the agreed analysis into a tree diagram, during the above process, and certainly at the end of it
- alternatively, introduce a tree diagram by identifying the three most important aspects of a chosen and known topic
- take these main ideas separately and identify the three most important aspects of each
- repeat the process until there is agreement that the topic has been adequately represented.

closely related visual tools

You will find that model maps most closely relate to tree diagrams.

	Similarities	Differences
model maps	Main ideas are identified and subsequently broken down hierarchically into constituent parts.	The main differences are graphic in nature: ■ model maps radiate out from the centre and tree diagrams work down from the top ■ model maps use 'free form' arcs to link constituent parts, while tree diagrams use straight lines ■ tree diagrams have items of similar levels within the hierarchy shown at the same horizontal level, while model maps do not.
concept maps	Both formats have the main ideas identified and subsequently broken down hierarchically into constituent parts. Both tree diagrams and concept maps start from the top and have the content displayed in descending order of the hierarchy.	Concept maps identify the nature of the relationships between higher and lower linked elements through propositional statements, while tree diagrams do not.

6 model map | SVT

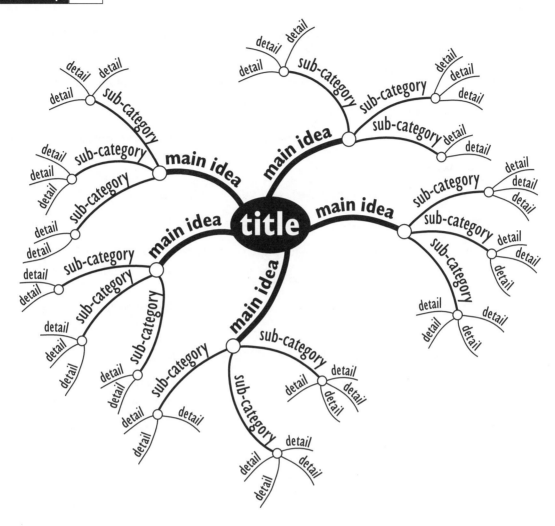

what it is

A model map shows the structure of any idea or topic. It gives you the 'lie of the land', as does any geographical map. It offers you the 'big picture'. It shows the organisation of the content, revealing both the detail and the overall view. A model map, most clearly of all visual tools, represents your mental model of the topic under focus.

why it has this name

The ideas you have about a topic are not real – 'the map is not the territory'. They are simply the ideas you have. They are a model of the real thing. You can represent your model, graphically, as a map. These maps are therefore called model maps.

other names

Model maps are also known as:

- mind maps®
- memory maps
- learning maps
- cognitive maps
- semantic maps
- brain maps
- webbing maps.

how to make it

To make a model map, follow these steps.

1   Write the name of your topic in the centre of a piece of paper placed in landscape orientation (widthways).

2   Draw a picture or symbol that illustrates that topic in the centre (not obligatory).

3   Mark out some main branches radiating out from the centre.

4   Write a key word on top of each of these branches for the main organising ideas of your topic.

5   Focus on one such branch at a time.

6   Mark out several other smaller branches from the end of the main branch.

7   Write a key word on each of these smaller branches for the ideas that form part of your main branch.

8   Repeat this sub-branching until you have given as much detail about that main branch as is needed.

9   Repeat the above process for each main branch.

10   Return to each main branch and decide which key words can easily be illustrated with icons, drawings or symbols.

11   Look over the whole map and talk it through to yourself.

12   Start at the centre and follow each main branch out to the edges along the smaller branches, explaining in full what each key word represents and how it relates to other branches.

13   Add to, amend or change any key words or branch arrangements that didn't stand up to common sense when you talked through your map.

14   Add colour to the map by colour coding each branch, idea or segment.

benefits

A model map gives you the primary map of the content under focus. It makes clear what is being studied, revealing the underlying meaning. As such, it is the perfect start before any further use of other visual tools. Uniquely, a model map can incorporate all other visual tools.

Using model maps develops both organisational skills and creativity. Organisational skills are developed when you are forced to decide where things belong and under which category. Creativity is developed when you are prompted to organise the content in novel ways, especially when mapping a new topic.

when to use it

Use a model map when you want to:

- find out what exactly you are about to study
- get clear about the main organising principles of the topic
- understand what is central and what is peripheral
- identify the main points in a piece of text
- explain your topic to others
- plan a piece of writing
- review a topic
- memorise and recall a topic.

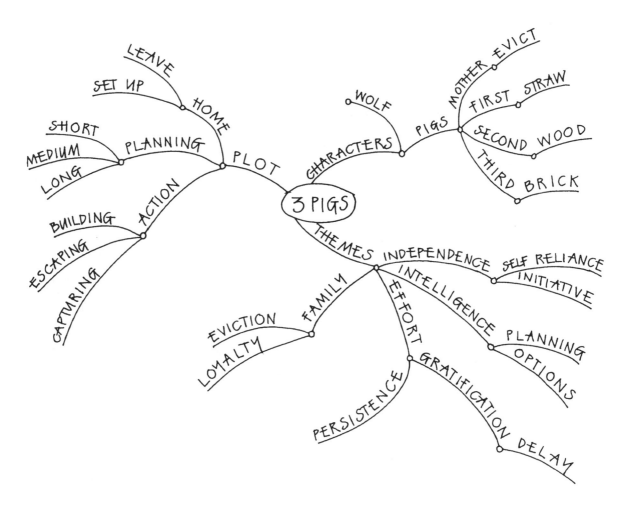

prompt questions

- What is the meaning behind this content?
- How can I make sense of this?
- What is the writer really saying?
- What are the main points?
- How can I summarise this?
- How can I see what he is saying?

how to introduce it to students

You can introduce model maps to students from a very early age. Many nurseries are using model maps with children to introduce and develop new topics. The nursery children themselves start model mapping by drawing links between key words that can be supported by images or symbols.

There are many strategies you can use to introduce model maps:

- Start with a fully completed map and talk it through.
- Use a partially completed map, with some branches having no key words, which you use as a sort of cloze procedure exercise (filling in the gaps).
- Collect all the information a class has about a new topic, before you have given your input about it, in a random list of key words (their prior knowledge). Negotiate with your students the best groupings of these words. Map them out.
- Build up a map collaboratively with students as you add more information.
- Give students the main branches, allotting one branch to each group to research and report back to the whole class. Construct the complete map.

closely related visual tools

You will find that tree diagrams, concept maps and clustering most closely relate to model maps.

	Similarities	Differences
tree diagrams	Structurally, tree diagrams are exactly the same as model maps, with their hierarchical breakdown of categories.	Tree diagrams do not radiate from the centre but stem from the top down. The lines in a tree diagram are drawn straight, rather than forming organic arcs as in model maps.
concept maps	The hierarchical and connected nature of the content is made visually clear.	Concept maps are drawn from the top down, while model maps radiate from the centre. The actual nature of the relationships between the key words is made more explicit in concept maps through the use of propositional statements.
clustering	The interconnected nature of the content is used as a stimulus for generating more novel and expanded connections.	There is no attempt to show the hierarchical relationship between the links in clustering diagrams.

7 concept map® SVT

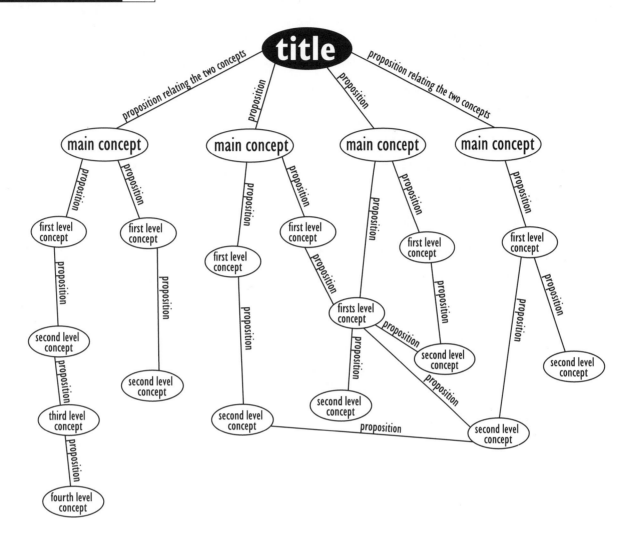

what it is

A concept map, like a model map, reveals the organisational structure of the content of any topic under focus. The content is organised hierarchically. Relationships between the separate items of the content are explained through propositional statements.

why it has this name

The items that make up a concept map and the relationships between them represent a schema or overall concept of the topic under study. A concept map is, therefore, a graphic display of the overall concept and the organisation of its constituent concepts.

other names

Concept maps are also known as:

- semantic networks
- concept webs
- webbing maps
- knowledge maps.

how to make it

To make a concept map, follow these steps.

1 List all the elements, or concepts, of the topic using, perhaps, sticky notes.

2 Group the sticky notes into rough categories based on the main concepts.

3 Rank order the sticky notes into a hierarchical order, in descending scale of importance for each category.

4 Draw out the chosen location of the elements on to paper.

5 Tidy up the elements by capturing them within a drawn ellipse (or rectangle).

6 Draw links between the elements.

7 Identify the nature of each links between elements.

8 Write down these linking relationships as propositional statements along the lines themselves.

9 All links that go downwards are taken to be read in that direction. If a link flows upwards, or sideways, an arrow is drawn to identify such a change of direction.

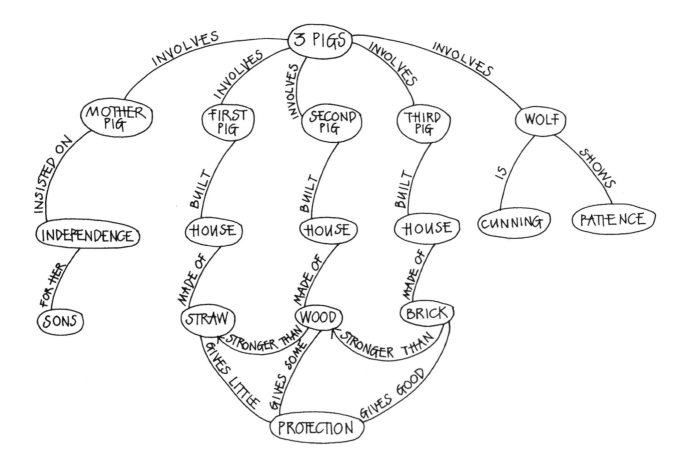

benefits

Concept maps enable you to explain fully the conceptual organisation of any topic. Put another way, they reveal the very knowledge structure of the topic itself. Through this transparent display of knowledge, a fundamental understanding of the topic can be achieved. Consequently, concept maps are a very rigorous way of assessing a student's conceptual grasp of any topic. Not only are the constituent concepts made apparent, but also the relationships between them.

when to use it

Use a concept map when you want to:

- understand a topic

- explore your understanding of a new topic

- check out, or test, your understanding

- demonstrate your understanding to someone else.

prompt questions

- What do I understand of this topic?

- What meaning can I make of this topic?

- What is the conceptual structure of this topic?

- How can I best explain this topic to someone else?

how to introduce it to students

As with model maps, there are many strategies you can use to introduce concept maps:

- Start with a fully completed map and talk it through.

- Use a partially completed map, with some links having no propositional statements, which you use as a prompt for discussion.

- Collect all the information a class has about a new topic, before you have given your input about it, in a random list of key words (their prior knowledge). Negotiate with your students the best groupings of these words. Map them out.

- Build up a map collaboratively with students as you add more information.

- Give students the main concepts, allotting one concept for each group to research and report back to the whole class. Construct the complete map by establishing the links between concepts.

closely related visual tools

You will find that model maps and tree diagrams most closely relate to concept maps.

	Similarities	Differences
concept maps	Model maps and concept maps both graphically represent the structure of a topic in a hierarchical way.	Concept mapping explicitly explains the nature of the relationships between the constituent parts, with propositional statements written along the links.
tree diagrams	Tree diagrams and concept maps both graphically represent the knowledge structure of a topic in a hierarchical way. Both concept maps and tree diagrams start with the main concept at the top and work downwards.	Tree diagrams do not explain the nature of the sub-categorical links with propositional statements, as concept maps do.

8 Vee map SVT

CONCEPTS

METHODS

WORLD VIEW
the overall belief system and knowledge structure that shape the nature of the enquiry

PHILOSOPHY
the beliefs about the nature of knowledge and 'how we know' that guide the enquiry

THEORY
the general principles that guide the enquiry through explanations of what is observed

PRINCIPLES
the statements of relationships between concepts that help to predict future observations

CONSTRUCTS
the ideas that show specific relationships between concepts abstracted from actual events or objects

CONCEPTS
the perceived regularity in events or objects observed

FOCUS QUESTIONS
the questions that serve to focus the enquiry about the events and objects to be observed and studied

VALUE CLAIMS
the statements based on the knowledge claims that assert the value of the enquiry

KNOWLEDGE CLAIMS
the statements that answer the focus question/s and the interpretations of the recorded observations

TRANSFORMATIONS
the visual tools and statistics or other forms of organisation of the recorded observations

RECORDS
the observations made and recorded from the events and objects studied

EVENTS & OBJECTS
the description of the events and objects to be observed and studied in order to answer the focus question

what it is

A Vee map is a way of showing and integrating the theoretical and methodological elements in research. The theoretical issues are ranked in order of abstraction, as are the methodological activities. Vee maps were originally devised by Joseph Novak (1998).

why it has this name

The diagram makes a V shape.

other names

There are no other names used for Vee maps.

how to make it

To make a Vee map it is best if you are competent in constructing concept maps. When you are, follow these steps.

1 Construct a focus question relating to the topic to be observed and studied.

2 Answer the focus question with regard to the different conceptual levels.

3 Answer the focus question with regard to the different methodological levels.

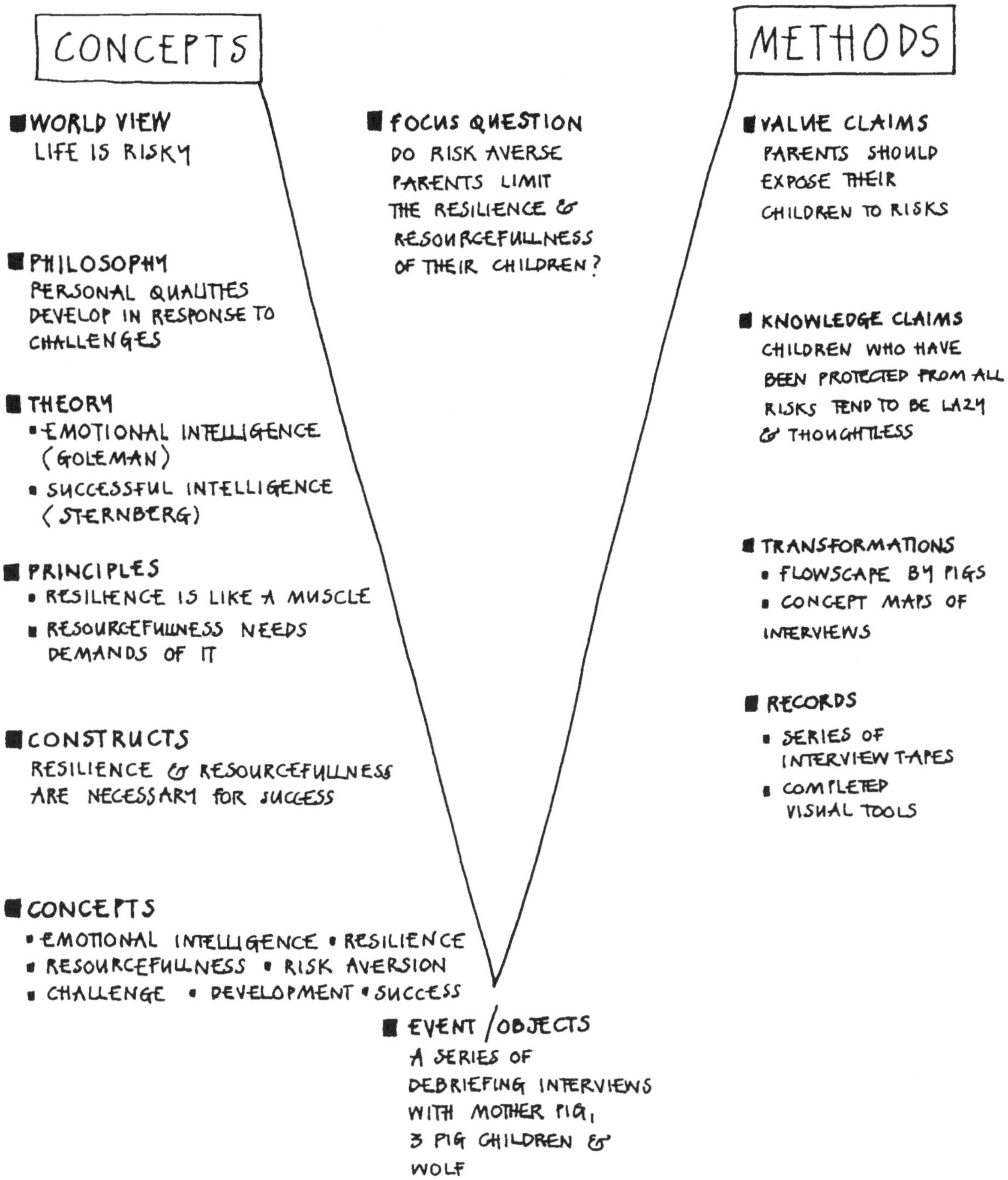

CONCEPTS   METHODS

■ WORLD VIEW
LIFE IS RISKY

■ PHILOSOPHY
PERSONAL QUALITIES
DEVELOP IN RESPONSE TO
CHALLENGES

■ THEORY
• EMOTIONAL INTELLIGENCE
  (GOLEMAN)
• SUCCESSFUL INTELLIGENCE
  (STERNBERG)

■ PRINCIPLES
• RESILIENCE IS LIKE A MUSCLE
• RESOURCEFULNESS NEEDS
  DEMANDS OF IT

■ CONSTRUCTS
RESILIENCE & RESOURCEFULNESS
ARE NECESSARY FOR SUCCESS

■ CONCEPTS
• EMOTIONAL INTELLIGENCE • RESILIENCE
• RESOURCEFULNESS • RISK AVERSION
• CHALLENGE • DEVELOPMENT • SUCCESS

■ FOCUS QUESTION
DO RISK AVERSE
PARENTS LIMIT
THE RESILIENCE &
RESOURCEFULLNESS
OF THEIR CHILDREN?

■ EVENT / OBJECTS
A SERIES OF
DEBRIEFING INTERVIEWS
WITH MOTHER PIG,
3 PIG CHILDREN &
WOLF

■ VALUE CLAIMS
PARENTS SHOULD
EXPOSE THEIR
CHILDREN TO RISKS

■ KNOWLEDGE CLAIMS
CHILDREN WHO HAVE
BEEN PROTECTED FROM ALL
RISKS TEND TO BE LAZY
& THOUGHTLESS

■ TRANSFORMATIONS
• FLOWSCAPE BY PIGS
• CONCEPT MAPS OF
  INTERVIEWS

■ RECORDS
• SERIES OF
  INTERVIEW TAPES
• COMPLETED
  VISUAL TOOLS

benefits

Vee diagrams help you to see how:

- there is a hierarchy to the theoretical frameworks that shape our thinking
- there is a need to judge the validity and reliability of our methodology
- our concepts, principles and theories match
- gathering different records and transforming data for display is dependent on the focus question
- our knowledge claims are shaped by our concepts, principles and theories
- our world view ultimately motivates the nature of our research
- your thinking differs from others', if you are able to compare your Vee map with theirs.

when to use it

Use a Vee map when you want to:

- conduct some research
- understand what shapes the nature and orientation of the research
- ensure coherence between your previously unstated theories and your methodology.

prompt questions

- What are the best questions to ask?
- What are the key concepts?
- What methods of enquiry best suit the research?
- What are the major knowledge claims?
- What are the value claims?

how to introduce it to students

Firstly, ensure that students are comfortable, confident and competent with concept maps. Next:

- use an experimental activity to stimulate students' questions
- discuss these questions and agree on one to be the agreed focus question
- go through the theoretical positions as a result of addressing the question
- go through and decide the most appropriate methodology in order to conduct the research.

Finally, when reading other research papers, ask these five questions:

- What are the telling questions?
- What are the major concepts?
- What methods of enquiry are used?
- What are the major knowledge claims?
- What are the value claims?

closely related visual tools

You will find that concept maps most closely relate to Vee map.

	Similarities	Differences
concept maps	Concept maps and Vee maps dissect the concepts and their inter-relationships.	The formats are completely different – in Vee maps, conceptual relationships are not graphically linked. Vee maps are specifically related to research issues in a way that concept maps are not.

differential visual tools DVT

DVT
Ranking order

DVT
Venn diagram

DVT
Double bubble map

DVT
Priorities grid

DIFFERENTIAL
DVT
VISUAL TOOLS

DVT
Matrix

DVT
Continuum line

DVT
Force field analysis

DVT
Bridge map

DVT
SWOT analysis

purpose

The main purposes of the visual tools in this category are to:

■ identify the similarities between two topics or ideas

■ identify the differences between two topics or ideas

■ compare and contrast elements related to two items or topics.

I Venn diagram DVT

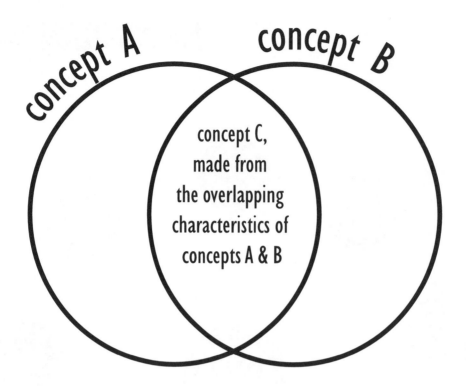

what it is

A Venn diagram is a graphic representation of the overlapping characteristics, or membership, of sets (or groups).

why it has this name

It is called a Venn diagram because it was invented by nineteenth century mathematician called Venn.

other names

Venn diagrams are not known by other names.

how to make it

To make a Venn diagram (with only two sets), follow these steps.

1 Construct a target map of a topic (page 150)

2 Construct a target map for a second topic

3 Draw two overlapping circles, representing the two content circles from the two target maps.

4 Identify which characteristics or elements of the two target maps (now known as sets) are common to both.

5 Write these down in the overlapping section of the two circles.

6 Write down the characteristics, or elements, related solely to one or other of the two sets in the respective circles where they do not overlap.

benefits

Venn diagrams are well known from work in mathematics. They are known from early work in infants schools. Because of their familiarity, you can easily incorporate the notions of commonality represented in this graphic format. This format allows a clear visual understanding of the notions of being both within a boundary of one concept and yet also being within a boundary of another.

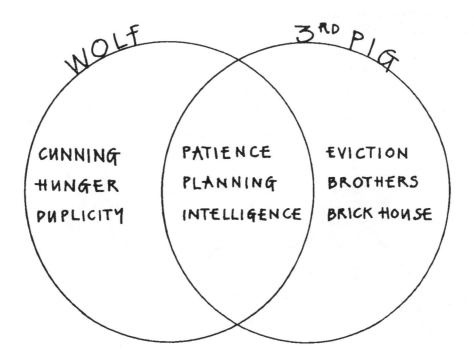

when to use it

Use a Venn diagram can when you want to:

- identify commonalities between and within two separate topics or issues

- illustrate the similarities and differences between two issues.

prompt questions

- In what ways are these two issues, or topics, similar?

- In what ways are these two issues, or topics, different?

- How are these two separate concepts related?

- What do these two sets of characteristics have in common?

how to introduce it to students

You can:

- ask pairs of students to construct a target map for an issue directed by you

- put pairs of students together and ask them, using sticky notes, to explore the similarities and differences between their two target maps by agreeing which characteristics, if any, they have in common

- ask these groups of students to present their findings to another group as a Venn diagram, explaining and justifying the locations of the sticky notes.

closely related visual tools

You will find that double bubble maps and matrix diagrams most closely relate to Venn diagrams.

	Similarities	Differences
double bubble maps	Both formats identify the similarities between two separate topics.	Each use a different graphic format to illustrate the similarities. Double bubble maps limit themselves to comparing two topics, whereas Venn diagrams can compare two or more.
matrix diagrams	Both formats identify the similarities between two separate topics.	Each use a different graphic format to illustrate the similarities.

2 double bubble map DVT

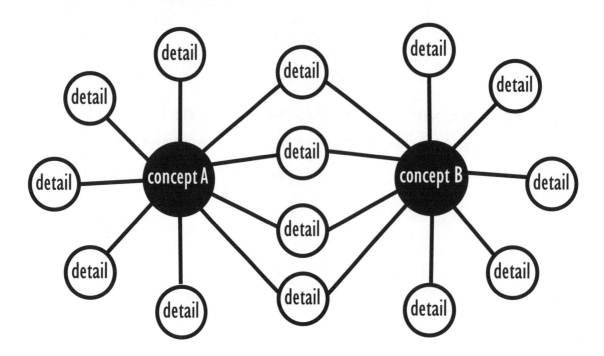

what it is

A double bubble map is the joining together of two single bubble maps.

why it has this name

The title describes the two-bubble formation.

other names

Double bubble maps are not known other names.

how to make it

To make a double bubble map, follow these steps.

1   Construct two separate bubble maps for the two issues or topics you want to compare and contrast.

2   Place the two bubble maps side by side.

3   Study the radiant characteristics of each topic and note any that are identical.

4   Next, identify any that are similar but which use a different wording.

5   Redraw the two bubbles on one sheet of paper, placing the similar characteristics between the two bubbles.

6   Join these similarities to both central bubbles.

7   Place the non-similar characteristics in radiant fashion, as in the original bubbles.

benefits

Double bubble maps are very useful in identifying commonalities between two concepts or topics. They do so seamlessly after the construction of separate bubble maps. Their graphic format is also less subject to possible confusion than the overlapping areas of Venn diagrams (students sometimes consider the size of the overlap of the circles to represent the degree of overlap of the concepts).

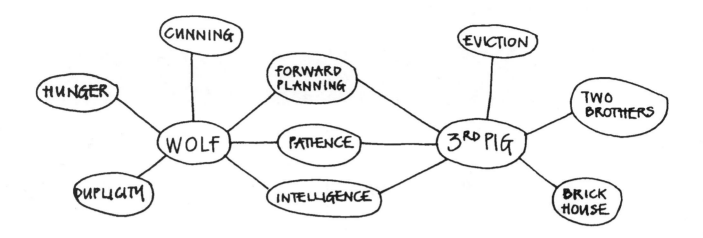

when to use it

Use a double bubble map when you want to:

- identify commonalities between and within two separate topics or issues
- illustrate the similarities and differences between two issues.

prompt questions

- In what ways are these two issues, or topics, similar?
- In what ways are these two issues, or topics, different?
- How are these two separate concepts related?
- What do these two sets of characteristics have in common?

how to introduce it to students

You can:

- ask individuals to construct a bubble map of a topic given by you
- get the students, in pairs, to construct a double bubble map from their two separate bubble maps using the technique described above.

closely related visual tools

You will find that Venn diagrams and matrix diagrams most closely relate to double bubble maps.

	Similarities	Differences
Venn diagrams	Both formats identify the commonalities between two separate topics.	Each use a different graphic format to illustrate the commonalities.
matrix diagrams	Both formats identify the commonalities between two separate topics.	Each use a different graphic format to illustrate the commonalities. Double bubble maps are limited to comparing two topics, whereas matrix diagrams can compare accommodate many more.

3 matrix diagram DVT

	detail one	detail two	detail three	detail four	detail five
A	◆		◆	◆	
B	◆	◆			◆
C		◆	◆		◆
D	◆		◆		

what it is

A matrix diagram is a chart that tabulates characteristics of two or more topics for direct comparison and contrast.

why it has this name

It is called a matrix because it is drawn as a table in which information is located, and can be read from, both horizontal and vertical axes.

other names

Matrix diagrams are also known as:

- tables
- decision charts
- compare-and-contrast charts
- gathering grids.

how to make it

To make a matrix diagram, follow these steps.

1 Identify the characteristics of the two (or more) topics to be compared.

2 List these characteristics along a horizontal axis at the top of the table.

3 Put the titles of the two topics along the vertical axis.

4 Where the horizontal reading of one topic row intersects with the column for each characteristic, identify with a tick if that characteristic is related to that topic.

5 Repeat this process for the second topic row.

6 Analyse the ticks to show how many of the characteristics are common to both topics.

benefits

Matrix diagrams concisely summarise a great deal of information onto one graphic format. This simplification of information encourages a grasp of the detail involved without risk of confusion or of feeling overwhelmed. Because of the tabulation of characteristics, matrix diagrams are frequently used as tools for decision making.

	1ST PIG	2ND PIG	3RD PIG
STRAW HOUSE	✓		
WOODEN HOUSE		✓	
BRICK HOUSE			✓

when to use it

Use a matrix diagram when you want to:

■ identify commonalities between and within two separate topics or issues

■ illustrate the similarities and differences between two issues.

prompt questions

■ In what ways are these two issues, or topics, similar?

■ In what ways are these two issues, or topics, different?

■ How are these two separate concepts related?

■ What do these two sets of characteristics have in common?

how to introduce it to students

You can:

■ use double bubble maps already constructed by pairs of students to identify the characteristics of two topics or issues

■ give the students ready-prepared blank template matrix diagrams

■ ask the students to transfer the information from their double bubble maps onto the matrix diagram templates

■ ask pairs of students to check the work of other pairs, looking for inconsistencies

■ ask the students to judge the relative merits of each form of diagram.

closely related visual tools

You will find that Venn diagrams and double bubble maps most closely relate to matrix diagrams:

	Similarities	Differences
Venn diagrams	Both formats identify the commonalities between two separate topics. Both formats can accommodate more than two topics for comparison.	Each use a different graphic format to illustrate the commonalities.
double bubble maps	Both formats identify the commonalities between two separate topics.	Each use a different graphic format to illustrate the commonalities. Double bubble maps are limited to comparing two topics, whereas matrix diagrams can compare accommodate many more.

4 force field analysis DVT

what it is
A force field analysis is a way of showing graphically the relative power of 'forces' that can either help or hinder change.

why it has this name
The visual display shows the analysis of the opposing 'forces' within a designated field of operation.

other names
Force field analysis is not known by other names.

how to make it
To construct a force field analysis, follow these steps.

1 Define the current situation within the scope of your focus.

2 Define the situation you want in the future – now your target situation. Write a brief summary of this target at the top of the page, and draw a vertical line downwards, dividing the page in two.

3 Think of all the forces that might be considered to be 'driving forces' – those that will take you towards your target situation.

4 Write these down on the left hand side of the vertical divide with an arrow for each force pointing towards the divide.

5 Think of all the forces that might resist your target situation.

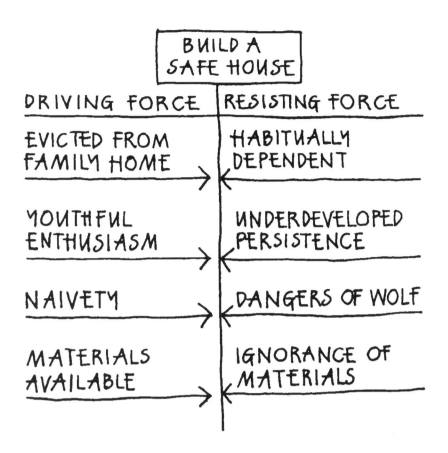

6 Write these 'resisting forces' down on the right hand side with an arrow for each pointing towards the divide, matching up any possible links between driving and resisting forces.

7 As a development, you can demonstrate the relative strength of each force by drawing the arrows in proportion to the perceived strength.

benefits
Force field analysis allows you to:

- search systematically all forces that might impinge on your action
- reduce anxiety by seeing and containing on paper worries about the future
- consider the potential situation facing others (when constructed from their point of view).

when to use it
Use a force field analysis when you want to:

- analyse the present situation
- make objective your subjective hunches about the future
- prepare for an action plan.

prompt questions
- What will drive us towards our target?
- What might restrain us from achieving our target?
- How do driving and resisting forces line up against each other?

how to introduce it to students

You can:

- get groups of students to identify something they would like to change in the school
- direct them to describe in detail their ideal situation, even to draw it
- ask them to brainstorm the forces that will help them to achieve their target
- ask them to brainstorm the forces that might restrain them from achieving the target
- direct them to match opposing forces
- pair up groups of students
- direct groups to present their force field analysis, requesting any additions from their audience.

closely related visual tools

You will find that SWOT analyses most closely relate to a force field analysis.

	Similarities	Differences
SWOT analyses	Both tools identify situations that are judged to be positive or negative with regard to achieving a target.	A SWOT analysis breaks both the positive and negative forces into two sub-categories, while the force field analysis matches up the opposing forces. Each uses a different graphic format.

5 SWOT analysis DVT

what it is

A SWOT analysis is a way of graphically representing the various positive and negative aspects of projects or organisations.

why it has this name

The name SWOT includes the major components of the tool – the focus on Strengths, Weaknesses, Opportunities and Threats.

other names

SWOT analyses are not known by other names.

how to make it

To construct a SWOT analysis, follow these steps.

1   Write the name of the focus of the analysis in the centre of the diagram.

2   Identify strengths – those positive characteristics and behaviours that are related to the topic under focus – and write them down in the appropriate quadrant.

3   Identify weaknesses – those negative characteristics and behaviours that are related to the topic under focus – and write them down in the appropriate quadrant.

4   Identify opportunities – those external events, openings and changes that are positive – and write them down in the appropriate quadrant.

5   Identify threats – those external events, openings and changes that are negative – and write them down in the appropriate quadrant.

benefits

SWOT analyses allow you to:

■   become clear about the aspects that can hinder or help your cause

■   stimulate discussion about perceptions regarding the future.

STRENGTHS	WEAKNESSES
• FAMILY BONDS • YOUTHFUL ENTHUSIASM	• NAIVETY • IGNORANCE OF MATERIALS • LAZINESS
OPPORTUNITIES **(3 PIGS)** THREATS	
• CREATE NEIGHBOURHOOD WOLF WATCH • INVENT NEW SECURITY WARNING SYSTEM	• WOLF'S CUNNING

when to use it

Use a SWOT analysis when you want to:

- summarise the various forces that might affect the achievement of the target
- prepare an action plan.

prompt questions

- How good is the project?
- Where are the project's weaknesses?
- What outside forces might affect the success of the project?

how to introduce it to students

You can:

- split the class up into four groups, allotting one each to 'strengths', 'weaknesses', 'opportunities' and 'threats'
- direct each group to brainstorm items for that section, regarding an agreed contentious or motivating project, and write them down
- pair up the 'strengths group' with the 'weaknesses' group and ask them to compare notes and suggest additions or changes to the other group
- pair up the 'opportunities' and 'threats' groups in the same way
- pair up the 'strengths' and 'opportunities' groups, asking them to brainstorm more items for both foci
- pair up the 'weaknesses' and 'threats' groups, asking them to double check to see if any items have been left out
- bring together the work of the four groups, as a whole class activity
- ask participants to compare the experiences of working solely within a positive boundary (strengths and opportunities) or within a negative one (weaknesses and threats)
- gather views of the limitations and dangers of working solely within one type of thinking.

closely related visual tools

You will find that force field analyses most closely relate to SWOT analyses.

	Similarities	Differences
force field analyses	Both tools identify situations that are judged to be positive or negative with regard to achieving a target.	A SWOT analysis breaks both the positive and negative forces into two sub-categories, while the force field analysis matches up the opposing forces. Each uses a different graphic format.

6 bridge map DVT

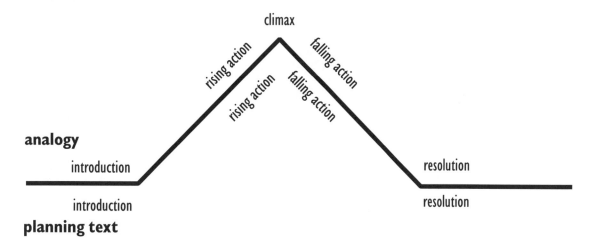

what it is

A bridge map is a graphic display of an extended analogy used to support the structuring (for the author) or understanding (for the reader) of a piece of text.

why it has this name

The development of the analogy (the known story) is depicted by a series of rises and descents (like hump-back bridges) representing the changing rhythm of the plot.

other names

Bridge maps are also known as plot diagrams.

how to make it

To make a bridge map, follow these steps.

1 Think of a story that is similar in many ways to the one you are about to write.

2 Consider the rhythm of this story and depict it as a line with crests representing climaxes in the plot.

3 Write key words representing these significant moments in the plot on top of the corresponding section of the plot line

4 Below the line, write key words representing those significant moments of your own text that will mirror the plot line of the analogy.

benefits

Bridge maps allow you to:

■ use a known story to structure your writing

■ use a known story to understand a piece of reading.

when to use it

Use a bridge map when you want to:

■ encourage creative writing

■ support understanding of difficult or new types of text.

BUILD STRAW HOUSE BLOWN DOWN BY WOLF
COPY OTHER'S WORK CAUGHT CHEATING

EVICTED   SAFETY IN BROTHER'S HOUSE
HOMEWORK SET   DO WORK ALONE & FEEL GOOD

prompt questions

- What kind of story do I want to write?
- What types of plot lines do I find attractive and may be useful to model?
- What does this piece of writing remind me of?

how to introduce it to students

You can:

- introduce students to a plot line you have already constructed for a well known story
- ask the students, as you read the text, to shout out when the story changes rhythm in accordance with the plot line
- direct students to write down the key words of each of these above moments onto their own plot line, copied from the board, or given as a photocopied template
- ask pairs of students to read a new, unknown story whose plot mirrors the rhythm of the known story
- ask the pairs to identify and write down key words representing the moments that mirror the changes in rhythm of the analogy plot line
- put pairs of students together and direct them to compare bridge maps and construct a new, agreed bridge map
- construct a master, whole-class bridge map from the groups' work.

closely related visual tools

There are no closely related visual tools.

7 continuum line DVT

the lower end

the higher end

item C   item A   item E   item D   item B

what it is

A continuum line is a visual display of the spectrum of values of a characteristic under focus and the relative positions of items against this benchmarked range.

why it has this name

The graphic format displays the positions of items within the continuum of the characteristic under focus.

other names

Continuum lines are also known as:

- continuum graphs.

how to make it

To make a continuum line, follow these steps.

1 Identify the two extremes of the characteristic under focus.

2 Draw a horizontal line to represent the distance from one extreme to the other.

3 Mark out regular segments along the continuum line.

4 Place the two extreme examples at the ends of the continuum line.

5 Place the other examples along the continuum line in accordance with the marked out measures between the two ends.

benefits

Continuum lines allow you to:

- arrive at a new perspective of the items being compared
- create a criterion for judgement – that is, make explicit the measure against which you are judging the items placed in the continuum.

STRENGTH OF MATERIALS

| STRAW | WOOD | BRICK |
| LEAST | | MOST |

when to use it

Use a continuum line when you want to:

- assess the reasons given for judging the relative merits of certain characteristics
- more objective in making judgements
- understand how judgements are made.

prompt questions

- How extreme is this?
- Is this normal?
- What is the relative strength of this?

how to introduce it to students

You can:

- find out the heights of the tallest and shortest students
- draw a line representing this range
- calculate the difference in centimetres between the two extreme heights
- mark out the continuum line at regular intervals in relation to the centimetre range
- ask students to identify and record their places on the continuum line
- transfer this new skill to unfamiliar, more abstract characteristics.

closely related visual tools

You will find that ranking lists most closely relate to continuum lines.

	Similarities	Differences
ranking lists	Both rank items with respect to a particular characteristic.	Continuum lines show the relative positions of the items both in relation to each other and also in relation to the continuum itself. Ranking lists display only the position of the items in relation to each other.

8 priorities grid DVT

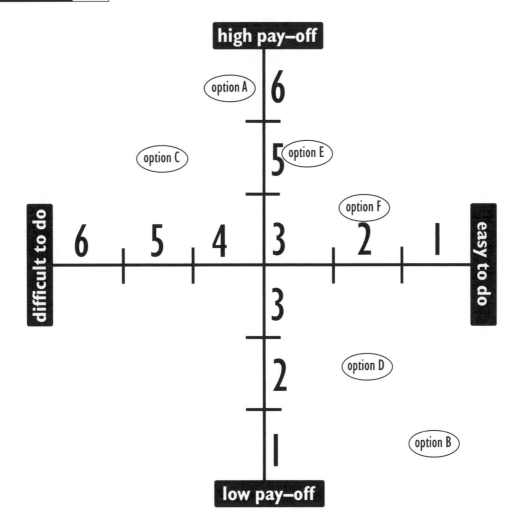

what it is

A priorities grid is a visual tool for decision making that displays the relative pay-off and ease of implementation of several options.

why it has this name

The visual display of judgements is structured around four priority quadrants.

other names

Priority grids are not known by other names.

how to make it

To make a priority grid, follow these steps.

1 Draw out two perpendicular continuum lines, dissecting one another in the middle.

2 Mark out each line into six sections.

3 Label the vertical line 'high pay-off' at the top, and 'low pay-off' at the bottom.

4 Label the horizontal line 'difficult to do' to the left, and 'easy to do' to the right.

5 Take each possible course of action in turn and assess it in relation to the two continuum lines.

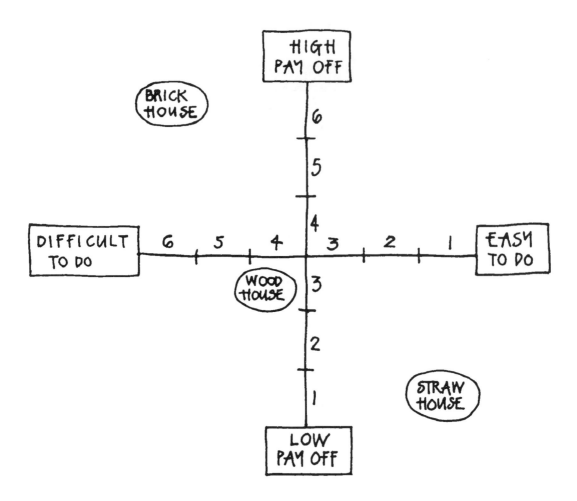

6 Using a sticky note to represent that option, place it in accordance with the judgements made in (5).

7 Repeat the process for the other possible courses of action.

8 Move the sticky notes around until you are happy that they best represent your views and judgements.

9 Transfer the information on the sticky notes by writing the options onto the grid itself.

benefits

Priorities grids allow you to:

- consider clearly the two main distinctions that influence decision making

- keep track of the discussion among team members when making decisions

- force team members to justify their judgements regarding the two distinctions.

when to use it

Use a priorities grid when you want to:

- illuminate the thinking behind the 'delayed gratification' of mature and positive actions within PSHE contexts

- support students in constructing personal study, or life, plans

- bring history lessons alive by considering the options open to, and the decisions made by, historical figures

- identify with literary figures by introducing possible alternative plots dependent on different choices made.

prompt questions

- What is the best course of action we can take?

- What are the relative strengths and weaknesses of each option?

- What is the option we must take, and why?

how to introduce it to students

You can:

- consider a recent showing of a popular soap on television

- identify several difficult decisions that characters had to take

- assign a character to a pair of students

- ask the pairs to complete a priorities grid for their character, analysing the decision options available from the character's perspective on the situation and the future

- ask the pairs then to construct another priorities grid from their own perspective, having seen the outcome of the character's decision

- arrange for pairs of students to explain their two priorities grids to another pair.

closely related visual tools

You will find that continuum lines most closely relate to priority grids.

	Similarities	Differences
continuum lines	Both use the visual display of a continuum.	Continuum lines only work within one dimension. Continuum lines are not specifically designed to aid decision making.

9 ranking order DVT

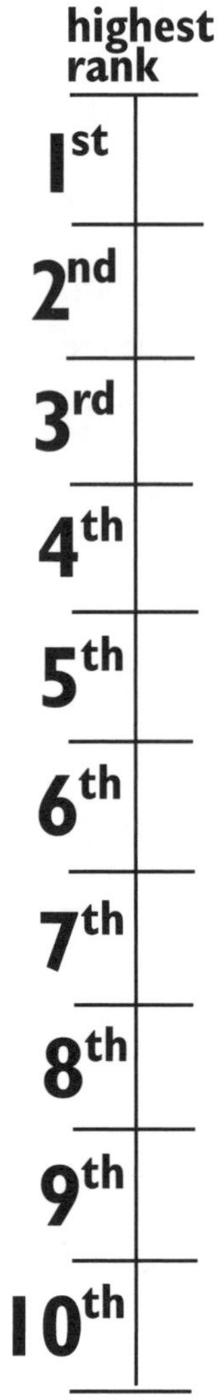

highest
rank

1st

2nd

3rd

4th

5th

6th

7th

8th

9th

10th

what it is

A ranking order is a list of ranked items.

why it has this name

The items are ranked in order of value, with respect to a chosen characteristic.

other names

Ranking orders are also known as:

■ ranking lists.

how to make it

To make a ranking order, follow these steps.

1 Consider and agree on the criterion, or characteristic, against which the items, people or events will be judged and ranked.

2 Write the name of the items, people or events onto separate sticky notes.

3 Place the sticky notes in a ranking order.

4 Review and reshuffle the sticky notes as required.

5 Write down the agreed ranking order.

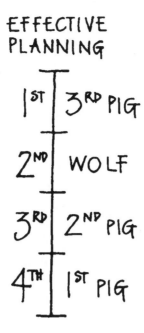

benefits

Ranking orders allow you to:

- make evaluations against a tightly defined criterion
- make alternative evaluations of the same content against a different criterion.

when to use it

Ranking orders can be used when you want to:

- extract information from a mass of text regarding a single criterion
- summarise performance or characteristics.

prompt questions

- Who has the most/least of this quality?
- How well did they do?
- What do we think of these?

how to introduce it to students

You can:

- ask your students to place themselves in a line according to height
- explain that they have just created a ranking order in relation to the criterion of height
- continue this process by looking at different criteria on which to base a ranking order – age, distance from home to school, and so on – gradually addressing more abstract characteristics.

closely related visual tools

You will find that continuum lines most closely relate to ranking order.

	Similarities	Differences
continuum lines	Both rank items with respect to a particular characteristic.	Continuum lines show the relative positions of the items both in relation to each other and also in relation to the continuum itself. Ranking lists display only the position of the items in relation to each other.

representational visual tools RVT

---

purpose

The main purposes of the visual tools in this category are to:

- illustrate key surface physical features
- reveal hidden physical structures
- highlight details
- project a variety of visual perspectives
- identify key aspects of action
- represent a simplified version of reality.

1 picture RVT

what it is

A picture is a two dimensional representation of reality.

why it has this name

It is called a picture because it differs from more stylised, conceptual diagrams.

other names

Pictures are also known as:

- drawings
- sketches.

how to draw picture

To make a picture, decide whether you are going to:

- let your imagination free
- follow what you eyes see
- draw your thoughts.

benefits

Pictures allow you to:

- show what you want to communicate
- summarise a situation concisely
- represent several concepts
- stimulate thinking.

when to use it

Use a pictures when you want to:

- see what you are thinking
- stimulate creative writing
- focus discussion.

prompt questions

- What does that look like?
- How would others see it?

how to introduce it to students

To introduce pictures to students as vehicles for thinking, you can:

- ask students questions about the motives, causes and consequences of what the picture is suggesting
- ask students to draw their fears or hopes, or other concepts.

closely related visual tools

You will find that cross sections most closely relate to pictures.

	Similarities	Differences
cross sections	Both are visual representations of physical reality.	Pictures represent the surface, exterior reality, while cross sections represent the internal, hidden structures and features.

2 cross section RVT

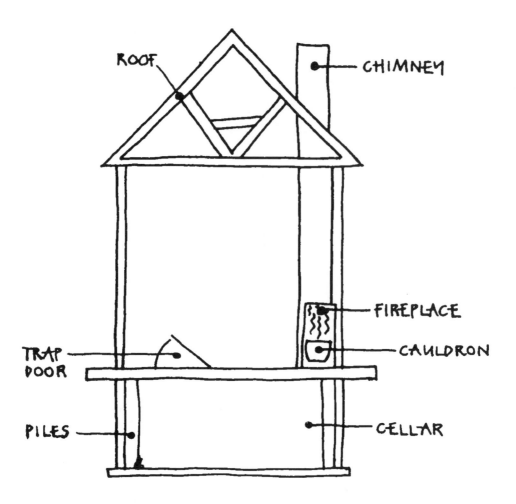

what it is

A cross section is an interior view of something physical.

why it has this name

It is called a cross section because it displays what would be visible if the physical item were 'cut across'.

other names

Cross sections are not known by other names.

how to make it

To draw a cross section, follow these steps.

1 List the constituent parts of an object, starting from the outside layer and gradually travelling deeper into the core of it and out the other side.

2 Draw the outside shape of the object under study.

3 Consider the next word on your list and imagine its outline and depth in relation to the outside layer – then draw it.

4 Continue this process until you have reached the end of your list.

5 Using arrows, label clearly the features you have drawn.

benefits

Cross sections reveal what is normally hidden and, therefore, enable you to:

- analyse the object
- discuss the constituent parts of the object
- understand how the object is structured
- demonstrate how the object works.

when to use it

Cross sections can be used when you want to:

- clarify what something consists of
- explain the structure of an object
- summarise the constituent parts of an object
- illustrate the working parts of an object

prompt questions

- How does it work?
- Why does it look like this?
- What is inside this?

how to introduce it to students

You can:

- show good examples of cross sections from the variety of children's books now available on the subject
- cut through an orange and show what is revealed.

closely related visual tools

You will find that pictures and diagrams most closely relate to cross sections.

	Similarities	Differences
pictures	Both are visual representations of physical reality.	Pictures represent the surface, exterior reality, while cross sections represent the internal, hidden structures and features.
diagrams	Both use explanatory labels for objects and their parts.	Cross sections always reveal the inner content and structures of objects, while diagrams mostly focus on outer appearances.

3 diagram RVT

FALL DOWN
CHIMNEY

WOLF

INTO
CAULDRON

BOILING
WATER

FIRE

what it is

A diagram is a very stylised, simplified drawing of physical objects.

why it has this name

It is called a diagram as it is halfway between a picture and a word-oriented visual conception. It is a simplified representation of the essential information relating to objects. It is more accurate than a sketch with regard to containing all the important information, but may not be as accurate with regard to scale.

other names

Diagrams are also known as:

- illustrations
- sketches
- schematic drawings.

how to draw a diagram

To draw a diagram, follow these steps.

1 Consider the essential parts of the objects to be illustrated and list them.

2 Draw the basic outlines of the objects – don't worry about the irrelevant detail not listed.

3 Label the parts of the diagram with the list created at the start.

benefits

Diagrams simplify the visual information needed to explain objects and events related to them.

when to use it

Diagrams can be used when you want to:

- explain an action or the parts of an object
- simplify a complex situation
- focus on the essential parts or a process.

prompt questions

- What goes on in this process?
- What are the different parts to this object?

how to introduce it to students

You can:

- carry out a simple action
- ask pairs of students to draw a diagram of the action, using the process described above
- ask pairs of students to compare their diagrams with other pairs, identifying any surplus details or missing information.

closely related visual tools

You will find that pictures most closely relate to diagrams.

	Similarities	Differences
pictures	Both visually represent physical appearances.	Pictures contain more information than is necessary for the visual explanation of a process or an object. Diagrams do not pay regard to objective scale.

4 plan RVT

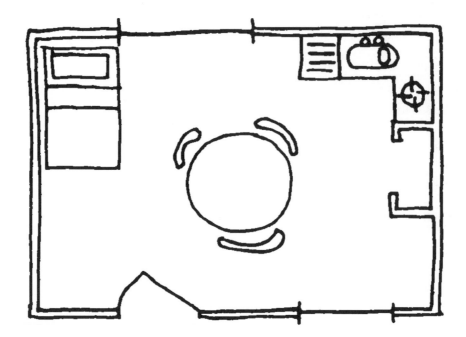

what it is

A plan illustrates the layout or design of something.

why it has this name

It is called a plan because it is drawn from the perspective directly above the object under focus.

other names

Plans are also known as:

- diagrams
- figures
- charts
- arrangements.

how to make it

To draw a plan, follow these steps.

1 Draw the outside boundary of the object as if seen from above.

2 Consider what are the constituent parts of the object and their spatial relationships to the drawn boundary.

3 Draw the plan piece-by-piece, fitting the parts into the overall view.

4 Monitor, as you make your plan, whether the constituent parts are in the correct orientation with respect to the boundary and to each other.

benefits

Plans allow you to:

■ convert a linear experience, as in walking, into a visual gestalt (whole) perception

■ see how things relate to each other spatially.

when to use it

Plans can be used when you want to:

■ record the spatial arrangements of an environment or object

■ find your way around a new environment or object

■ understand the design of objects

■ record the design of objects

■ replicate the manufacture of objects, or construction of environments.

prompt questions

■ Where are we?

■ How can we remember where we were?

■ How is this designed?

■ How can we record where this is?

how to introduce it to students

You can:

■ Use the traditional method of starting with a plan of the students' desks, moving out to the classroom itself, and so on.

■ Map out the journey of a Turtle (robot).

■ Ask a student to direct a blindfolded partner to various parts of the school. The blindfolded student then describes her spatial movements to a third student, who records them as a plan. The plan is later studied and compared to reality.

closely related visual tools

You will find that diagrams most closely relate to plans.

	Similarities	Differences
diagrams	Both visual formats display essential information. Both do not represent the objects as seen by the eye – they are stylised.	Diagrams can view the object from many perspectives, while plans are always drawn as if seen from above.

temporal visual tools TVT

Time line

Story board

Flow chart

GANTT chart

Cycle

---

purpose

The main purposes of the visual tools in this category are to:

■ capture the chronology of events

■ represent the sequence of events.

---

time line TVT

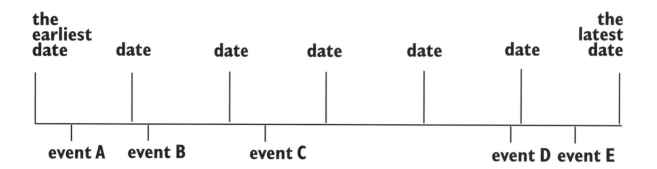

what it is

A time line is a model, or metaphor, of time as if it progressed along a line.

why it has this name

The visual format is literally a line, which represents the progression of time.

other names

Time lines are not known by other names.

how to make it

To construct a time line, follow these steps.

1 Draw a line, either vertical or horizontal.

2 Consider the time scale to be studied.

3 Label the ends of the line in accordance with the end points in time, ensuring that vertical time lines will be read from bottom to top, and horizontal time lines from left to right.

4 Mark out equally the time intervals between the two ends.

5 Plot the events within the time line and write them down in their correct chronological place.

benefits

Time lines enable you to:

■ work with the abstract concept of time in a visual, spatial and, therefore, concrete fashion.

■ compare the different time spans between events

■ understand the passing of time

■ record the sequence of events

■ appreciate the temporal distance between the present and historical events in the past.

0	2yo	4yo	5yo	7yo	9yo
BORN	PIG SCHOOL	EVICTED FROM HOME	BUILT HOUSE	STARTED PIGS' CO-OP.	RETIRED

when to use it

Use a time line when you want to:

- plot historical events

- place historical events in perspective relative to the present

- plot the sequence of events of a process.

prompt questions

- In what order did things happen?

- How long ago was that?

how to introduce it to students

You can:

- start with a time line of the school day

- move on to a time line of the students' lives

- extend students' time lines in relation to the past century

- plot students' time lines in relation to the past two millennia.

closely related visual tools

You will find that plot diagrams most closely relate to time lines.

	Similarities	Differences
plot diagrams	Both map out the sequence of events.	Plot diagrams do not refer to dates. Plot diagrams do not attempt to represent the time intervals between events spatially.

2 flow chart TVT

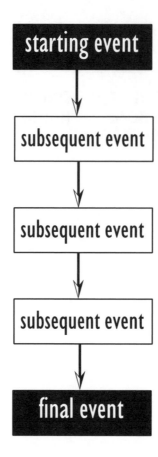

what it is
A flow chart is a visual representation of the sequence of events within a given time frame.

why it has this name
It is called a flow chart because it charts the 'flow' of events.

other names
Flow charts are also known as:

- chains of events
- plot diagrams
- flow maps
- sequence charts.

how to make it
To make a flow chart, follow these steps.

1 Decide whether your flow chart will be read from top to bottom or from left to right.

2 Start with the first action of a process, and write it down inside a box.

3 Decide on the next event, and write it down inside another box joined by an arrow from the first box.

4 Continue until the complete process has been charted.

benefits
Flow charts enable you to:

- represent very clearly the sequence of events.

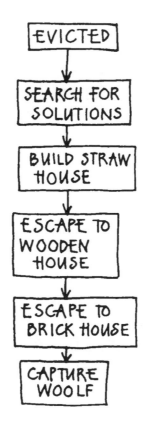

when to use it

Use a flow chart when you want to:

- analyse and determine a sequence of events that is, as yet, unknown
- represent and explain a sequence of events that have taken place.

prompt questions

- In what order did things happen?
- In what order should events be structured?
- How can we best record the stages of this process?

how to introduce it to students

You can:

- ask students, in pairs, to look at the actions involved in making a cup of tea
- ask them to identify the key actions, in sequence, and write them down in boxes joined by arrows
- ask each pair of students to evaluate another pair's flow chart for any superfluous information or omitted actions
- build up this skill by analysing more complex processes.

closely related visual tools

You will find that cycles and algorithms most closely relate to flow charts:

	Similarities	Differences
cycles	Both formats represent a sequence of events.	Flow charts represent a linear sequence of events, while cycles represent a sequence of events that repeat themselves in the same order.
algorithms	Both formats represent a sequence of events.	Flow charts represent a single sequence of events, while algorithms represent multiple sequences depending on responses to questions.

3 cycle TVT

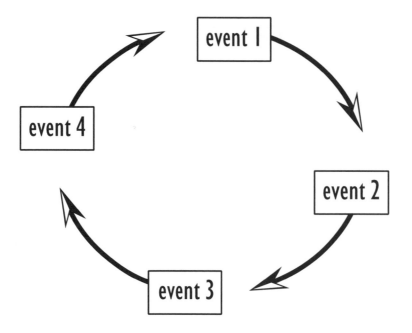

what it is

A cycle diagram is a graphic representation of a chain of events that repeat themselves.

why it has this name

It is called a cycle diagram because the diagram represents a cycle of repeating events.

other names

Cycle diagrams are also known as:

- cyclical maps
- cycle charts.

how to make it

To make a cycle diagram, follow these steps.

1 Starting at any point, list all the actions related to the perceived cycle on to sticky notes.

2 Arrange the sticky notes in circular sequence.

3 Study the proposed cycle, looking for correct sequencing, omitted or irrelevant events.

4 Draw out the cycle, putting each event into a box and joining the boxes by a series of arrows.

benefits

Cycle diagrams enable you to perceive a series of events as being cyclical rather than linear.

when to use it

Use a cycle diagram when you want to:

- understand the reappearance of repeated sequences of events
- explain sequences in the natural world.

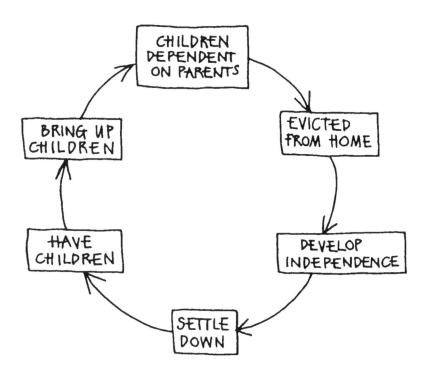

prompt questions

- Why does this seem to happen?

- Is there a pattern to these events?

how to introduce it to students

You can:

- introduce the seasons as a cycle

- ask pairs of students to identify the different events relating to rain (the water cycle)

- ask the pairs to sequence the events into a cycle

- arrange pairs of students to study, comment on and suggest corrections to each other's cycles

- ask the students to draw out their agreed cycle

- move on to more complex cycles.

closely related visual tools

You will find that flow charts and systems diagrams most closely relate to cycle diagrams.

	Similarities	Differences
flow charts	Both formats represent a sequence of events.	Flow charts represent a linear sequence of events, while cycles represent a sequence of events that repeat themselves in the same order.
systems diagrams	Both formats represent the cyclical nature of events.	Cycle diagrams represent a set, unchanging sequence of events, while system diagrams represent developments and consequences of diversions and digressions from the original cycle.

4 story board TVT

1 sketch of first scene	2 sketch of second scene	3 sketch of third scene
4 sketch of fourth scene	5 sketch of fifth scene	6 sketch of sixth scene

what it is

A story board is a pictorial plan and record of dramatic situations that will occur in a narrative, whether in film, theatre, radio or comic strip. In fact, it rather resembles a comic strip itself.

why it has this name

It is called a story board because it encapsulates the dramatic elements of a story.

other names

Story boards are not known by other names.

how to make it

To make a story board, follow these steps.

1   Divide your paper into eight sections.

2   Think of the three main dramatic situations of your proposed narrative and sketch them out (the first, last and middle sections).

3   Spend time considering what might be the intervening scenes in between those sketched out.

4   Start to sketch out those intermediate scenes, completing the sequence of events of your story board.

5   Review, and amend if necessary, the sequence of scenes for coherence and dramatic impact.

benefits

Story boards help stimulate and organise the imagination in the preparation of narrative writing for dramatic purposes.

when to use it

Use a story board when you want to:

■   write a story

■   write a play

■   plan a comic strip.

prompt questions

- What are the main scenes?

- What situations will cause the plot to move on?

- What kinds of dramatic tension can be built into the story?

- What does the story 'look' like?

how to introduce it to students

You can:

- read out a short story and ask the students to construct a four-section story board depicting the main scenes

- ask groups of four students to devise four scenes of a collaborative narrative, and to sketch out one each for subsequent sequencing

- get each group of four to join with another group, and invite each other to interpret their story boards.

closely related visual tools

There are no really closely related visual tools.

5 GANTT chart TVT

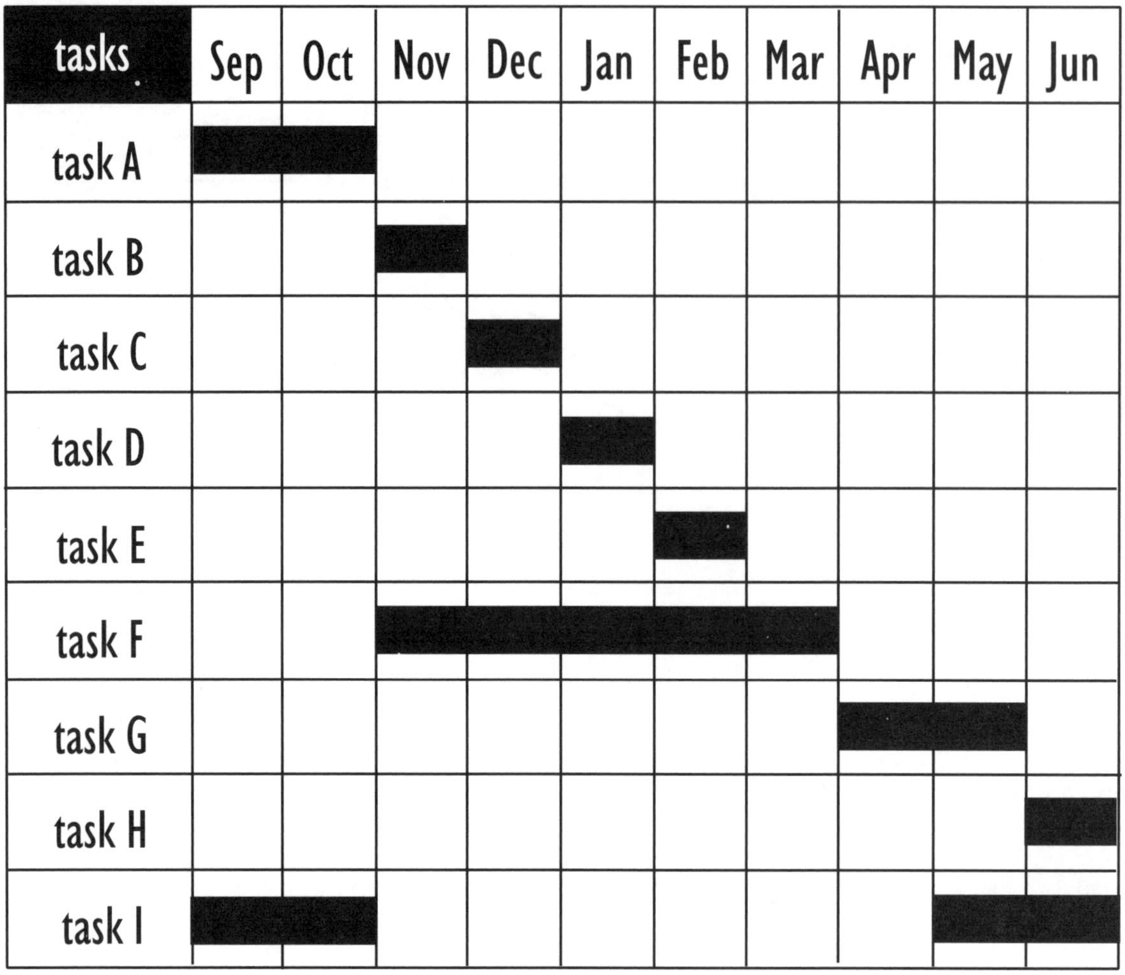

tasks	Sep	Oct	Nov	Dec	Jan	Feb	Mar	Apr	May	Jun
task A	■	■								
task B			■							
task C				■						
task D					■					
task E						■				
task F			■	■	■	■	■			
task G								■	■	
task H										■
task I	■	■							■	■

what it is

A GANTT chart is a table of scheduled action used for planning and subsequent monitoring.

other names

GANTT charts are also known as:

■ task schedules

■ planning tables.

how to make it

To make a GANTT chart, follow these steps.

1 Consider and note all the tasks to be undertaken.

2 Put them into a working sequence (see Critical path analysis, page 224, for help).

3 Evaluate how long each task will take to complete.

4 Place the actions on the GANTT chart, organising the start and end times of each task in relation to the calendar segments (decided by you).

	JAN	FEB	MAR	APR	MAY	JUN	JUL
FIND LOCATION	—						
RESEARCH MATERIALS	—						
OBTAIN MATERIALS	—						
ENLIST SUPPORT	—						
GROUND WORK		—					
BRICK WORK			——	—			
ELECTRICS					—		
PLUMBING					—		
PLASTERING						—	
PAINTING							—

benefits

GANTT charts allow you to:

- identify the breakdown of tasks
- analyse the possible sequences of tasks
- place the tasks into a schedule of work
- monitor the completion of tasks in relation to time plans.

when to use it

Use a GANTT chart when you want to:

- ensure a project is planned, communicated, managed and completed.

prompt questions
- What needs to be done?
- How long will it take?
- Who is doing what?
- When is it taking place?
- How can we know if it going to plan?

how to introduce it to students

You can ask groups of four students to think of a project they want to complete, identifying:

- the tasks involved
- how long the project will take
- which tasks must be completed before others can begin
- who will be responsible for which tasks.

Ask the students to draw out a table with:

- the top horizontal axis to represent the time scale, broken down into weeks
- the vertical axis to represent the titles of the tasks to be completed.

Ask the students to place the agreed information about the project tasks onto the chart.

closely related visual tools

You will find that critical path analyses most closely relate to GANTT charts.

	Similarities	Differences
flow charts	Both rely on the identification of which tasks are dependent on each other – which should be completed before others can start.	Critical path analysis makes clear graphically the core, critical sequence of tasks in relation to more peripheral tasks, while GANTT charts imply this information only. GANTT charts schedule tasks in time, while critical path analysis does not.

casual visual tools CVT

---

purpose

The main purposes of the visual tools in this category are to:

- identify the causes of events
- identify possible alternative causal sequences
- create a baseline for action planning.

1 fishbone diagram CVT

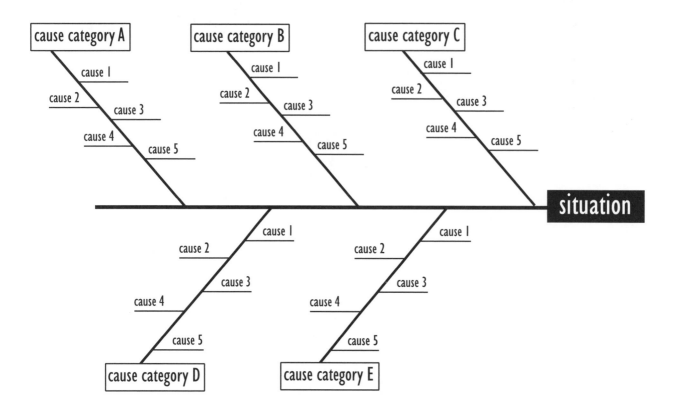

what it is

A fishbone diagram is a graphic representation of the categorisation of causes relating to an event or situation.

why it has this name

It is called a fishbone diagram because the graphic arrangement resembles the structure of the bones on a fish.

other names

Fishbone diagrams are also known as:

- Ishikawa diagrams (after the originator)
- cause and effect analyses.

how to make it

To make a fishbone diagram, follow these steps.

1 Identify a situation whose causes are not known to you.

2 Consider and list all possible causes.

3 Put the contents of the list of causes into categories, possibly using an affinity diagram as a supportive tool (page 157)

4 Draw the fishbone diagram with as many 'bones' as there are categories of causes, and the identified situation to be analysed as the 'head' of the 'fish'.

5 Decide on a title for each category of causes and write it at the end of the relevant bone.

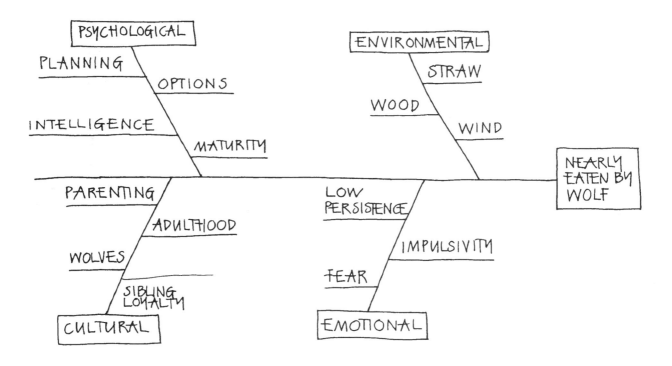

6 Write the causes horizontally on lines (smaller bones) joined to both sides of the appropriate bone.

7 Some causes can be attached to more than one bone/category.

8 If needed, further clarification can be created by asking questions of each cause such as 'what?', 'why?', 'how?' and 'where?'.

benefits

Fishbone diagrams enable you to:

- identify the causes of a given situation
- represent visually the reasons for what is happening
- form the basis for further investigation of causes.

when to use it

Use a fishbone diagram when you want to:

- investigate the causes of historical events
- analyse the causes of physical conditions
- enquire into social and emotional situations that have emerged from circle time.

prompt questions

- What could have caused this?
- What is happening?
- How could this have happened?
- What was the main cause of this situation?

how to introduce it to students

You can:

- choose a dramatic situation from a story well known to the students

- ask pairs of students to think of a list of all possible causes

- ask students, in double pairs, to make an affinity diagram (page 157) to establish categories

- ask them, in groups of eight (four of the original pairs), to compare, exchange and finalise both the categories and causes

- ask them, back in pairs, to draw out the fishbone diagram.

closely related visual tools

You will find that relations diagrams most closely relate to fishbone diagrams.

	Similarities	Differences
cycles	Both are visual answers to questions about causes.	Relations diagrams identify the inter-relationships of causes, while fishbone diagrams do not. Fishbone diagrams categorise causes while relations diagrams do not.

2 relations diagram CVT

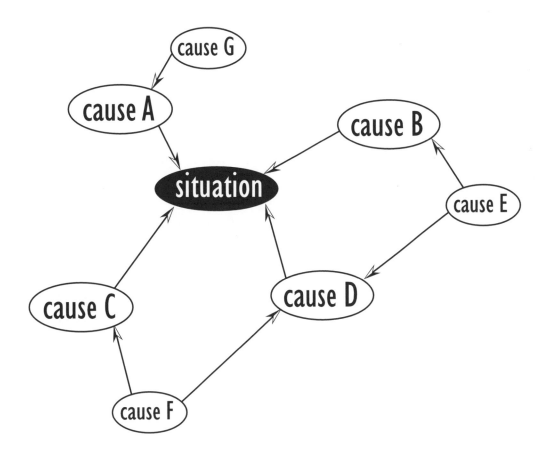

what it is

A relations diagram is a visual method of identifying and representing the inter-relationships of causes, often in a complex pattern.

why it has this name

It is called a relations diagram because the visual format of the diagram illustrates the inter-relations of causes.

other names

Relations diagrams are also known as:

- multi-flow maps
- process mapping.

how to make it

To make a relations diagram, follow these steps.

1 Identify the situation or problem you want analysed.

2 Write it in the middle of the paper.

3 Ask 'why?' regarding the situation.

4 Write down your answers cvn radiant fashion around the centre, as if joined by spokes.

5 Ask 'why?' of each cause, as if they were themselves an effect.

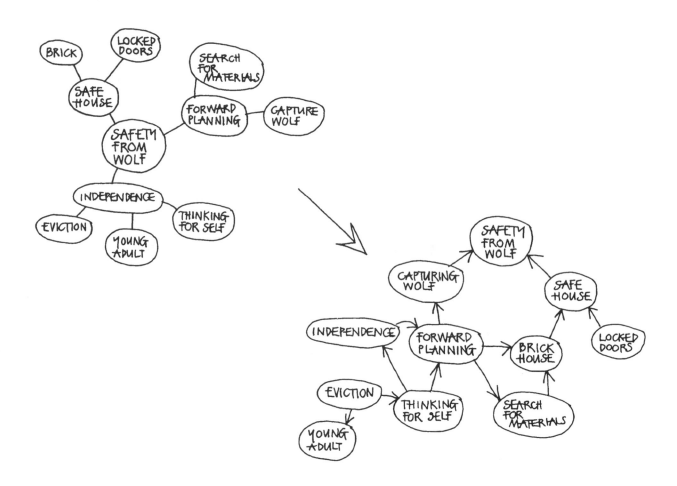

6 Write down the causes in radiant fashion around the primary cause questioned, and join them with lines as described above.

7 Look for cross links between any of the causes and represent the links with lines. Add arrows to represent the flow of causation.

8 Study the diagram, consider and identify graphically which are the root causes.

benefits

Relations diagrams allow you to:

- obtain clarity from apparently complex situations
- appreciate the multi-causal background to particular problems
- observe your reasoning as you create causal links between items on the diagram.

when to use it

Use a relations diagram when you want to:

- understand the reasons for the emergence of difficult situations
- prepare a plan of action to remedy a problem
- consider the complex inter-relationships of causes behind historical events.

prompt questions

- Why is this happening?
- How can we find out how to remedy this problem?

how to introduce it to students

You can:

- identify a current social problem known to the students

- working from the board, OHP or computer projector, ask the students 'why?'

- write down the main answers around the centre title, as described above

- allot one of these causes to each groups of four students

- ask the students to write the cause in the centre of their page, asking of it the question 'why?'

- ask the students to write down their answers in radiant fashion around their primary cause, as you modelled earlier

- gather and write down the groups' work on the original relations diagram you started

- ask the students to make any additions

- encourage the students to spot any cross links between causes and draw in the appropriate linking lines.

closely related visual tools

You will find that fishbone diagrams and flowscapes most closely relate to relations diagrams.

	Similarities	Differences
fishbone diagrams	Both are visual answers to questions about causes.	Relations diagrams identify the inter-relationships of causes, while fishbone diagrams do not. Fishbone diagrams categorise causes while relations diagrams do not.
flowscapes	Both use similar graphic formats to represent the inter-relationships between factors that influence one another.	Relations diagrams focus on actual events while flowscapes focus on perceptions. Each causal link of a relations diagram is constructed piece by piece, while the links of the flowscape are constructed as a final summary of paired relationships made between individual perceptions.

3 critical path analysis CVT

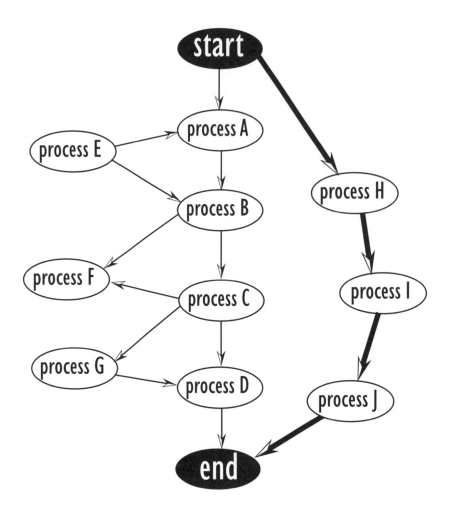

what it is

A critical path analysis is a graphic way of identifying the ordering of tasks according to dependencies.

why it has this name

It is called a critical path analysis because, among many possible sequences of tasks, the core and essential (critical) sequence is identified based on an analysis of which tasks need to be completed before others can start.

other names

Critical path analyses are also known as:

- arrow diagrams
- process decision programme charts
- network diagrams.

how to make it

To construct a critical path analysis, follow these steps.

1 Think of all the tasks to be completed.

2 Evaluate how long each task will take.

3 Write each task on a sticky note and identify any linked tasks in terms of dependencies.

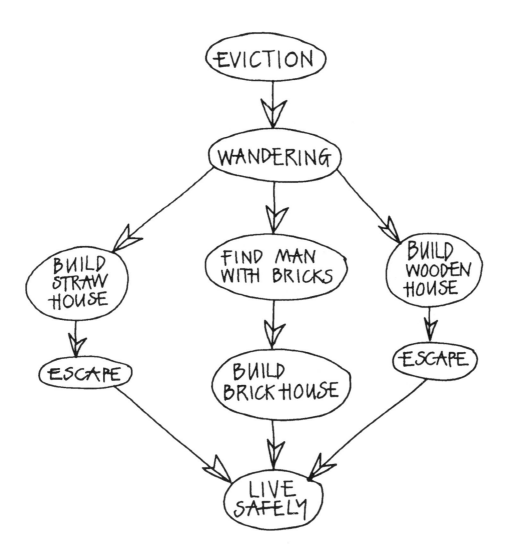

4   Arrange the sticky notes into sequences, joining them with lines.

5   Number the sticky notes in case they move and you forget the sequences.

6   Draw out the sequences, identifying the critical path and other parallel paths – the critical path will take the shortest amount of time to complete.

7   Identify the critical path with a different set of graphic arrows to those used for the parallel paths.

benefits
Critical path analyses allow you to:

- identify the minimum amount of time to complete a project
- organise the most efficient way of sequencing the tasks.

when to use it
Use a critical path analysis when you want to:

- plan a project.

prompt questions
- What does this project entail?
- Which tasks are most important?
- What is the quickest time in which the project can be completed?

how to introduce it to students

You can:

- choose a project such as building a house

- brainstorm the tasks involved

- allot one task to each student, identified with an A4 label

- ask students to find a partner whose task is in some way dependent on their own

- note these groupings, as described above

- agree which group of tasks is the essential, critical one, and which are not

- ask the groups to note down their own and others' tasks, and to sequence them, forming a critical path analysis.

closely related visual tools

You will find that GANTT charts and algorithms most closely relate to critical path analyses.

	Similarities	Differences
GANTT charts	Both rely on the identification of which tasks are dependent on each other – which should be completed before others can start.	Critical path analysis makes clear graphically the core, critical sequence of tasks in relation to more peripheral tasks, while GANTT charts imply this information only. GANTT charts schedule tasks in time, while critical path analysis does not.
algorithms	Both formats identify the route to successful completion of a process among possible alternative or peripheral tasks.	Critical path analysis represents all the tasks to be completed, identified through analysing dependencies, while algorithms represent all possible eventualities from a user's point of view and redirects all diversions back towards the completion of the process.

4 algorithm CVT

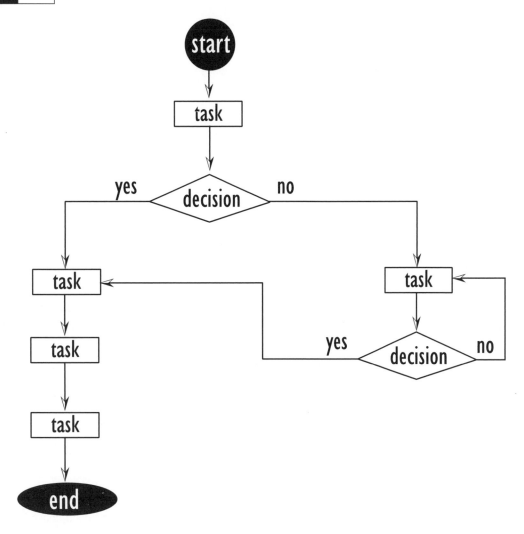

what it is

An algorithm is a graphic format used to represent possible alternative routes through a variety of options.

why it has this name

The word algorithm comes from the name of a ninth century Persian mathematician called al-Kuwarizmi.

other names

Algorithms are also known as:

- decision trees
- flow charts
- tree diagrams
- process mapping.

how to make it

To make construct an algorithm, follow these steps.

1   Decide on a process whose parts you want to analyse.

2   List all the component actions of the process and write each down on a sticky note.

3   Arrange the sticky notes in a sequence, from top to bottom, that mirrors the sequence of actions in the process.

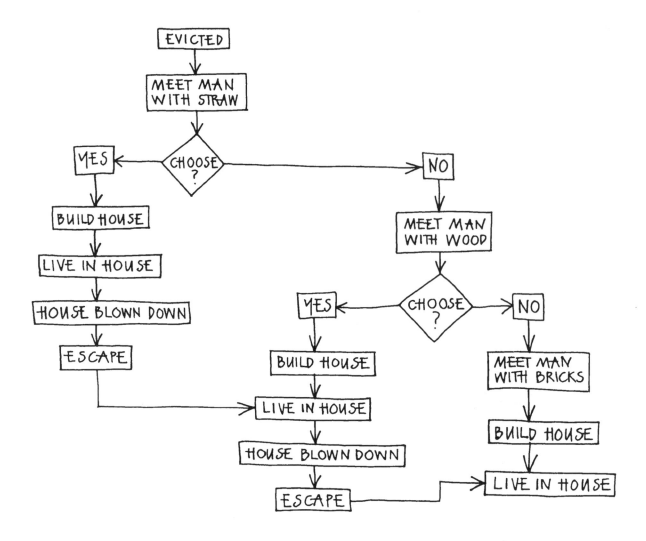

4   Starting from the top, ask yourself questions relating to the necessary conditions of satisfaction for the completion of the first task.

5   If there are conditions needed in order to start the task, write the question down before the task and draw a diamond around it (all questions are framed by diamonds).

6   Write answers to the question, which will probably be 'yes' or 'no', in boxes and join the boxes to the question.

7   Join the 'yes' box to the first task.

8   Create a statement to direct an action arising from the 'no' answer that will result in you being able to now answer 'yes' to the first question (this starts the first loop).

9   Continue posing questions of the original list of tasks and arranging loops as a result of positive or negative answers such that you form a successful route to the completion of the process.

10 Ensure that you consider the consequence of negative answers to the questions by building in loops that return you back to the route of successful completion.

benefits

Algorithms allow you to:

- analyse all possible conditions needed for the successful completion of a process
- shape users of the algorithm to achieve a successful completion of a process
- identify where possible problems might occur in completing a desired process and, therefore, build in solutions.

when to use it

Use an algorithm when you want to:

- introduce a new process to a group of users
- train users to complete a process or skill
- analyse where mistakes are being made among a group of users of a process.

prompt questions

- What is involved in completing this process?
- How can we ensure everyone succeeds?
- How can we identify and rectify possible mistakes or failures?

how to introduce it to students

You can:

- start with simple, known processes such as making a cup of tea, making a telephone call, catching a bus, having a bath
- put students into groups of three, allotting one process to each group
- ask each group to create an algorithm for their process, using the steps described above
- ask pairs of groups to 'test drive' each other's algorithm and make suggestions regarding the ease of reading, and the logic of the loops leading you back on course.

closely related visual tools

You will find that flow charts and critical path analyses most closely relate to algorithms.

	Similarities	Differences
flow charts	Both formats represent a sequence of events.	Flow charts represent a single sequence of events, while algorithms represent multiple sequences depending on responses to questions.
critical path analyses	Both formats identify the route to successful completion of a process among possible alternative or peripheral tasks.	Critical path analysis represents all the tasks to be completed, identified through analysing dependencies, while algorithms represent all possible eventualities from a user's point of view and redirects all diversions back towards the completion of the process.

5 systems diagram CVT

reinforcing loop template

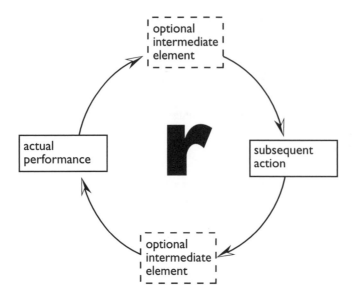

balancing loop template

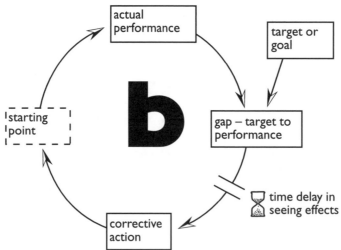

based on P. Senge and co-workers (1994)

what it is

A systems diagram is a visual representation of a system in operation. There are many variations based on the basic two types – the reinforcing loop and the balancing loop.

why it has this name

It is called a systems diagram because the visual format illustrates the inter-relationships of the key components that represent a system. All systems diagrams outline causal links, but there is an acknowledgement that cause and effect will not necessarily be closely related in time and space. Systems diagrams, therefore, chart the indirect causal links and the repercussions of the subsequent effects on other components.

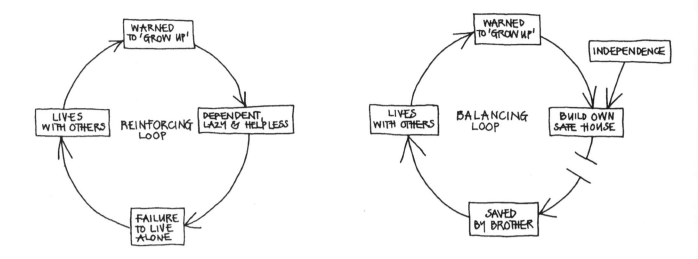

other names

The variations of the basic two looped systems diagrams are:

- success to the successful
- limits to growth
- accidental adversaries
- fixes that backfire
- escalation
- drifting goals
- shifting the burden
- tragedy of the commons
- growth and under-investment
- the attractiveness principle.

how to make it

To make a systems diagram, follow these steps.

1 Choose a situation you want to understand.

2 Identify the elements.

3 Write them separately onto sticky notes.

4 Pick one element of the situation that is causing concern.

5 Describe what this element is doing, noticing a sense of movement.

6 Describe the impact of this movement on another element.

7 Continue identifying causal inter-relationships.

8 Represent these hypothesised relationships by placing the sticky notes in cyclical fashion.

9 Now study the two archetypal systems diagrams – the reinforcing loop and the balancing loop.

10 Experiment with blank templates of the two loops and identify which of the two best describes your perceived situation.

11 Complete the system loop templates with the information you have identified from your earlier work.

benefits

Systems diagrams allow you to:

- reach, rather than jump, to conclusions
- identify underlying trends of causes
- see past immediate time frames, which supply only surface causal links
- understand why certain situations are kept in place and remain.

when to use it

Use a systems diagrams when you want to:

- solve a recurring problem
- look beyond superficial, surface explanations
- stop repeating limiting actions
- identify key leveraging elements that keep certain situations in place.

prompt questions

Ask 'why is this happening?' and ask it again of the answer, repeating the process until the question has been asked five times.

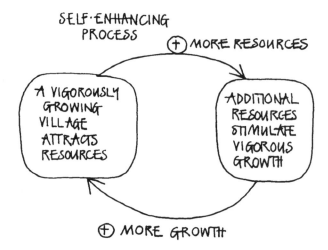

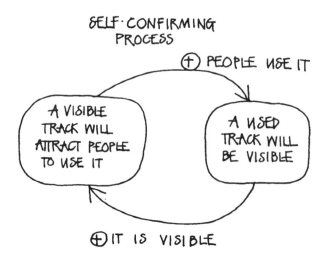

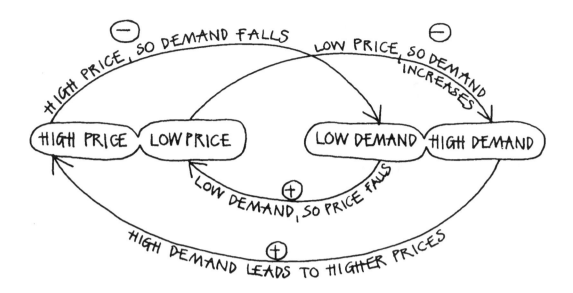

R. Carter, J. Martin, B. Mayblin and M. Munday (1984)

how to introduce it to students

You can:

- tell students a story that illustrates how situations can often remain despite much effort to change them

- analyse the story by introducing the two basic systems diagram loop templates

- repeat this process with other stories and incidents from the students' lives, school life or television soaps

- alternatively, illustrate the nature of a system with a simple example, such as turning the cold tap in the shower in immediate response to being scalded, ignoring the time element in the causal link between turning the tap and experiencing a change in temperature.

closely related visual tools

You will find that cycles most closely relate to systems diagrams.

	Similarities	Differences
cycles	Both are non-linear representations of causal links. Both use similar graphic formats.	Cycles identify simple, one-process-at-a-time, systems, while systems diagrams identify simultaneous processes and their effects on more than one direct element. There are archetypal systems that represent types of systemic structures.

6 flowscape CVT

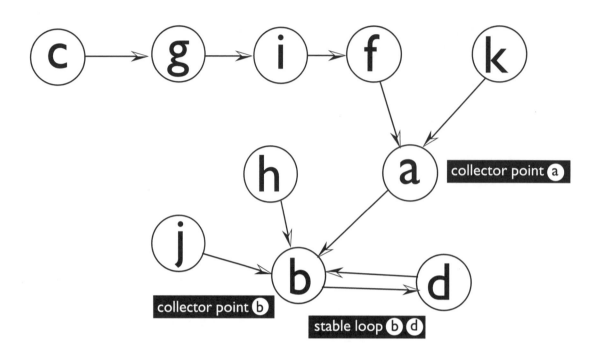

chain **c** **g** **i** **f**

collector point **a**

collector point **b**

stable loop **b** **d**

what it is

A flowscape is a diagram representing the relationships between perceptions a person may have of a situation. It is what its originator, Edward de Bono, called a map of your perceptions, of your inner world.

why it has this name

It is called a flowscape because the nature of the relationships do not conform to rational logic (which de Bono described as 'rock logic'). Flowscapes are formed from internal, personal, fluid and changing logic (which de Bono termed 'water logic').

other names

Flowscapes are not known by other names.

how to make it

To make a flowscape, follow these steps.

1 Choose a subject or situation you want to investigate.

2 Make a list of all the factors relating to this situation, 'off the top of your head'.

3 Give each of these factors a letter, in alphabetical order.

4 Consider each factor in turn, identifying which other factor is immediately brought to mind (this is the 'flow' of your natural associations), and write these 'partner' letters.

5 Identify the most frequently chosen factor.

6 Draw the flowscape based on these partner factors, starting with the most commonly linked factors.

1. FORWARD PLANNING

2. DELAYED GRATIFICATION

3. INDEPENDENCE

4. COURAGE

5. LEAVING HOME

6. HUNGER

7. NAIVETY

8. TECHNICAL KNOWLEDGE

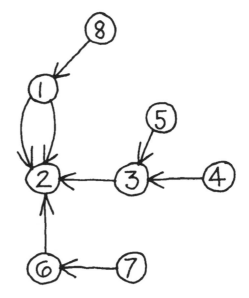

7 Redraw your flowscape, if needed, rearranging the linked factors into the best graphic format to illustrate the relationships.

8 Study your flowscape, searching for:

- 'stable loops', which show reciprocal flows of relationships

- 'collector points', which are factors on the receiving end of several other factors

- 'links', which can join stable loops and collector points.

benefits

Flowscapes make it possible to investigate your perceptions in an objective, visual way, according validity to them. They become the means by which you can communicate and explain your feelings and thoughts, and the reasons behind your actions.

when to use it

Use a flowscape when you want to:

- gain insights into your perceptions

- identify what may be the best course of action.

prompt questions

- What do I feel about this?

- What is shaping my feelings?

- What should I do about this situation?

- What are my core perceptions?

how to introduce it to students

You can:

- introduce a controversial situation in either a school, local or national context
- identify the feelings and thoughts of the students regarding this situation
- introduce the process of constructing a flowscape to the students
- ask the students to discuss their flowscapes with partners
- subsequently, when the students are familiar with the technique, ask them to construct a flowscape from the perspective of a chosen character of a novel being studied, or a character from a soap on television.

closely related visual tools

You will find that relations diagrams most closely relate to flowscapes.

	Similarities	Differences
relations diagrams	Both use similar graphic formats to represent the inter-relationships between factors that influence one another.	Relations diagrams focus on actual events while flowscapes focus on perceptions. Each causal link of a relations diagram is constructed piece by piece, while the links of the flowscape are constructed as a final summary of paired relationships made between individual perceptions.

numerical visual tools NVT

purpose

The main purpose of the visual tools in this category is to represent a quantitative evaluation that compares:

- components – the size of each part as a percentage of the total
- items – the ranking order
- trends – the change over time
- frequency – the items within ranges
- correlation – the relationship between variables

●	component	item	time series	frequency	correlation
pie chart	(pie chart)				
bar chart		(bar chart)			(bar chart)
column chart			(column chart)	(column chart)	
line chart			(line chart)	(line chart)	
dot chart					(dot chart)

Numerical visual tools are familiar to us all. As such, they do not need the depth of explanation devoted to the other visual tools.

Gene Zelazny, in his best-selling book *Say It With Charts* (1996), makes the following points about the five charts.

▌ pie chart NVT

- the most popular of all charts
- the least practical of all charts
- should account for only 5% of charts used
- the best chart for showing the components of a single total

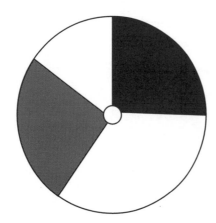

2 bar chart NVT

- the most versatile of all charts
- the least appreciated
- deserve more attention
- should account for at least 25% of charts used
- use scales at the top or bottom, or numbers at the ends of the bars, but not both

There are six variations of the bar chart:

1 the deviation bar chart

2 the range bar chart

3 the grouped bar chart

4 the sliding bar chart

5 the paired bar chart

6 the sub-divided bar chart.

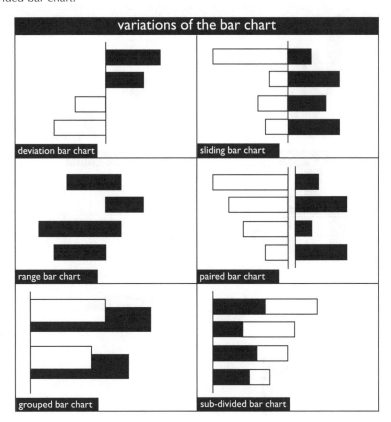

Keep bar charts horizontal rather than vertical to:

- avoid confusion with column charts (bar charts show item comparison; column charts show changes over time)
- accommodate the lengthy labels (often proper nouns) found with items.

3 column chart NVT

- very reliable
- tend to emphasise levels of magnitude occurring within a set time period
- keep column charts vertical (not horizontal) as in the West we 'read' time from left to right
- should account for 25% of charts used
- use only if there are less than around 10 points in time to plot

There are five variations of the column chart:

1 the deviation column chart
2 the range column chart
3 the grouped column chart
4 the sub-divided column chart
5 the step–column chart.

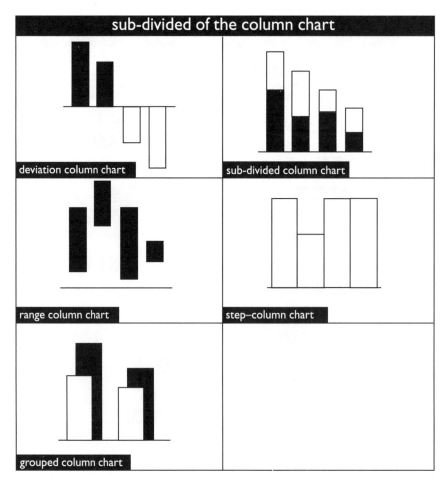

sub-divided of the column chart

deviation column chart

sub-divided column chart

range column chart

step–column chart

grouped column chart

4 line chart NVT

- the 'workhorse' of charts
- should account for 25% of charts used
- tend to emphasise movement and abrupt changes
- the most compact chart
- the easiest to draw
- the easiest with which to identify trends

There are two variations of the line chart:

1 the grouped line chart

2 the sub-divided line chart.

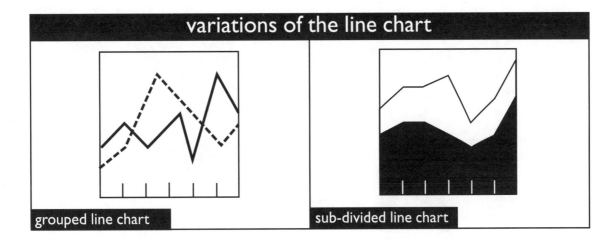

variations of the line chart

grouped line chart

sub-divided line chart

5 dot chart NVT

- sometimes known as a scatter diagram
- should account for 10% of charts used

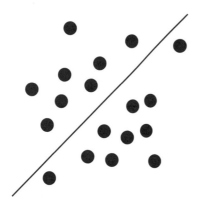

There are three variations of the dot chart:

1 the grouped dot chart

2 the bubble chart

3 the time dot chart.

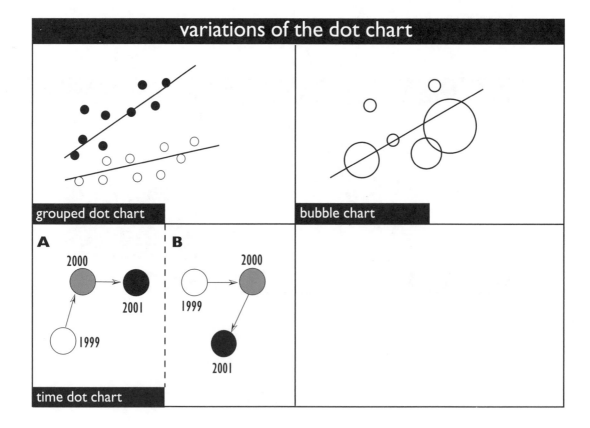

organisational visual tools | OVT

Writing frame

PMI

Compare & contrast

ORGANISATIONAL OVT VISUAL TOOLS

Arch diagram

Interaction outline

Problem solution frame

purpose

The main purposes of the visual tools in this category are to:

- direct the content of your focus
- direct the sequence of your thoughts
- direct what you will write
- direct where you will write
- direct how much you will write.

Characteristics of organisational visual tools

Organisational visual tools, compared to the other categories, have limitations and tend to:

- be set by the teacher
- be templates
- give students little choice
- allow students very limited possibilities for creativity
- not be very transferable to contexts other than the one for which they were set.

Structurally, most organisational visual tools:

- are no more than boxes in which students have to contain their writing
- have little visual logic – the locations of the boxes are not spatially meaningful
- resemble work sheets.

The limitations of organisational visual tools, however, mean they offer:

- an easy introduction to visual tools for students
- a graded progression to more complex visual tools
- a quick and easy set of tools to use for teachers new to this way of working
- a structured way of thinking that produces immediate results for students
- a known sequence of working that reassures students.

 **writing frame** OVT

recount genre

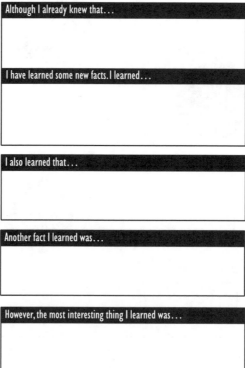

Although I already knew that...

I have learned some new facts. I learned...

I also learned that...

Another fact I learned was...

However, the most interesting thing I learned was...

what it is

A writing frame is a set formula of what to write and in what sequence.

why it has this name

It is called a writing frame because frames form the structure in which the work is ordered.

how to make it

Simply construct boxes that represent the aspect of writing you want your students to complete. Join the boxes by arrows to indicate the sequence in which you want the writing to occur.

2 compare and contrast organiser OVT

what it is

A compare and contrast organiser is a framework for directing your students to look at similarities and differences.

why it has this name

It is called a compare and contrast organiser because it directs students to identify the similarities and differences between two items.

how to make it

Draw out boxes to indicate what two items are to be studied, the ways in which they are similar, and (with regard to what criteria) the ways in which they are different.

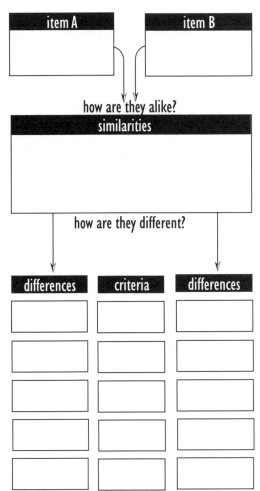

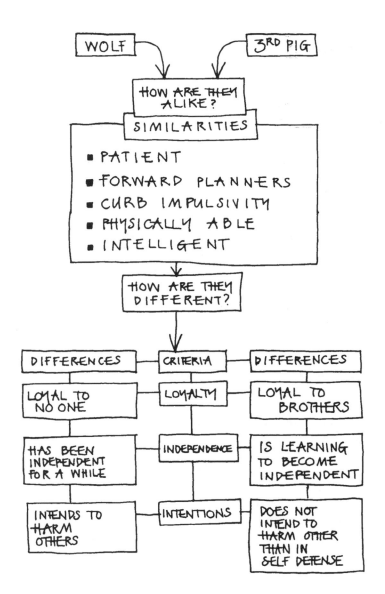

3 interaction outline OVT

goal	goal

interaction
action

outcome	outcome

what it is

An interaction outline is a way of guiding attention on the development of events.

why it has this name

It is called an interaction outline because the interaction between two goals is summarised and the outcomes identified.

how to make it

Draw boxes to identify the two separate goals, their interaction and the outcomes. Join the boxes to direct the flow of the development.

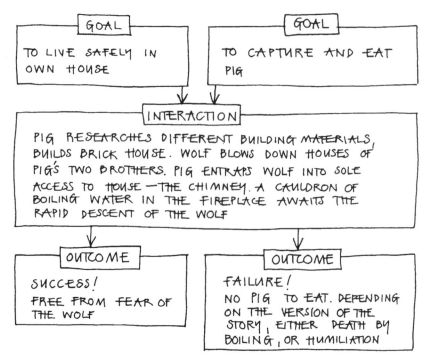

GOAL
TO LIVE SAFELY IN OWN HOUSE

GOAL
TO CAPTURE AND EAT PIG

INTERACTION
PIG RESEARCHES DIFFERENT BUILDING MATERIALS, BUILDS BRICK HOUSE. WOLF BLOWS DOWN HOUSES OF PIG'S TWO BROTHERS. PIG ENTRAPS WOLF INTO SOLE ACCESS TO HOUSE — THE CHIMNEY. A CAULDRON OF BOILING WATER IN THE FIREPLACE AWAITS THE RAPID DESCENT OF THE WOLF

OUTCOME
SUCCESS!
FREE FROM FEAR OF THE WOLF

OUTCOME
FAILURE!
NO PIG TO EAT. DEPENDING ON THE VERSION OF THE STORY, EITHER DEATH BY BOILING, OR HUMILIATION

4 problem–solution frame OVT

```
┌─────────────────────────────┐
│           problem           │
│                             │
│                             │
└─────────────────────────────┘
              │
              ▼
┌─────────────────────────────┐
│          solution           │
│                             │
│                             │
└─────────────────────────────┘
              │
              ▼
┌─────────────────────────────┐
│            result           │
│                             │
│                             │
└─────────────────────────────┘
```

what it is

A problem–solution frame is a way of directing students to pay attention to both aspects of a situation and to consider their relationship.

why it has this name

It is called a problem–solution frame because it offers a basic framework in which to focus on a problem and its solution.

how to make it

Simply draw three boxes into which students will write separately about the problem, the solution and the result.

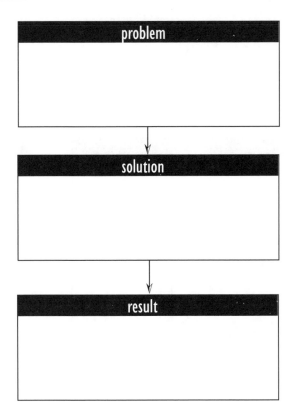

PROBLEM

3 PIGS ARE VULNERABLE TO THE CUNNING WAYS OF THE HUNGRY AND POWERFUL WOLF

SOLUTION

LURE WOLF INTO THE ONLY ACCESS INTO THE HOUSE (CHIMNEY) IN ORDER TO CAPTURE AND DISABLE HIM (BOILING WATER IN FIREPLACE CAULDRON)

RESULT

SAFETY & NEW CAREER IN HOME SECURITY SYSTEMS

5 arch diagram OVT

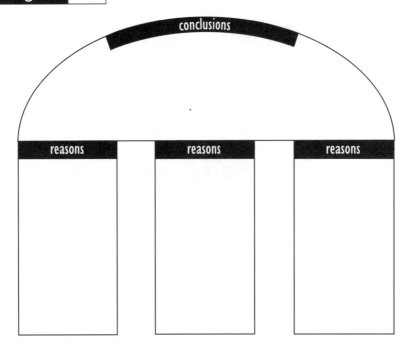

what it is

An arch diagram is a graphic way of showing the reasons supporting a conclusion.

why it has this name

It is called an arch diagram because of the visual metaphor it uses – the conclusion is the top section of an arch and the three columns are the reasons that support it.

how to make it

Draw an arch in which the conclusion is to be written, and underneath it draw three large boxes to represent the columns in which the reasons will be described.

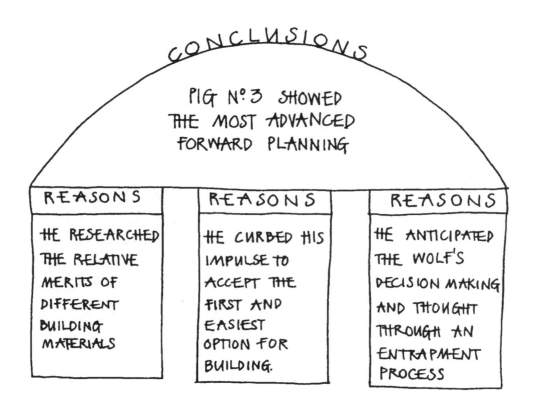

6 'PMI' OVT

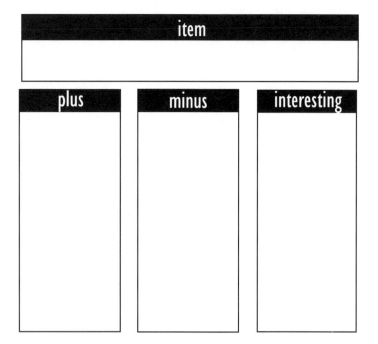

what it is

A 'PMI' is a way of delaying conclusions by forcing you to look at optional viewpoints. It was originally devised by Edward de Bono.

why it has this name

It is called a 'PMI' because this visual tool focuses on the Plus, Minus and Interesting aspects of a situation in preparation for decision making.

how to make it

Simply fill in the three boxes that represent the three perspectives.

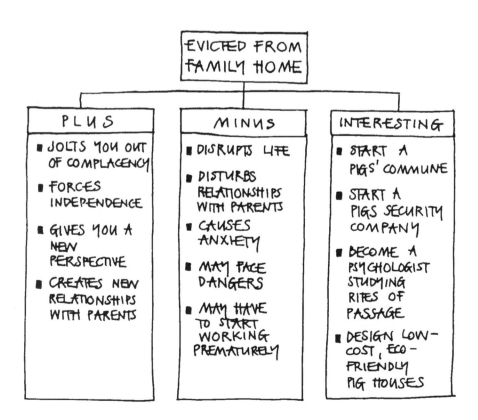

individual visual tools | IVT

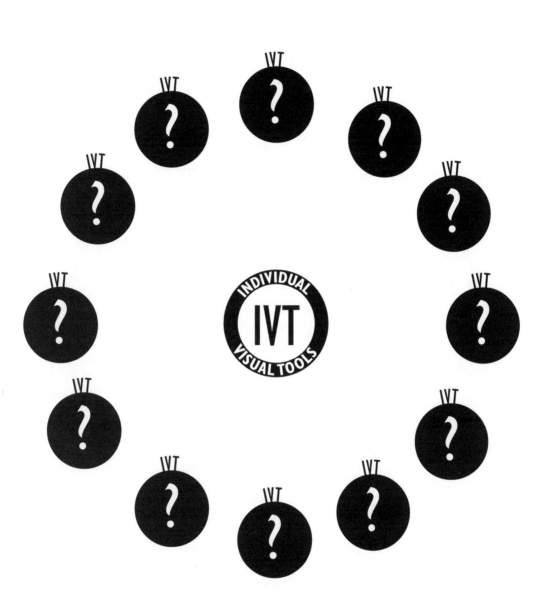

purpose	The main purposes of the visual tools in this category are to:

- suit the individual requirements of a particular piece of work
- allow for exploration and development of your thinking
- create new hybrids of visual tools.

This section comprises examples of visual tools that have been customised and developed for specific, individual needs.

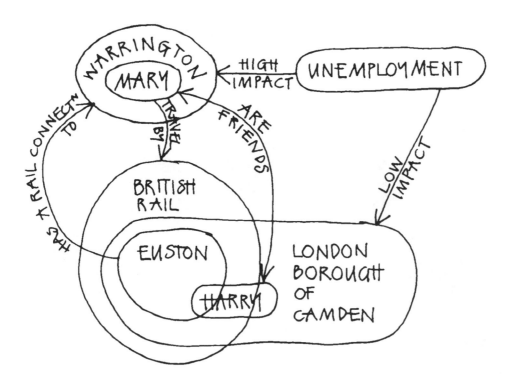

based on R. Carter, J. Martin, B. Mayblin and M. Munday (1984)

This example illustrates how individual visual tools are very often – if not always – hybrids of other visual tools. In this particular example, you can see how it consists of:

■ a concept map with propositional statements linking one idea to another

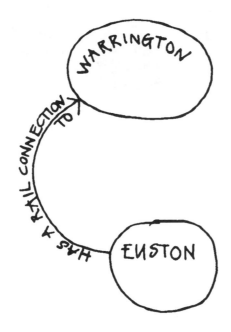

■ a systems diagram with arrows depicting the flow of causation or influence in a way that holds the whole in place

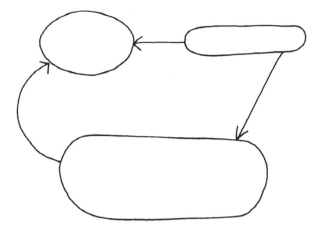

■ a Venn diagram with its overlapping sets indicating the relationships between parts of the content.

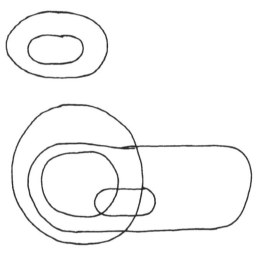

See if you can identify the constituent visual tools within the following examples in this category of visual tools.

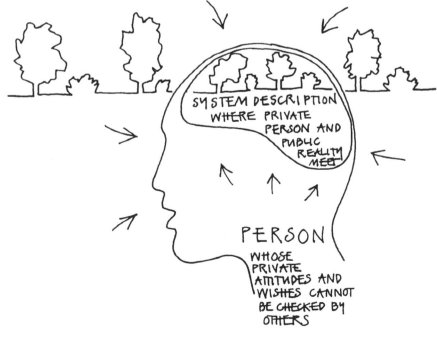

based on R. Carter, J. Martin, B. Mayblin and M. Munday (1984)

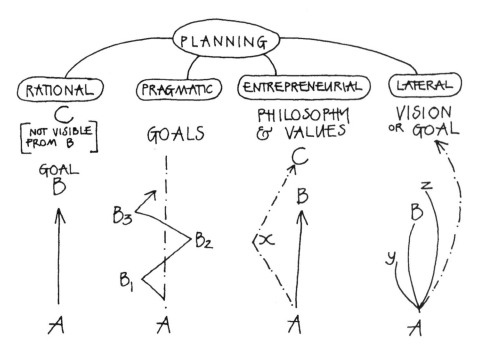

based on O. Caviglioli (2001)

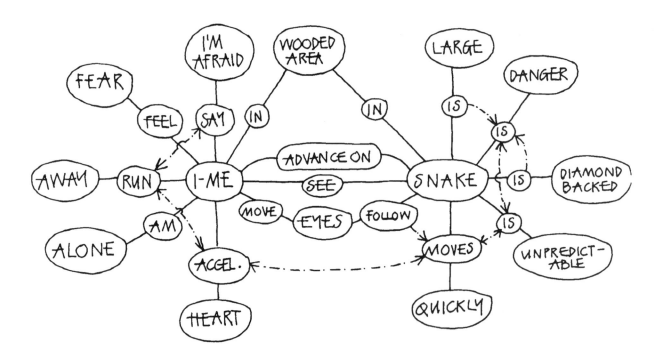

based on J. Ledoux (1996)

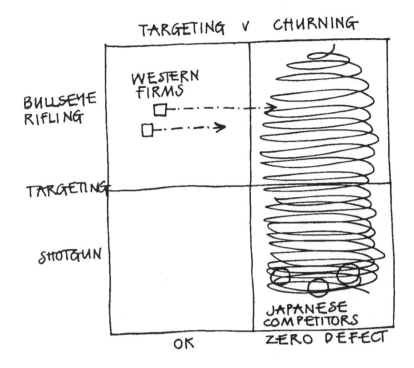

TARGETING V CHURNING

WESTERN FIRMS

BULLSEYE RIFLING

TARGETING

SHOTGUN

JAPANESE COMPETITORS

OK   ZERO DEFECT

based on J. K. Johansson and I. Nonaka (1996)

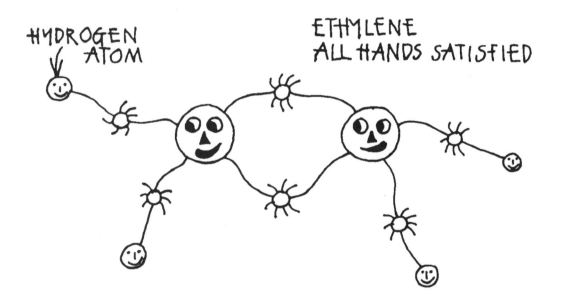

HYDROGEN ATOM

ETHYLENE ALL HANDS SATISFIED

based on C. Burgess and co-workers (1973)

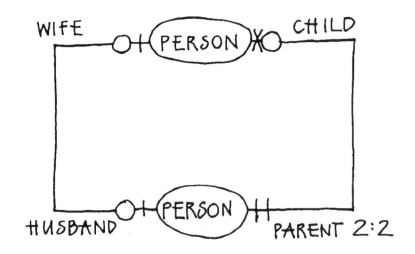

based on J. Halé (1998)

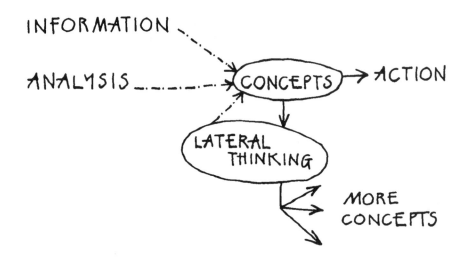

based on E. de Bono (1987)

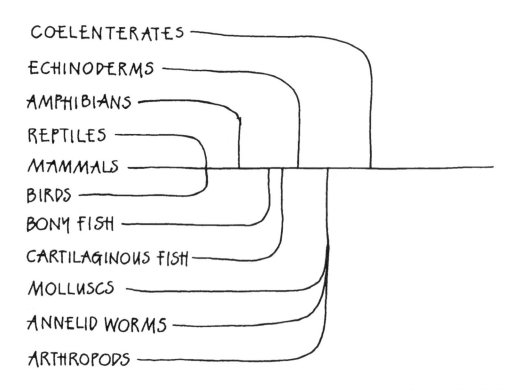

based on D. E. Harding (1998)

References

■ Ainscow. M. (1994) *Special Needs in the Classroom*: A Teacher Education Guide, Jessica Kingsley, London

■ Andrews, F. and Andrews, G. (1996) Clear English, Bloomsbury, London

■ Argyris, C. (1982) *Reasoning, Learning and Action: Individual and Organisational*, Jossey-Bass, San Francisco

■ Baddeley, A. (1994) *Your Memory*, Penguin, London

■ Barker, P. and Van Schank, P. (2000) 'Icons in the Mind', in Yazdani, M. and Barker, P. (eds) (2000) *Iconic Communication*, Intellect Books, Bristol

■ Barley, S. D. (1971) *A New Look at the Loom of Visual Literacy*, Eastman Kodak Company, Rochester, quoted in Moore, D. M. and Dwyer, F. M. (1994) *Visual Literacy*, Educational Technology Publications, Englewood, California

■ Bartlett, F. C. (1968) 'Adventurous Thinking', in Watson, P. C. and Johnson-Laird (eds) *Thinking and Reasoning*, Penguin, London

■ Bigge, M. L. and Shermis, S. S. (1999) *Learning Theories for Teachers*, Longman, New York

■ Boak, G. and Thompson, D. (1998) *Mental Models for Managers,* Century, London

■ Bowers, S. (2001) 'Modern visions and the old school of thought', *Guardian Education*, 29 February 2001

■ Braden, R. A. (1983) 'Visualizing the Verbal and Verbalizing the Visual', in Braden, R. A. and Walker, A. W. (eds) (1983) *Seeing Ourselves: Visualizing in a Social Context*, International Visual Literacy Association, Blacksbury, VA

■ Britton, J. (1982) 'Shaping at the Point of Utterance' in Pradl, G. M. (ed) *Prospect and Retrospect: Selected Essays of James Britton*, Boynton Cook, New Jersey

■ Brophy, J. (1998) *Motivating Students to Learn*, McGraw-Hill, New York

■ Brown, G. and Wragg, E. C. (1993) *Questioning*, Routledge, London

■ Bruner, J. S. (1968) 'The Course of Cognitive Growth', in Watson, P. C. and Johnson-Laird (eds) *Thinking and Reasoning*, Penguin, London

■ Bruner, J. S. (1971) *Towards a Theory of Instruction*, OUP, Oxford

■ Bruner, J. S. (1988) quoted in Healy, J. M. (1999) *Endangered Minds,* Touchstone, New York

■ Burgess, C. and coworkers (1973) *Understanding Children's Writing*, Penguin, London

■ Caine, R. N. and Caine, G. (1991) *Making Connections: Teaching and the Human Brain*, Addison-Wesley, Menlo Park, California

■ Carter, R., Martin, J., Mayblin, B. and Munday, M. (1984) *Systems, Management and Change*, Harper and Row, London

■ Caviglioli, O. (2001) Personal notes on financial planning

■ Caviglioli, O. and Harris, I. (2000) *MapWise*, Network Educational Press, Stafford

■ Clarke, T. and Clegg, S. (2000) *Changing Paradigms*, Harper Collins, London

■ Claxton, G. (1990) *Teaching to Learn*, Cassell, London

■ Claxton, G. (1997) *Hare Brain, Tortoise Mind*, Fourth Estate, London

■ Claxton, G. (1999) *Wise Up*, Bloomsbury, London

■ Cooper, P. and McIntyre, D. (1993) 'Commonality in teachers' and pupils' perceptions of effective classroom learning', *British Journal of Educational Psychology*, No 63.

■ Costa, A. L. (1996) 'Introduction' in Hyerle, D. (1996) *Visual Tools for Constructing Knowledge*, Association for Supervision and Curriculum Development, Virginia

■ Coughlan, S. (2000), 'Book of the Week' (a review of Barrington Atlas of the Greek and Roman World), *Times Educational Supplement*, 2.10.2000

■ Counsell, C. (2000) 'Why Was Becket Murdered?', *Teaching Thinking*, Issue 1, Summer 2000

■ Craig, M. (2000) *Thinking Visually*, Continuum, London

■ Crystal, D. (1995) *The Cambridge Encyclopedia of the English Language*, Cambridge University Press, Cambridge

■ Csikszentmihalyi, M. (1990) *Flow: The Psychology of Optimal Experience*, Harper and Row, New York

■ Czerniawska, F. (1997) *Corporate Speak*, Macmillan, Basingstoke

■ Davitt, J. (1990) personal communication

■ De Bono, E. (1987) *Letters to Thinkers*, Penguin, London

■ De Bono, E. (1992) *Serious Creativity*, HarperBusiness, New York

■ De Bono, E. (1996) introduction in McAlhone, B. and Stuart, D., *A Smile in the Mind, Phaidon*, London

■ Desforges, C. and Lings, P. (1998) 'Teaching Knowledge Application: Advances in Theoretical Conceptions and their Professional Implications', *British Journal of Educational Studies*, ISSN 0007–1005, Vol 46, December 1998

■ Dillon, J. T. (1988) *Questioning and Teaching: A Manual of Practice*, Croom Helm, London

■ Dweck, C. S., Chin, C. and Hong, Y. (1995) 'Implicit theories and their role in judgements and reactions: A world from two perspectives', *Psychological Inquiry*, 6, 267–285

■ Eastwood, C. (2000) 'WordImage', *British Journal of Special Education*, Vol 27, No 4, December 2000

■ Edmiston, A. (2000) 'A term in the life', *Teaching Thinking*, Issue 2, Autumn 2000

■ Elhelou, M-W., A. (1997) 'The Use of Concept Mapping in Learning Science Subjects by Arab Students', *Educational Research*, Vol 39, No 3, winter 1997

■ Eysenck, M. W. (ed) (1994) *The Blackwell Dictionary of Cognitive Psychology*, Blackwell, Oxford

■ Feuerstein, R., Rand, Y., Hoffman, M. and Miller, R. (1980) *Instrumental Enrichment*, University Park Press, Baltimore, USA

■ Fisher, R. (1992) 'Questions for Thinking', *Multi-Mind*, summer 1992

■ Fisher, R. (1995) *Teaching Children to Learn*, Stanley Thornes, Cheltenham

■ Flory, J. (1978) *Visual Literacy: A Vital Skill in the Process of Rhetorical Critism*, Southern Speech Communication Association, Atlanta, GA

■ Foley, J. (1998) *The Guinness Encyclopedia of Signs and Symbols*, Guinness Publishing, Enfield

■ Funes, M. and Johnson, N. (1998) *Honing Your Knowledge Skills*, Butterworth-Heinemann, Oxford

■ Gaarder, J. (1996) *Hello? Is Anybody There?*, Orion Children's Books, London

■ Gauvain, M. (1998) 'Thinking in Niches – Sociocultural Influences on Cognitive Development', *Human Development*, 38, 25–45

■ Galloway, D., Rogers, C., Armstrong, D. and Leo, E. (1998) *Motivating The Hard To Teach*, Longman, London

■ Gardner, H. (1983) *Frames of Mind*, Fontana, London

■ Getner, D. and Stevens, A. L. (1983) *Mental Models*, Lawrence Erlbaum, New Jersey

■ Gilster, P. (1997) *Digital Literacy*, J. Wiley and Sons, Chichester

■ Gipps, C. V. (1994) *Beyond Testing – Towards a Theory of Educational Assessment. Falmer*, London

■ Goleman, D. (1985) *Vital Lies, Simple Truths,* Bloomsbury, London

■ Gopnik, A., Meltzoff, A. and Kuhl, P. (1999) *How Babies Think*, Weidenfeld and Nicholson, London

■ Greenfield, S. (2000) *The Private Life of the Brain*, Penguin, London

■ Halé, J. (1998) *From Concepts to Capabilities,* J. Wiley, London

■ Harding, D. E. (1998) appendix 'On Diagrams, and Some Aspects of Symbolism' in Harding, D. E. (1998) *The Hierarchy of Heaven and Earth*, The Sholland Trust, London

■ Harding, D. E. (1998) *The Hierarchy of Heaven and Earth*, The Sholland Trust, London

■ Hargreaves, D. H. (1999) 'The Knowledge-Creating School', *British Journal of Educational Studies*, ISSN 0007–1005, Vol 47, No 2, June 2000

■ Healy, J. M. (1999) *Endangered Minds,* Touchstone, New York

■ Hodgson, T. and Tait, F. (2000) *Crashing into the present: facilitating decision through fast scenario thinking,* www.metabridge.com

■ Hoffman, D. (1998) *Visual Intelligence,* Norton, New York

■ Holt, J. (1983) *How Children Learn*, Penguin, London

■ Hortin, J. (1980) 'Symbol Systems and Mental Skills Research: Their Emphasis and Future', in *Media Adult Learning*, 2, (2), 3–6

■ Hyerle, D. (1996) *Visual Tools for Constructing Knowledge*, Association for Supervision and Curriculum Development, Virginia

■ Hyerle, D. (2000) *A Field Guide to Using Visual Tools*, Association for Supervision and Curriculum Development, Virginia

■ Jeffries, M. (2000) quoted in Constantine, A., 'Let's Think Laterally', *Times Educational Supplement,* 2 June 2000

■ Jensen, E. (2000) *Brain-Based Learning*, Brain Store Inc., San Diego, CA

■ Johansson, J. K. and Nonaka, I. (1996) *Relentless – The Japanese Way Of Marketing*, Butterworth-Heinemann, Oxford

■ Kelly, G. (1955) *The Psychology of Personal Constructs*, Norton, New York

■ Kinchin, I. M., Hay, D. B. and Adams, A. (2000) 'How a Qualitative Approach to Concept Map Analysis Can be Used to Aid Learning by Illustrating Patterns of Conceptual Development', *Educational Research*, Vol 42, No 1, spring 2000

■ Lake, M. (1990), 'Unfold Your Arms and Start Talking', *Special Children*, June/July 1990

■ Lake, M. (1994) 'Narrative, Pictures and Imagination', in *Centre for Thinking Skills Information Pack*, Vol 3, No 2

■ Lakoff, G. and Johnson, M. (1980) *Metaphors We Live By*, University of Chicago Press, Chicago

■ Lawless, C., Smee, P. and O'Shea, T. (1998) 'Using Concept Sorting and Concept Mapping in Business and Public Administration, and in Education: An Overview', *Educational Research*, Vol 40, No 2, summer 1998

■ LeDoux, J. (1996) *The Emotional Brain: The Mysterious Underpinnings of Emotional Life*, Simon & Schuster, New York

■ Light, P., Sheldon, S. and Woodhead, M. (1991) *Learning to Think*, Routledge, London

■ Lissack, M. and Roos, J. (1999) *The Next Common Sense*, Nicholas Brealey, London

■ Lloyd, R. (2000) 'Understanding Learning', in Kitchen, R. and Freundschuh, S. (eds) *Cognitive Mapping*, Routledge, London

■ Manguel, A. (1996) *A History of Reading,* Harper Collins, London

■ Marzano, R. J., Pickering, D. J. and Pollock, J. E. (2001), *Classroom Instruction That Works*, Association for Supervision and Curriculum Development, Virginia

■ McAleese, R. (1998) *A Theoretical View of Concept Mapping*, website www.icbl.hw.ac.uk

■ McBer, H. (2000) *A Model of Teacher Effectiveness*, report to the Department for Education and Employment, London

■ McCabe, D. (1999) *The Concept Mapping Workshop*, website www.CncptMapp.Wkshp

■ McCaskey, M. B. (1991) 'Mapping: creating, maintaining, and relinquishing conceptual frameworks', in Henry, J. (ed) *Creative Management,* Sage, London

■ McGuiness, C. (1999) *From Thinking Skills to Thinking Classrooms: A Review and Evaluation of Approaches for Developing Pupils' Thinking*, DfEE, London

■ McKenzie, M. (1996) 'Grazing the Net, From Now On', *The Educational Technology Journal*, 5, 5, January/February 1996

■ McKim, R. H. M. (1972) *Experience in Visual Thinking*, Brookes College, California

■ McPeck, J. (1990) *Teaching Critical Thinking*, Routledge, London

■ Meier, D. (2000) *The Accelerated Learning Handbook*, McGraw-Hill, New York

■ Minto, B. (1995) *The Pyramid Principle*, Pitman, London

■ Moll, L. C. and Whitmore, K. F. (1998) 'Vygotsky in Classroom Practice', in Moll, L. C. and Whitmore, K. F. (eds) (1998) *Learning Relationships in the Classroom*, Routledge, London

■ Moore, D. M. and Dwyer, F. M. (1994) *Visual Literacy*, Educational Technology Publications, Englewood Cliffs

■ Murris, K. (1992) *Teaching Philosophy with Picture Books*, Infonet Publications, London

■ Nonaka, I. and Takeuchi, H. (1995) *The Knowledge Creating Company*, OUP, Oxford

■ Novak, J. D. (1993) 'Human constructivism: a unification of psychological and epistemological phenomena in meaning making.' *International Journal of Personal Constructive Psychology*, 6, 167–93

■ Novak, J. D. (1998) *Learning, Creating and Using Knowledge*, Lawrence Erlbaum, New York

■ Nutbrown, C. (1999) *Threads of Thinking*, Paul Chapman, London

■ O'Connor, J. and McDermott, I. (1997) *The Art of Systems Thinking*, Thorsons, London

■ Ornstein, R. and Ehrlich, P. (1991) *New World, New Mind*, Paladin, London

■ Paine, N. (2000) in Walker, D. 'A Prophet in Open Learning', *TES Online*, 13 October 2000

- Palmer, S. (2000) 'Can't Write, Won't Write?', *Times Educational Supplement*, Curriculum Special, spring 2000

- Parks, S. and Black, H. (1992) *Organising Thinking*, Critical Thinking Books and Software, Pacific Grove, California

- Peacock, A. (2000) 'What is Visual Literacy?' in *Times Educational Supplement, Curriculum Special (Science and Technology)*, Spring 2000

- Petterson, R. (1989) Visuals for information: research practice, *Educational Technology Publications*, Englewood Cliffs, NJ

- Piaget, J. (1960) *Language and Thought of the Child*, Routledge, London

- Pinker, S. (1997) *How the Mind Works*, Penguin, London

- Pinker, S. (1999) *Words and Rules,* Phoenix, London

- Pollard, A. (1999) 'Towards a New Perspective on Children's Learning', *Education*, October 1999

- Postman, N. (1990) *Teaching as a Conserving Activity*, Delecorte, New York

- Postman, N. (1992) *Technopoly*, Knopf, New York

- Poyner, N. (1996) *Typography Now Two*, Booth-Clibborn, London

- Pumfrey, P. and Stamboltizis, A. (2000) 'Reading Across Genres: A Review of Literature', *Support for Learning*, Vol 15, No 2

- Riding, R. and Rayner, S. (1998) *Cognitive Styles and Learning Styles*, David Fulton, London

- Robinson, K. (2001) *Out of our minds,* Capstone, Oxford

- Roszak, T. (1986) *The Cult of Information*, Pantheon, New York

- Saljo, R. (1998) 'Thinking With and Through Artefacts', in Faulkner, D., Littlejon, K. and Woodhead, M. (eds) (1998) *Learning Relationships in the Classroom*, Routledge, London

- Saljo, R. (1998) 'Thinking With and Through Artefacts', in Faulkner, D., Littleton, K. and Woodhead, M. (eds) (1998) *Learning Relationships in the Classroom*, Routledge, London

- Senge, P. (1990) *The Fifth Discipline*, Nicholas Brealey, London

- Senge, P., Ross, R., Smith, B., Roberts, C. and Kleiner, A. (1994) *The Fifth Discipline Fieldbook*, Nicholas Brealey, London

- Sharron, H. (1987) *Changing Children's Minds*, Souvenir Press, London

- Sharron, H. (1999) 'Teaching Thinking Skills – Changing the Role of Teachers', *Professional Development Today*, autumn term

- Sherwood, D. (1998) *Unlock Your Mind*, Gower, Aldershot

- Siler, T. (1996) *Think Like A Genius*, Bantam, New York

- Smith, F. (1990) *Writing and the Writer*, Heinemann, Oxford

- Smith, F. (1992) *To Think,* Routledge, London

- Smitsman, A. W. (2000) 'Slumbering Talents: Where Do They Reside?' in Lieshout, F. M. V. and Heymans, P. G. (eds) (2000) *Developing Talent Across the Lifespan*, Psychology Press, Hove

- Stewart, T. A. (1998) *Intellectual Capital*, Nicholas Brealey Publishing, UK

- Stigler, J. W. (1984) 'Mental Abacus: the Effect of Abacus Training on Chinese Children's Mental Calculations', *Cognitive Psychology*, 16, 145–176

- Stigler, J. W., Chalip, L. and Miller, K. F. (1986) 'Consequences of Skill: The Case of Abacus Training in Taiwan', *American Journal of Education*, 94, 447–479

■ Sylwester, R. (1995) *A Celebration of Neurones*, Association for Supervision and Curriculum Development, Virginia

■ Trent, S. C., Pernell Junior, E., Mungai, A. and Chimedza, R. (1998) 'Using Concept Maps to Measure Conceptual Change in Preservice Teachers Enrolled in a Multicultural Education/Special Education Course', *Remedial and Special Education*, Vol 19, No 1, January/February 1998

■ Tufte, E. (1990) *Envisioning Information*, Graphics Press, Connecticut

■ Tulving, E. (1983) *Elements of Episodic Memory*, Oxford Univeristy Press, Oxford

■ Uttal, D. and Tan, L. S. (2000) 'Cognitive Mapping in Childhood', in *Cognitive Mapping* (eds. ???)

■ Vygotsky, L. S. (1962) *Thought and Language*, MIT Press, Cambridge, MA

■ Wandersee, J. H. (1990) 'Concept Mapping and the Cartography of Cognition', *Journal of Research in Science Teaching*, 27, 10

■ Watson, J. (2000) 'Constructive Instruction and Learning Difficulties', *Support for Learning*, Vol 15, No 3

■ Wells, G. (1986) *The Meaning Makers*, Hodder and Stoughton, London

■ Wenger, W. (1980) *The Einstein Factor*, Prima, California

■ Wheton, D., Cameron, K. and Woods, M. (1996) *Effective Problem Solving*, Harper Collins, London

■ Winston, R. (1998) *The Human Body*, BBC video

■ Wittgenstein, L. (1953) *Philosophical Investigations*, Oxford University Press, Oxford

■ Woditsch, G. A. (1991) *The Thinking Teacher's Guide to Thinking Skills*, Lawrence Erlbaum, New Jersey

■ Wurman, R. S. (1990) *Information Anxiety*, Pan, London

■ Zelazny, G. (1996) *Say it with Charts*, McGraw-Hill

Index

ability range 137–41
Adams, A. 66, 128
affinity diagrams 157–9
Ainscow, M. 138
algorithms 227–9
Andrews, F. and G. 94, 95
arch diagrams 248
Argyris, C. 59

Baddeley, A. 24
Ball, C. 23
bar charts 239
Barker, P. 96
Bartlett, F. C. 102
Bigge, M. L. 90
Black, H. 102
Boak, G. 118
Bowers, S. 37
bridge maps 185–6
Britton, J. 94
Brophy, J. 23, 24
Brown, G. 109
Bruner, J. S. 24, 37, 49, 51, 71
Burgess, C. et al. 255

Caine, R. N. and G. 31, 67, 90, 103, 135
Cameron, K. 109
Carlyle, T. 51
Carter, R. et al. 233, 252, 253

categorisation 70–1, 78–9, 144–5, 157–9
Causal Visual Tools 145, 217–36
Caviglioli, O. 114, 254
Clarke, T. 30
classification 144
Claxton, G. 17, 18, 24, 30, 34, 44, 51, 59, 117
Clegg, S. 30
clustering 154–6
cognition 18, 24, 55–6, 78–9, 106, 141
collaboration 139, 141
column charts 240
compare and contrast organisers 245
computers 33–7
concept maps 128, 167–9, 252
concepts 56, 66, 71, 102, 103
connections 22, 25, 66, 127, 154
constructivism 16, 17, 70–1, 73, 139
continuum lines 187–8
Cooper, P. 62
Costa, A. L. 24, 141
Coughlan, S. 18
Counsell, C. 18
Craig, M. 66, 135
critical path analysis 224–6
cross sections 198–9
Crystal, D. 114
curriculum subjects 114, 116, 117
cycles 210–11
Czerniawska, F. 28
Czikszentmihalyi, M. 126

Davitt, J. 138
de Bono, E. 18, 234, 249, 256
Desforges, C. 73
diagrams 109, 200–1
Differential Visual Tools 145, 173–93
Dillon, J. T. 109
dot charts 242
double bubble maps 176–7
Dweck, C. 23
Dwyer, F. M. 41, 135

Eastwood, C. 82
Edmiston, A. 16
effective education 24, 58, 72, 106
Elhelou, M-W. A. 82
Eysenck, M. W. 128

Feuerstein, R. 62, 65, 71, 100
fishbone diagrams 218–20
Fisher, R. 103, 109
Flory 43
flow charts 208–9
flowscapes 234–6
force field analysis 180–2
Fuller, B. 49
Funes, M. 30, 74

Gaarder, J. 107
Galloway, D. et al. 139
GANTT charts 214–16
Gardner, H. 116
Gauvain, M. 48, 139
genres 114–15, 117, 118t, 119t, 145
Getner, D. 66
Gilster, P. 37
Gipps, C. V. 128
Goleman, D. 141
Gopnik, A. 55
Greenfield, S. 55

Halé, J. 256
Harding, D. E. 3, 18, 41, 256
Hargreaves, D. H. 73
Harris, I. 114
Hay, D. B. 66, 128
Healy, J. M. 24, 34, 35, 36, 44
hierarchies 71, 114, 160–2, 167–9
Hodgson, T. 128
Holt, J. 66
Hortin, J. 41
Hyerle, D. 31, 40, 70, 71, 82, 90, 96, 128, 135, 141, 146

iDesk model 21, 23–4
Individual Visual Tools 145, 146, 251–6
information 25, 28, 30, 31, 134
intellectual capital 29, 30
intelligence 116
interaction outlines 246

Jeffries, M. 96
Jensen, E. 48, 132
Jobs, S. 51
Johansson, J. K. 255
Johnson, M. 42, 101
Johnson, N. 30, 74

Kelly, G. 55
Kinchin, I. M. 66, 128
knowledge 25, 27–31, 69–74, 117
   structures 18, 23, 59, 66, 71, 72, 73
   theories 70–1, 73
   workers 15–16, 29, 70
Kuhl, P. 55

Lake, M. 31, 128
Lakoff, G. 42, 101
language
   acquisition 56, 78–9

self-talk 80–1
spatial relationships 79, 80, 81, 101
structure 72–3
support for 77–82, 128
vocabulary 78, 80, 108, 114
Lawless, C. 103
learning 64
Accelerated Learning 16–17
   active learning 123–8
   adults 118
   collaborative 139, 141
   discovery learning 71–2
   episodic 65
   holistic view 22
   models 22–4
   questions 105–9, 120t, 127
   skills 133–5
   styles 131–5
   support for 138–40
   theory 16–17, 139, 140
Ledoux, J. 254
line charts 241
Lings, P. 73
Lissack, M. 31, 58, 70, 73
literacy 15, 18, 117
Lloyd, R. 103

MacUser 36
Manguel, A. 90
Marzano, R. J. et al. 43
matrix diagrams 178–9
McBer, H. 58
McCabe, D. 141
McCaskey, M. B. 72
McDermott, J. 58, 82
McGuiness, C. 141
McIntyre, D. 62
McKenzie, M. 31
McKim, R. H. M. 41
McPeck, J. 114
meaning making 22, 70–1, 72, 73, 74, 117, 139, 141
   see also schemas
Meier, D. 65
Meltzoff, A. 55
memory 43, 54, 64, 67, 101, 128, 134
mental maps 63, 102, 103
mental models see schemas
mind 43, 55
Minto, B. 73
misunderstanding 19
model maps 163–6
Moll, L. C. 117
Moore, D. M. 41, 135
Murris, K. 40

Nin, A. 44
Nonaka, I. 15–16, 28, 255
Novak, J. D. 22, 70, 170
Numerical Visual Tools 145, 237–42
Nutbrown, C. 58

O'Connor, J. 58, 82
Organisational Visual Tools 145, 243–9
Ornstein, R. 8, 132
O'Shea, T. 103

Paine, N. 37
Palmer, S. 96
Parks, S. 102
Peacock, A. 37
personal construct theory 55
Petterson, R. 42
Piaget, J. 71, 80
Picasso, P. 44
pictures 196–7
pie charts 238
Pinker, S. 41, 70, 71, 144
plans 202–3

'PMI' 249
Postman, N. 37, 72
Poyner, N. 44
priorities grids 189–91
problem–solution frames 247
Pumfrey, P. 90

questions and answers 105–9, 120t, 127

ranking order 192–3
Rayner, S. 133
reading 9–11, 85–90
    decoding 87, 88
    problems 87, 90
    purpose 89
    understanding 86, 87, 88–90
    visual tools for 86–7, 90
reasoning 100–1, 248
relations diagrams 221–3
Representational Visual Tools 145, 195–203
Rico, G. 154
Riding, R. 133
Robinson, K. 65
Roos, J. 31, 58, 70, 73
Roszak, T. 24, 30, 37, 109

Saljo, R. 24, 117
schemas 53–9, 64, 80, 86, 102, 103, 135, 141
    see also understanding: holographic–linear
Schopenhauer, A. 44
self-esteem 57, 58
Senge, P. et al. 49, 51
Shermis, S. S. 90
Sherwood, D. 58, 109, 141
Siler, T. 100
single bubble maps 152–3
Smee, P. 103
Smith, F. 64, 96
Smitsman, A. W. 48, 49, 50
space 42–3, 44, 67, 79, 100, 101, 103
special educational needs 138
Stamboltizis, A. 90
Stevens, A. L. 66
Stewart, T. A. 29
Stigler, J. W. 50
story boards 212–13
Structural Visual Tools 145, 149–72
SWOT analysis 183–4
Sylwester, R. 40
systems diagrams 230–3, 253

Tait, F. 128
Takeuchi, H. 15–16, 28
Tan, L. S. 18
target maps 150–1
Temporal Visual Tools 145, 205–16
texts 64, 65, 66, 126, 185–6
    see also genres
thinking 99–103, 117
    in action 113–18
    aloud 80–1, 128
    modelling 141

modes 43, 62, 67
skills 34, 37, 70, 116, 120t, 121t, 145
thought-objects 81, 100–1, 115, 116
types of 115
visual tools for 65–6, 81, 101–3, 114, 117, 118t, 119t, 121t
    see also genres; questions; understanding
Thompson, D. 118
time lines 206–7
tools 47–51
tree diagrams 160–2
Trent, S. C. et al. 135
Tufte, E. 66
Tulving, E. 54

understanding 23–4, 138
    and explanation 66, 139–40
    holographic–linear 61–7, 133
    misunderstanding 19
    reading 86, 87, 88–90
Uttal, D. 18

Van Schank, P. 96
Vee maps 170–2
Venn diagrams 51, 174–5, 253
visual displays 41–2
visual literacy 36–7, 39–44
visual processing 14–15, 18, 40
visual tools 14, 17, 18, 25, 28–9
    categories 144–5
    Causal (CVT) 145, 217–36
    Differential (DVT) 145, 173–93
    examples 146
    Individual (IVT) 145, 146, 251–6
    Numerical (NVT) 145, 237–42
    Organisational (OVT) 145, 243–9
    Representational (RVT) 145, 195–203
    Structural (SVT) 145, 149–72
    templates 146
    Temporal (TVT) 145, 205–16
    theory 49
Vygotsky, L. S. 80

Wandersee, J. H. 73
Watson, J. 117
Wells, G. 106
Wenger, W. 95
Wheton, D. 109
Whitmore, K. F. 117
Wittgenstein, L. 72, 144
Woditsch, G. A. 24, 132
Woods, M. 109
worksheets 146
Wragg, E. C. 109
writing 93–6
    modelling 95
    organisation 94, 96, 244
    visual tools 94–6, 212–13
writing frames 244
Wurman, R. S. 67

Zelazny, G. 238